JOHN W. GARDNER

ON LEADERSHIP

JOHN W. GARDNER attended Stanford University (A.B., 1935; M.A., 1936) and the University of California (Ph.D., 1938). He taught psychology at the University of California, Connecticut College and Mount Holyoke College. He was an officer in the U.S. Marine Corps in World War II.

He was president of the Carnegie Corporation and the Carnegie Foundation for the Advancement of Teaching (1955–1965); U.S. Secretary of Health, Education, and Welfare (1965–1968); chairman of the National Urban Coalition (1968–1970); founding chairman of Common Cause (1970–1977); and a co-founder of Independent Sector (1980). Mr. Gardner served on President Kennedy's Task Force on Education and was chairman of President Kennedy's Commission on International Educational and Cultural Affairs. He was chairman of President Johnson's Task Force on Education, served on President Carter's Commission on an Agenda for the '80s, and chaired (1976–1980) the President's Commission on White House Fellowships. He served on President Reagan's Task Force on Private Sector Initiatives.

Mr. Gardner has been a director of a number of corporations, including Shell Oil Company, the New York Telephone Company, American Airlines and Time, Inc. Among other organizations he has served as a board member are Stanford University and the Scientific Advisory Board of the Air Force.

Mr. Gardner was the editor of President John F. Kennedy's book *To Turn the Tide* and the author of *Excellence, Self-Renewal, No Easy Victories, The Recovery of Confidence, In Common Cause* and *Morale*. He is the coeditor, with Francesca Gardner Reese, of *Quotations of Wit and Wisdom*.

In 1964 Mr. Gardner was awarded the Presidential Medal of Freedom, the highest civil honor in the United States. Among other awards he has received are the U.S. Air Force Exceptional Service Award, and the Distinguished Achievement Medal of the Stanford Athletic Board.

John W. Gardner

ON LEADERSHIP

THE FREE PRESS
A Division of Macmillan, Inc.
NEW YORK

The Free Press
A Division of Macmillan, Inc.
866 Third Avenue, New York, N.Y. 10022

Collier Macmillan Canada, Inc.

Printed in the United States of America

printing number
3 4 5 6 7 8 9 10

Library of Congress Cataloging-in-Publication Data

Gardner, John William
On leadership / John W. Gardner.
p. cm.
Includes bibliographical references.
ISBN 0-02-911311-3
1. Political leadership. I. Title.
JC330.3.G37 1990 89-16894
303.3'4—dc20 CIP

TO
Brian O'Connell

CONTENTS

ACKNOWLEDGMENTS

I have been writing on leadership for twenty-five years and have accumulated intellectual debts extending over many fields:

- to the great early sociologists whom I have read and reread since graduate school—Max Weber, Georg Simmel, C. H. Cooley, and others; and to the later contributors who were my friends and mentors—Talcott Parsons, Robert Merton, and others.
- to the historians and biographers who have taught me so much: Alan Bullock, Henry Steele Commager, James Flexner, Elisabeth Griffith, Arthur Link, Dumas Malone, Samuel Eliot Morison, Allan Nevins, Jaroslav Pelikan, Arthur Schlesinger, Jr., Barbara Tuchman, and many others.
- to those political scientists who have helped me understand the presidency and the political process: James MacGregor Burns, Thomas Cronin, Fred Greenstein, Richard Neustadt, Nelson Polsby, David Truman, Aaron Wildavsky, and others.
- to those behavior scientists who have devoted themselves to the study of group functioning, from the pioneers who were colleagues and friends of mine (Kurt Lewin, Rensis Likert, Ron Lippitt, Douglas McGregor, et al.) to more recent contributors such as B. M. Bass, F. E. Fiedler, Edwin P. Hollander, James March, Victor H. Vroom, Philip W. Yetton, and others.
- to distinguished colleagues all over the country who are working on one or another aspect of leadership: Bruce Adams, Kenneth Clark, Harlan Cleveland, Ann De Busk, Peter Drucker, Madeleine F. Green,

Robert Greenleaf, Joseph Jaworski, Barbara Kovach, Harold Leavitt, Bruce Payne, Howard Prince, Donna Shavlik, Irving Spitzberg, Judith G. Touchton, Walt Ulmer; and to my beloved friends John Macy and Frank Pace, whose recent untimely deaths were a great loss to the field.

• and, finally to the leaders I have had the good fortune to know or work with during one or another phase of an action-filled career.

This book is the product of a five-year study. I thank the donors who have made it possible. Their generosity has given me the time and resources to explore broadly and deeply the literature on leaders and leadership, to interview contemporary leaders, to visit the centers in which significant work on leadership is taking place, and to consult with scholars who are addressing themselves to the subject. Specifically, my thanks go to the Carnegie Corporation of New York; the Commonwealth Fund; the Ford Foundation; the George Gund Foundation; the Miriam and Peter Haas Fund; the Evelyn and Walter Haas Jr. Fund; the William and Flora Hewlett Foundation; the Lilly Endowment, Inc.; Mrs. John D. Rockefeller 3rd; the Rockefeller Foundation; the Seaver Institute; and the Spencer Foundation. The work would not have been undertaken had it not been for the generous friendship of Brian O'Connell, president of Independent Sector, who worked out the funding of the program and has provided encouragement at every step of the journey. And the work could not have prospered without the vigorous and intelligent support of my executive assistant, Cynthia Hahn, and the valuable editorial counsel of my friend and associate, Harold R. Levy. John G. Trimble, William Trimble, Jennifer Reese, and Bill Davis provided help with the series of leadership papers that preceded the book.

Richard Van Wagenen and Jacqueline Goodwin reviewed the manuscript and made invaluable suggestions. I am grateful for their skill and for their friendship. Finally, my thanks to Caryl and Edna Haskins for intellectual and moral support at every stage.

INTRODUCTION

The Cry for Leadership

Why do we not have better leadership? The question is asked over and over. We complain, express our disappointment, often our outrage; but no answer emerges.

When we ask a question countless times and arrive at no answer, it is possible that we are asking the wrong question—or that we have misconceived the terms of the query. Another possibility is that it is not a question at all but simply convenient shorthand to express deep and complex anxieties. It would strike most of our contemporaries as old-fashioned to cry out, "What shall we do to be saved?" And it would be time-consuming to express fully our concerns about the social disintegration, the moral disorientation, and the spinning compass needle of our time. So we cry out for leadership.

To some extent the conventional views of leadership are shallow, and set us up for endless disappointment. There is an element of wanting to be rescued, of wanting a parental figure who will set all things right. Such fantasies for grown-up children should not lead us to dismiss the need for leaders nor the insistent popular expression of that need. A great many people who are not given to juvenile fantasies want leaders—leaders who are exemplary, who inspire, who stand for something, who help us set and achieve goals.

Unfortunately, in popular thinking on the subject, the mature need and the childlike fantasies interweave. One of the tasks of this book is to untangle them, and to sketch what is realistically possible.

Leadership is such a gripping subject that once it is given center stage it draws attention away from everything else. But attention to leadership alone is sterile—and inappropriate. The larger topic of which leadership is a subtopic is *the accomplishment of group purpose*, which is furthered not only by effective leaders but also by innovators, entrepreneurs and thinkers; by the availability of resources; by questions of morale and social cohesion; and by much else that I discuss in this book. It is not my purpose to deal with either leadership or its related subjects comprehensively. I hope to illuminate aspects of the subject that may be of use in facing our present dilemmas—as a society and as a species.

The Issues Behind the Issues

We are faced with immensely threatening problems—terrorism, AIDS, drugs, depletion of the ozone layer, the threat of nuclear conflict, toxic waste, the real possibility of economic disaster. Even moderately informed citizens could extend the list. Yet on none of the items listed does our response acknowledge the manifest urgency of the problem. We give every appearance of sleepwalking through a dangerous passage of history. We see the life-threatening problems, but we do not react. We are anxious but immobilized.

I do not find the problems themselves as frightening as the questions they raise concerning our capacity to gather our forces and act. No doubt many of the grave problems that beset us have discoverable, though difficult, solutions. But to mobilize the required resources and to bear what sacrifices are necessary calls for a capacity to focus our energies, a capacity for sustained commitment. Suppose that we can no longer summon our forces to such effort. Suppose that we have lost the capacity to motivate ourselves for arduous exertions in behalf of the group. A discussion of leadership cannot avoid such questions.

Could it be that we suppress our awareness of problems—however ominous—because we have lost all conviction that we can do anything about them? Effective leaders heighten both motivation and confidence, but when these qualities have been gravely diminished, leaders have a hard time leading.

Suppose that fragmentation and divisiveness have proceeded so far in American life that we can no longer lend ourselves to any worthy common purpose. Suppose that our shared values have disintegrated to the point that we believe in nothing strongly enough to work for it as a group. Shared values are the bedrock on which leaders build the edifice of group achievement. No examination of leadership would be complete without attention to the decay and possible regeneration of the value framework.

Suppose that our institutions have become so lacking in adaptiveness that they can no longer meet new challenges. All human institutions must renew themselves continuously; therefore, we must explore this process as it bears on leadership.

I think of such matters—motivation, values, social cohesion, renewal—as the "issues behind the issues," and I shall return to them often in the pages that follow.

Our Dispersed Leadership

In this society, leadership is dispersed throughout all segments of the society—government, business, organized labor, the professions, the minority communities, the universities, social agencies, and so on. Leadership is also dispersed down through the many levels of social functioning, from the loftiest levels of our national life down to the school principal, the local union leader, the shop supervisor.

We have always associated both kinds of dispersion with our notions of democracy and pluralism. But as our understanding of the principles of organization has developed, we have come to see that there is really no alternative to such dispersal of leadership if large-scale systems are to retain their vitality. The point is relevant not only for our society as a whole but also for all the organized subsystems (corporations, unions, government agencies, and so forth) that compose it.

Most leadership today is an attempt to accomplish purposes through (or in spite of) large, intricately organized systems. There is no possibility that centralized authority can call all the shots in such systems, whether the system is a corporation or a nation. Individuals in all segments and at all levels must be prepared to exercise leaderlike initiative and responsibility, using their local knowledge to solve problems at their level. *Vitality at middle and lower levels of leadership can produce greater vitality in the higher levels of leadership.*

In addition to all people down the line who may properly be called leaders at their level, there are in any vital organization or society a great many individuals who *share leadership tasks* unofficially, by behaving responsibly with respect to the purposes of the group. Such individuals, who have been virtually ignored in the leadership literature, are immensely important to the leader and to the group. (And as I point out later, even the responsible dissenter may be sharing the leadership task.)

Understanding Leadership

I have seen a good many leaders in action. My first chore for a president was for Eisenhower, whom I had known earlier when he headed Columbia University. Of the seven presidents since then, I have worked with all but two. But I have learned powerful lessons from less lofty leaders—from a top sergeant in the Marine Corps, from university presidents, corporate chief executive officers, community leaders, bankers, scientists, union leaders, school superintendents, and others. I have led, and have worked in harness with other leaders.

The development of more and better leaders is an important objective that receives a good deal of attention in these pages. But this is not a how-to-do-it manual. The first step is not action; the first step is understanding. The first question is how to think about leadership. I have in mind not just political buffs who want more and better leaders on the political scene, nor just CEOs who wonder why there are not more leaders scattered through their huge organizations. I have in mind citizens who do not want to be victimized by their leaders, neighborhood organizations that want to train their future leaders, the young people who dream of leadership, and all kinds of people who just want to comprehend the world around them.

Citizens must understand the possibilities and limitations of leadership. We must know how we can strengthen and support good leaders; and we must be able to see through the leaders who are exploiting us, playing on our hatred and prejudice, or taking us down dangerous paths.

Understanding these things, we come to see that much of the responsibility for leaders and how they perform is in our own hands. If we are lazy, self-indulgent, and wanting to be deceived; if we willingly follow corrupt leaders; if we allow our heritage of freedom to decay; if we fail to be faithful monitors of the public process—then we shall get and deserve the worst.

Accountability

The concept of accountability is as important as the concept of leadership. Humankind has spent thousands of years trying to figure out how to hold power accountable. And we have come a long way in devising the strategies that make that difficult task possible. The rule of law, trial by jury, the secret ballot, a free press and other principles have contributed importantly to that end. But it is still difficult. And that, too, is a part of the conversation about leaders.

Leadership Development

How many dispersed leaders do we need? When one considers all the towns and city councils, corporations, government agencies, unions, schools and colleges, churches, professions and so on, the number must be high. In order to have a target to think about, and setting precision aside, let us say that it is 1 percent of the population—2.4 million men and women who are prepared to take leaderlike action at their levels. How can we ever find that many leaders?

Fortunately, the development of leaders is possible on a scale far beyond anything we have ever attempted. As one surveys the subject of leadership, there are depressing aspects but leadership development is not one of them. Although our record to date is unimpressive, the prospects for improvement are excellent.

Many dismiss the subject with the confident assertion that "leaders are born not made." Nonsense! Most of what leaders have that enables them to lead is learned. Leadership is not a mysterious activity. It is possible to describe the tasks that leaders perform. And the capacity to perform those tasks is widely distributed in the population. Today, unfortunately, specialization and patterns of professional functioning draw most of our young potential leaders into prestigious and lucrative nonleadership roles.

We have barely scratched the surface in our efforts toward leadership development. In the mid-twenty-first century, people will look back on our present practices as primitive.

Most men and women go through their lives using no more than a fraction—usually a rather small fraction—of the potentialities within them. The reservoir of unused human talent and energy is vast, and learning to tap that reservoir more effectively is one of the exciting tasks ahead for humankind.

Among the untapped capabilities are leadership gifts. For every effectively functioning leader in our society, I would guess that there are five or ten others with the same potential for leadership who have never led or perhaps even considered leading. Why? Perhaps they were drawn off into the byways of specialization . . . or have never sensed the potentialities within them . . . or have never understood how much the society needs what they have to give.

We can do better. Much, much better.

1

THE NATURE OF LEADERSHIP

Leadership is a word that has risen above normal workaday usage as a conveyor of meaning. There seems to be a feeling that if we invoke it often enough with sufficient ardor we can ease our sense of having lost our way, our sense of things unaccomplished, of duties unfulfilled.

All of that simply clouds our thinking. The aura with which we tend to surround the words *leader* and *leadership* makes it hard to think clearly. Good sense calls for demystification.

Leadership is the process of persuasion or example by which an individual (or leadership team) induces a group to pursue objectives held by the leader or shared by the leader and his or her followers.

In any established group, individuals fill different roles, and one of the roles is that of leader. Leaders cannot be thought of apart from the historic context in which they arise, the setting in which they function (e.g., elective political office), and the system over which they preside (e.g., a particular city or state). They are integral parts of the system, subject to the forces that affect the system. They perform (or cause to be performed) certain tasks or functions that are essential if the group is to accomplish its purposes.

All that we know about the interaction between leaders and constituents or followers tells us that communication and influence flow in both directions; and in that two-way communication, nonrational, nonverbal, and unconscious elements play their part. In the process leaders shape and are shaped. This is true even in systems that appear to be led in quite autocratic fashion. In a state governed by coercion, followers cannot prevent the leader from violating their customs and beliefs, but they have many ways of making it more costly to violate than to honor their norms, and leaders usually make substantial accommodations. If Julius Caesar had been willing to live more flexibly with the give-and-take he might not have been slain in the Senate House. Machiavelli, the ultimate realist, advised the prince, "You will always need the favor of the inhabitants. . . . It is necessary for a prince to possess the friendship of the people."[1]

The connotations of the word *follower* suggest too much passivity and dependence to make it a fit term for all who are at the other end of the dialogue with leaders. I don't intend to discard it, but I also make frequent use of the word *constituent*. It is awkward in some contexts, but often it does fuller justice to the two-way interchange.

Elements of physical coercion are involved in some kinds of leadership; and of course there is psychological coercion, however mild and subtle, including peer pressure, in all social action. But in our culture, popular understanding of the leadership process distinguishes it from coercion—and places those forms involving the least coercion higher on the scale of leadership.

The focus of this book is leadership in this country today. Examples are drawn from other cultures and many of the generalizations are relevant for all times and places; but the focus is here and now. The points emphasized might be different were I writing fifty years ago or fifty years hence, or writing of Bulgaria or Tibet.

Distinctions

We must not confuse leadership with status. Even in large corporations and government agencies, the top-ranking person may simply be bureaucrat number 1. We have all occasionally encountered top persons who couldn't lead a squad of seven-year-olds to the ice cream counter.

It does not follow that status is irrelevant to leadership. Most positions of high status carry with them symbolic values and traditions that enhance the possibility of leadership. People expect governors and corporation presidents to lead, which heightens the possibility that they will. But the selection process for positions of high status does not make that a sure outcome.

Similarly, we must not confuse leadership with power. Leaders always have some measure of power, rooted in their capacity to persuade, but many people with power are without leadership gifts. Their power derives from money, or from the capacity to inflict harm, or from control of some piece of institutional machinery, or from access to the media. A military dictator has power. The thug who sticks a gun in your ribs has power. Leadership is something else.

Finally, we must not confuse leadership with official authority, which is simply legitimized power. Meter maids have it; the person who audits your tax returns has it.

Leadership requires major expenditures of effort and energy—more than most people care to make. When I outlined to a teenager of my acquaintance the preceding distinctions and then described the hard tasks of leadership, he said, "I'll leave the leadership to you, Mr. Gardner. Give me some of that power and status."

Confusion between leadership and official authority has a deadly effect on large organizations. Corporations and government agencies everywhere have executives who imagine that their place on the organization chart has given them a body of followers. And of course it has not. They have been given subordinates. Whether the subordinates become followers depends on whether the executives act like leaders.

Is it appropriate to apply to leaders the word *elite*? The word was once applied to families of exalted social status. Then sociologists adopted the word to describe any group of high status, whether hereditary or earned; thus, in addition to the elites of old families and old money, there are elites of performance and profession.

Some social critics today use the word with consistent negative overtones. They believe that elite status is incompatible with an equalitarian philosophy. But in any society—no matter how democratic, no matter how equalitarian—there are elites in the sociologist's sense: intellectual, athletic, artistic, political, and so on. The marks of an open society are that elite status is generally earned, and that those who have earned it do not use their status to violate democratic norms. In our society, leaders are among the many "performance elites."

Leaders and Managers

The word *manager* usually indicates that the individual so labeled holds a directive post in an organization, presiding over the processes by which the organization functions, allocating resources prudently, and making the best possible use of people.

Many writers on leadership take considerable pains to distinguish between leaders and managers. In the process leaders generally end up looking like a cross between Napoleon and the Pied Piper, and managers like unimaginative clods. This troubles me. I once heard it said of a man, "He's an utterly first-class manager but there isn't a trace of the leader in him." I am still looking for that man, and I am beginning to believe that he does not exist. Every time I encounter utterly first-class managers they turn out to have quite a lot of the leader in them.

Even the most visionary leader is faced on occasion with decisions that every manager faces: when to take a short-term loss to achieve a long-term gain, how to allocate scarce resources, whom to trust with a delicate assignment. So even though it has become conventional to contrast leaders and managers, I am inclined to use slightly different categories, lumping leaders and leader/managers into one category and placing in the other category those numerous managers whom one would not normally describe as leaders. Leaders and leader/managers distinguish themselves from the general run of managers in at least six respects:

1. They think longer term—beyond the day's crises, beyond the quarterly report, beyond the horizon.

2. In thinking about the unit they are heading, they grasp its relationship to larger realities—the larger organization of which they are a part, conditions external to the organization, global trends.

3. They reach and influence constituents beyond their jurisdictions, beyond boundaries. Thomas Jefferson influenced people all over Europe. Gandhi influenced people all over the world. In an organization, leaders extend their reach across bureaucratic boundaries—often a distinct advantage in a world too complex and tumultuous to be handled "through channels." Leaders' capacity to rise above jurisdictions may enable them to bind together the fragmented constituencies that must work together to solve a problem.

4. They put heavy emphasis on the intangibles of vision, values, and motivation and understand intuitively the nonrational and unconscious elements in leader–constituent interaction.

5. They have the political skill to cope with the conflicting requirements of multiple constituencies.

6. They think in terms of renewal. The routine manager tends to accept organizational structure and process as it exists. The leader or leader/manager seeks the revisions of process and structure required by ever-changing reality.

The manager is more tightly linked to an organization than is the leader. Indeed, the leader may have no organization at all. Florence Nightingale, after leaving the Crimea, exercised extraordinary leadership in health care for decades with no organization under her command. Gandhi was a leader before he had an organization. Some of our most memorable leaders have headed movements so amorphous that management would be an inappropriate word.

The Many Kinds of Leaders

One hears and reads a surprising number of sentences that describe leaders in general as having such and such attributes and behaving in such and such a fashion—as though one could distill out of the spectacular diversity of leaders an idealized picture of The Leader.

Leaders come in many forms, with many styles and diverse qualities. There are quiet leaders and leaders one can hear in the next county. Some find their strength in eloquence, some in judgment, some in courage. I had a friend who was a superior leader in outdoor activities and sports but quite incapable of leading in a bureaucratic setting.

The diversity is almost without limit: Churchill, the splendidly eloquent old warrior; Gandhi, the visionary and the shrewd mobilizer of his people; Lenin, the coldly purposeful revolutionary. Consider just the limited category of military leadership. George Marshall was a self-effacing, low-keyed man with superb judgment and a limitless capacity to inspire trust. MacArthur was a brilliant strategist, a farsighted administrator, and flamboyant to his fingertips. (Eisenhower, who had served under MacArthur, once said, "I studied dramatics under a master.") Eisenhower in his wartime assignment was an outstanding leader/administrator and coalition builder. General Patton was a slashing, intense combat commander. Field Marshal Montgomery was a gifted, temperamental leader of whom Churchill said, "In defeat, indomitable; in victory, insufferable." All were great leaders—but extraordinarily diverse in personal attributes.

The fact that there are many kinds of leaders has implications for leadership education. Most of those seeking to develop young potential leaders have in mind one ideal model that is inevitably constricting. We should give young people a sense of the many kinds of leaders and styles of leadership, and encourage them to move toward those models that are right for them.

Leaders and History

All too often when we think of our historic leaders, we eliminate all the contradictions that make individuals distinctive. And we further violate reality by lifting them out of their historical contexts. No wonder we are left with pasteboard portraits. As first steps toward a mature view of leaders we must accept complexity and context.

Thomas Jefferson was first of all a gifted and many-sided human, an enigmatic man who loved—among other things—abstract ideas, agriculture, architecture and statecraft. He was a man of natural aloofness who lived most of his life in public; a man of action with a gift for words and a bent for research; an idealist who proved himself a shrewd, even wily, operator on the political scene. Different sides of his nature came into play in different situations.

Place him now in the context of the exhilarating events and themes of his time: a new nation coming into being, with a new consciousness; the brilliant rays of the Enlightenment reaching into every phase of life; the inner contradictions of American society (e.g., slavery) already rumbling beneath the surface.

Finally, add the overpowering impulse of succeeding generations to serve their own needs by mythologizing, idolizing or debunking him. It turns out to be an intricately textured story—and not one that diminishes Jefferson.

It was once believed that if leadership traits were truly present in an individual, they would manifest themselves almost without regard to the situation in which the person was functioning. No one believes that any more. Acts of leadership take place in an unimaginable variety of settings, and the setting does much to determine the kinds of leaders that emerge and how they play their roles.

We cannot avoid the bewhiskered question, "Does the leader make history or does the historical moment make the leader?" It sounds like a seminar question but it is of interest to most leaders sooner or later. Corporate chief executive officers fighting a deteriorating trend in an industry feel like people trying to run up the down escalator. Looking across town at less able leaders riding an upward trend in another industry, they are ripe for the theory that history makes the leader.

Thomas Carlyle placed excessive emphasis on the great person, as did Sidney Hook ("all factors in history, save great men, are inconsequential.")[2] Karl Marx, Georg Hegel, and Herbert Spencer placed excessive emphasis on historical forces. For Marx, economic forces shaped history; for Spencer, societies had their evolutionary course just as species did, and the leader was a product of the process; for Hegel, leaders were a part of the dialectic of history and could not help what they did.

The balanced view, of course, is that historical forces create the circumstances in which leaders emerge, but the characteristics of the particular leader in turn have their impact on history.

It is not possible to understand Queen Isabella without understanding fifteenth-century Europe (when she was born, Spain as we know it did not exist), or without understanding the impact of the Reformation on the Catholic world and the gnawing fear stirred by the Muslim conquests. But many monarchs flourished on the Iberian Peninsula in that historical context; only Isabella left an indelible mark. Similarly, by the time Martin Luther emerged, the seeds of the Reformation had already sprouted in many places, but no one would argue that the passionate, charismatic priest who nailed his ninety-five theses to the church door was a puppet of history. Historical forces set the stage for him, but once there, he was himself a historical force.

Churchill is an even more interesting case because he tried out for leadership many times before history was ready for him. After Dunkirk, England needed a leader who could rally the British people to heroic exertions in an uncompromising war, and the eloquent, combative Churchill delivered one of the great performances of the century. Subsequently the clock of history ticked on and—with the war over—the voters dropped him unceremoniously. When a friend told him it was a blessing in disguise, he growled "If it is, the disguise is perfect."

Forces of history determined his rise and fall, but in his time on the world stage he left a uniquely Churchillian mark on the course of events.

Settings

The historical moment is the broadest context affecting the emergence and functioning of leaders; but immensely diverse settings of a more modest nature clearly affect leadership.

The makeup of the group to be led is, of course, a crucial feature of the context. According to research findings, the approach to leadership or style of leadership that will be effective depends on, among other things, the age level of the individuals to be led; their educational background and competence; the size, homogeneity and cohesiveness of the group; its motivation and morale; its rate of turnover; and so on.

Other relevant contextual features are too numerous and diverse to list. Leading a corporation is one thing, leading a street gang is something else. Thomas Cronin has pointed out that it may take one kind of leadership to start a new enterprise and quite another kind to keep it going through its various phases.[3] Religious bodies, political parties, government agencies, the academic world—all offer distinctive contexts for leadership. I discuss these contexts more fully in chapter 4.

Judgments of Leaders

In curious ways, people tend to aggrandize the role of leaders. They tend to exaggerate the capacity of leaders to influence events. Jeffrey Pfeffer says that people want to achieve a feeling of control over their environment, and that this inclines them to attribute the outcomes of group performance to leaders rather than to context.[4] If we were to face the fact—so the argument goes—that outcomes are the result of a complex set of interactions among group members plus environmental and historical forces, we would feel helpless. By attributing outcomes to an identifiable leader we feel, rightly or not, more in control. There is at least a chance that one can fire the leader; one cannot "fire" historical forces.

Leaders act in the stream of history. As they labor to bring about a result, multiple forces beyond their control, even beyond their knowledge, are moving to hasten or hinder the result. So there is rarely a demonstrable causal link between a leader's specific decisions and consequent events. Consequences are not a reliable measure of leadership. Franklin Roosevelt's efforts to bolster the economy in the middle-to-late-1930s were powerfully aided by a force that did not originate with his economic brain trust—the winds of war. Leaders of a farm workers' union fighting for better wages may find their efforts set at naught by a crop failure.

Frank Lloyd Wright said, "A doctor can bury his mistakes. An architect can only advise his client to plant vines." Unlike either doctor or architect, leaders suffer from the mistakes of predecessors and leave some of their own misjudgments as time bombs for successors.

Many of the changes sought by leaders take time: lots of years, long public debate, slow shifts in attitude. In their lifetimes, leaders may see little result from heroic efforts yet may be setting the stage for victories that will come after them. Reflect on the long, slow unfolding of the battles for racial equality or for women's rights. Leaders who did vitally important early work died without knowing what they had wrought.

Leaders may appear to have succeeded (or failed) only to have historians a generation later reverse the verdict. The "verdict of history" has a wonderfully magisterial sound, but in reality it is subject to endless appeals to later generations of historians—with no court of last resort to render a final judgment.

In the real world, the judgments one makes of a leader must be multidimensional, taking into consideration great strengths, streaks of mediocrity, and perhaps great flaws. If the great strengths correspond to the needs of a critical moment in history, the flaws are forgiven and simply provide texture to the biographies. Each leader has his or her own unique pattern of attributes, sometimes conflicting in curious ways. Ronald Reagan was notably passive with respect to many important issues, but vigorously tenacious on other issues.

Leaders change over the course of their active careers as do other human beings. In looking back, it is natural for us to freeze them in that moment when they served history's needs most spectacularly, but leaders evolve. The passionately antislavery Lincoln of the Douglas debates was not the see-both-sides Lincoln of fifteen years earlier. The "national unity" Churchill of 1942 was not the fiercely partisan, adversarial Churchill of the 1930s.

Devolving Initiative and Responsibility

I have already commented on our dispersed leadership and on its importance to the vitality of a large, intricately-organized system. Our most forward-looking business concerns are working in quite imaginative ways to devolve initiative downward and outward through their organizations to develop their lower levels of leadership.

There is no comparable movement in government agencies. But in the nation as a whole, dispersed leadership is a reality. In Santa Barbara County, California, Superintendent of Schools William Cirone is a leader in every sense of the word. A healthy school system requires a vital and involved citizenry. How does one achieve that? Given the aging population, fewer and fewer citizens have children in the schools. How do we keep them interested? Education is a lifelong process. How do we provide for that? These are questions to which Cirone has addressed himself with uncommon energy and imagination.[5]

The leaders of the Soviet Union did not launch the reforms of 1987 because they had developed a sudden taste for grass-roots democracy. They launched them because their system was grinding to a halt. Leader/managers at the lower levels and at the periphery of the system had neither the motivation nor the authority to solve problems that they understood better than the Moscow bureaucrats.

We have only half learned the lesson ourselves. In many of our large corporate, governmental, and nonprofit organizations we still make it all too difficult for potential leaders down the line to exercise initiative. We are still in the process of discovering how much vitality and motivation are buried at those levels awaiting release.

To emphasize the need for dispersed leadership does not deny the need for highly qualified top leadership. But our high-level leaders will be more effective in every way if the systems over which they preside are made vital by dispersed leadership. As I argued in *Excellence*, we must demand high performance at every level of society.[6]

Friends of mine have argued that in view of my convictions

concerning the importance of middle- and lower-level leaders, I lean too heavily on examples of high-level leaders. My response is that we know a great deal about the more famous figures, statements about them can be documented, and they are comfortably familiar to readers. No one who reads this book with care could believe that I consider such exalted figures the only ones worth considering.

Institutionalizing Leadership

To exercise leadership today, leaders must institutionalize their leadership. The issues are too technical and the pace of change too swift to expect that a leader, no matter how gifted, will be able to solve personally the major problems facing the system over which he or she presides. So we design an institutional system—a government agency, a corporation—to solve the problems, and then we select a leader who has the capacity to preside over and strengthen the system. Some leaders may be quite gifted in solving problems personally, but if they fail to institutionalize the process, their departure leaves the system crippled. They must create or strengthen systems that will survive them.

The institutional arrangements generally include a leadership team. Often throughout this book when I use the word *leader*, I am in fact referring to the leadership team. No individual has all the skills—and certainly not the time—to carry out all the complex tasks of contemporary leadership. And the team must be chosen for excellence in performance. Loyalty and being on the boss's wavelength are necessary but not sufficient qualifications. I emphasize the point because more than one recent president of the United States has had aides who possessed no other qualifications.

I am attempting in these early chapters to say what leadership is—and no such description would be complete without a careful examination of what leaders do. So next we look at the tasks of leadership.

2

THE TASKS OF LEADERSHIP

Examination of the tasks performed by leaders takes us to the heart of some of the most interesting questions concerning leadership. It also helps to distinguish among the many kinds of leaders. Leaders differ strikingly in how well they perform various functions.

The following nine tasks seem to me to be the most significant functions of leadership, but I encourage readers to add to the list or to describe the tasks in other ways. Leadership activities implicit in all of the tasks (e.g., communicating, relating effectively with people) are not dealt with separately.

Envisioning Goals

The two tasks at the heart of the popular notion of leadership are goal setting and motivating. As a high school senior put it, "Leaders point us in the right direction and tell us to get moving." Although we take a more complicated view of the tasks of leadership, it is appropriate that we begin with the envisioning of goals. Albert Einstein said, "Perfection of means and confusion of ends seems to characterize our age."

Leaders perform the function of goal setting in diverse ways. Some assert a vision of what the group (organization, community, nation) can be at its best. Others point us toward solutions to our problems. Still others, presiding over internally divided groups, are able to define overarching goals that unify constituencies and focus energies. In today's complex world, the setting of goals may have to be preceded by extensive research and problem solving.

Obviously, a constituency is not a blank slate for the leader to write on. Any collection of people sufficiently related to be called a community has many shared goals, some explicit, some unexpressed (perhaps even unconscious), as tangible as better prices for their crops, as intangible as a better future for their children. In a democracy, the leader takes such shared goals into account.

The relative roles of leaders and followers in determining goals varies from group to group. The teacher of first-grade children and the sergeant training recruits do not do extensive consulting as to goals; congressional candidates do a great deal. In the case of many leaders, goals are handed to them by higher authority. The factory manager and the combat commander may be superb leaders, but many of their goals are set at higher levels.

In short, goals emerge from many sources. The culture itself specifies certain goals; constituents have their concerns; higher authority makes its wishes known. Out of the welter, leaders take some goals as given, and making their own contribution, select and formulate a set of objectives. It may sound as though leaders have only marginal freedom, but in fact there is usually considerable opportunity, even for lower-level leaders, to put their personal emphasis and interpretation on the setting of goals.

There is inevitable tension between long- and short-term goals. On the one hand, constituents are not entirely comfortable with the jerkiness of short-term goal seeking, and they value the sense of stability that comes with a vision of far horizons. On the other hand, long-term goals may require them to defer immediate gratification on at least some fronts. Leaders often fear that when citizens enter the voting booth, they will remember the deferral of gratification more vividly than they remember the reason for it.

Before the Civil War, Elizabeth Cady Stanton saw virtually the whole agenda for women's rights as it was to emerge over the succeeding century. Many of her contemporaries in the movement were not at all prepared for such an inclusive vision and urged her to play it down.

Another visionary far ahead of his time was the South American liberator, Simon Bolívar. He launched his fight in that part of Gran Colombia which is now Venezuela, but in his mind was a vision not only of independence for all of Spain's possessions in the New World, but also a peaceful alliance of the new states in some form of league or confederation. Although he was tragically ahead of his time, the dream never died and has influenced generations of Latin American leaders striving toward unity.

Affirming Values

A great civilization is a drama lived in the minds of a people. It is a shared vision; it is shared norms, expectations, and purposes. When one thinks of the world's great civilizations, the most vivid images that crowd in on us are apt to be of the physical monuments left behind—the Pyramids, the Parthenon, the Mayan temples. But in truth, all the physical splendor was the merest by-product. The civilizations themselves, from beginning to end, existed in the minds of men and women.

If we look at ordinary human communities, we see the same reality: A community lives in the minds of its members—in shared assumptions, beliefs, customs, ideas that give meaning, ideas that motivate. And among the ideas are norms or values. In any healthy, reasonably coherent community, people come to have shared views concerning right and wrong, better and worse—in personal conduct, in governing, in art, whatever. They define for their time and place what things are legal or illegal, virtuous or vicious, good taste or bad. They have little or no impulse to be neutral about such matters. Every society is, as Philip Rieff puts it, "a system of moralizing demands."[1]

Values are embodied in the society's religious beliefs and its secular philosophy. Over the past century, many intellectuals have looked down on the celebration of our values as an unsophisticated and often hypocritical activity. But every healthy society celebrates its values. They are expressed in art, in song, in ritual. They are stated explicitly in historical documents, in ceremonial speeches, in textbooks. They are reflected in stories told around the campfire, in the legends kept alive by old folks, in the fables told to children.

In a pluralistic community there are, within the broad consensus that enables the community to function, many and vigorous conflicts over specific values.

The Regeneration of Values

One of the milder pleasures of maturity is bemoaning the decay of once strongly held values. *Values always decay over time. Societies that keep their values alive do so not by escaping the processes of decay but by powerful processes of regeneration.* There must be perpetual rebuilding. Each generation must rediscover the living elements in its own tradition and adapt them to present realities. To assist in that rediscovery is one of the tasks of leadership.

The leaders whom we admire the most help to revitalize our shared beliefs and values. They have always spent a portion of their time teaching the value framework.

Sometimes the leader's affirmation of values challenges entrenched hypocrisy or conflicts with the values held by a segment of the constituency. Elizabeth Cady Stanton, speaking for now-accepted values, was regarded as a thoroughgoing radical in her day.[2] Jesus not only comforted the afflicted but afflicted the comfortable.

Motivating

Chapter 16 is devoted to the task of motivating, so I deal with it briefly here.

Leaders do not create motivation out of thin air. They unlock or channel existing motives. Any group has a great tangle of motives. Effective leaders tap those that serve the purposes of collective action in pursuit of shared goals. They accomplish the alignment of individual and group goals. They deal with the circumstances that often lead group members to withhold their best efforts. They call for the kind of effort and restraint, drive and discipline that make for great performance. They create a climate in which there is pride in making significant contributions to shared goals.

Note that in the tasks of leadership, the transactions between leaders and constituents go beyond the rational level to the nonrational and unconscious levels of human functioning. Young potential leaders who have been schooled to believe that all elements of a problem are rational and technical, reducible to words and numbers, are ill-equipped to move into an area where intuition and empathy are powerful aids to problem solving.

Managing

Most managers exhibit some leadership skills, and most leaders on occasion find themselves managing. Leadership and management are not the same thing, but they overlap. It makes sense to include managing in the list of tasks leaders perform.

In the paragraphs that follow I focus on those aspects of leadership that one might describe as managing without slipping into a conventional description of managing as such. And I try to find terminology and phrasing broad enough to cover the diverse contexts in which leadership occurs in corporations, unions, municipalities, political movements, and so on.

1. *Planning and Priority Setting*. Assuming that broad goals have been set, someone has to plan, fix priorities, choose means, and formulate policy. These are functions often performed by leaders. When Lyndon B. Johnson said, early in his presidency, that education was the nation's number one priority, he galvanized the nation's educational leaders and released constructive energies far beyond any governmental action that had yet been taken. It was a major factor in leading me to accept a post in his Cabinet.

2. *Organizing and Institution Building*. We have all seen leaders enjoy their brilliant moment and then disappear without a trace because they had no gift for building their purposes into institutions. In the ranks of leaders, Alfred Sloan was at the other extreme. Though he sold a lot of automobiles, he was not primarily a salesman; he was an institution builder. His understanding of organization was intuitive and profound.

Someone has to design the structures and processes through which substantial endeavors get accomplished over time. Ideally, leaders should not regard themselves as indispensable but should enable the group to carry on. Institutions are a means to that end. Jean Monnet said, "Nothing is possible without individuals; nothing is lasting without institutions."[3]

3. *Keeping the System Functioning*. Presiding over the arrangements through which individual energies are coordinated to achieve shared goals sounds like a quintessential management task. But it is clear that most leaders find themselves occasionally performing one or another of the essential chores: mobilizing and allocating resources; staffing and ensuring the continuing vitality of the team; creating and maintaining appropriate procedures; directing, delegating and coordinating; providing a system of incentives; reporting, evaluating and holding accountable.

4. *Agenda Setting and Decision Making*. The goals may be clear and the organization well set up and smoothly operating, but there remain agenda-setting and decision-making functions that must be dealt with. The announcement of goals without a proposed program for meeting them is a familiar enough political phenomenon—but not one that builds credibility. There are leaders who can motivate and inspire but who cannot visualize a path to the goal in practical, feasible steps. Leaders who lack that skill must bring onto their team people who have it.

One of the purest examples of the leader as agenda setter was Florence Nightingale.[4] Her public image was and is that of the lady of mercy, but under her gentle manner, she was a rugged spirit, a fighter, a tough-minded system changer. She never made public appearances or speeches, and except for her two years in the Crimea, held no public position. Her strength was that she was a formidable authority on the evils to be remedied, she knew what to do about them, and she used public opinion to goad top officials to adopt her agenda.

5. *Exercising Political Judgment*. In our pluralistic society, persons directing substantial enterprises find that they are presiding over many constituencies within their organizations and contending with many outside. Each has its needs and claims. One of the tasks of the leader/manager is to make the political judgments necessary to prevent secondary conflicts of purpose from blocking progress toward primary goals. Sometimes the literature on administration and management treats politics as an alien and disruptive force. But Aaron Wildavsky, in his brilliant book, *The Nursing Father: Moses as a Political Leader*, makes the point that leaders are inevitably political.[5]

Achieving Workable Unity

A pluralistic society is, by definition, one that accepts many different elements, each with its own purposes. Collisions are inevitable and often healthy—as in commercial competition, in civil suits, and in efforts to redress grievances through the political process. Conflict is necessary in the case of oppressed groups that must fight for the justice that is due them. All our elective officials know the intense conflict of the political campaign. Indeed, one could argue that willingness to engage in battle when necessary is a sine qua non of leadership.

But most leaders most of the time are striving to diminish conflict rather than increase it. Some measure of cohesion and mutual tolerance is an absolute requirement of social functioning.

Sometimes the problem is not outright conflict but an unwillingness to cooperate. One of the gravest problems George Washington faced as a general was that the former colonies, though they had no doubt they were all on the same side, were not always sure they wanted to cooperate. As late as 1818, John Randolph declared, "When I speak of my country, I mean the Commonwealth of Virginia."[6]

The unifying function of leaders is well illustrated in the actions of George Bush after winning the presidential election of 1988. He promptly met with his defeated opponent, Michael Dukakis; with his chief rival for the nomination, Senator Robert Dole; and with Jesse Jackson and Coretta Scott King, both of whom had opposed his election.

He asked Jack Kemp, another of his rivals for the nomination, to be Secretary of Housing and Urban Development, and Senator Dole's wife, Elizabeth Hanford Dole, to be Secretary of Labor.

Leaders in this country today must cope with the fragmentation of the society into groups that have great difficulty in understanding one another or agreeing on common goals. It is a fragmentation rooted in the pluralism of our society, in the obsessive specialization of modern life, and in the skill with which groups organize to advance their concerns.

Under the circumstances, all our leaders must spend part of their time dealing with polarization and building community. There is a false notion that this is a more bland, less rigorous task than leadership of one of the combative segments. In fact, the leader willing to combat polarization is the braver person, and is generally under fire from both sides. I would suggest that Jean Monnet, the father of the European Common Market, is a useful model for future leaders. When there were conflicting purposes Monnet saw the possibility of shared goals, and he knew how to move his contemporaries toward those shared goals.

Trust

Much depends on the general level of trust in the organization or society. The infinitely varied and complex doings of the society—any society—would come to a halt if people did not trust other people most of the time—trust them to observe custom, follow the rules, and behave with some predictability. Countless circumstances operate to diminish that trust, but one may be sure that if the society is functioning at all, *some* degree of trust survives.

Leaders can do much to preserve the necessary level of trust. And the first requirement is that they have the capacity to inspire trust in themselves. In sixteenth-century Italy, where relations among the warring kingdoms were an unending alley fight, Machiavelli's chilling advice to the Prince—"It is necessary . . . to be a feigner and a dissembler," or, as another translator renders the same passage, "You must be a great liar and hypocrite"—may have been warranted.[7] And, under conditions of iron rule, Hitler and Stalin were able to live by betrayals. But in our society, leaders must work to raise the level of trust.

Explaining

Explaining sounds too pedestrian to be on a list of leadership tasks, but every leader recognizes it. People want to know what the problem is, why they are being asked to do certain things, why they face so many frustrations. Thurman Arnold said, "Unhappy is a people that has run out of words to describe what is happening to them."[8] Leaders find the words.

To be heard above the hubbub in the public forum today, explaining generally requires more than clarity and eloquence. It requires effective access to the media of communication or to those segments of the population that keep ideas in circulation—editors, writers, intellectuals, association leaders, advocacy groups, chief executive officers, and the like.

The task of explaining is so important that some who do it exceptionally well play a leadership role even though they are not leaders in the conventional sense. When the American colonies were struggling for independence, Thomas Paine was a memorable explainer. In the powerful environmentalist surge of the 1960s and 70s, no activist leader had as pervasive an influence on the movement as did Rachel Carson, whose book *Silent Spring* burst on the scene in 1963.[9] Betty Friedan's *The Feminine Mystique* played a similar role for the women's movement.[10]

Leaders teach. Lincoln, in his second inaugural address, provided an extraordinary example of the leader as teacher. Teaching and leading are distinguishable occupations, but every great leader is clearly teaching—and every great teacher is leading.

Serving as a Symbol

Leaders are inevitably symbols. Workers singled out to be supervisors discover that they are set apart from their old comrades in subtle ways. They try to keep the old camaraderie but things have changed. They are now symbols of management. Sergeants symbolize the chain of command. Parish religious leaders symbolize their churches.

In a group threatened with internal strife, the leader may be a crucial symbol of unity. In a minority group's struggle to find its place, combative leaders—troublesome to others—may be to their own people the perfect symbol of their anger and their struggle.

The top leader of a community or nation symbolizes the group's collective identity and continuity. For this reason, the death of a president produces a special reaction of grief and loss. Americans who were beyond childhood when John F. Kennedy was assassinated remember, despite the passage of decades, precisely where they were and what they were doing when the news reached them. Even for many who did not admire him, the news had the impact of a blow to the solar plexus. And those old enough to remember Franklin D. Roosevelt's death recognize the reaction.

For late eighteenth-century Americans, George Washington was the symbol of all that they had been through together. Thomas Jefferson became such a powerful symbol of our democratic aspirations that for generations politicians fought over his memory. Those who favored Hamiltonian views sought bitterly and unsuccessfully to shatter the Jefferson image. As Merrill Peterson has cogently argued, the man himself lost reality and the symbol took over.[11] In the dark days of the Great Depression, the American impulse to face events in a positive spirit found its symbol in the ebullient Franklin D. Roosevelt.

Outside the political area, Albert Schweitzer, the gifted theologian and musician who in 1913 gave up a comfortable and respected life in his native Germany to spend the remainder of his years presiding over a medical mission in Equatorial Africa, stands as the pristine example of leader as symbol.

Some individuals newly risen to leadership have a hard time adjusting to the reality that they are symbols. I recall a visit with a young college president who had just come into the job fresh from a professorship, with no prior administrative experience. He confided that he was deeply irked by an incident the preceding day. In his first speech before faculty, students, trustees and alumni he had simply been himself—a man of independent mind full of lively personal opinions—and many of his listeners were nonplussed and irritated. They were not interested in a display of idiosyncratic views. They had expected him to speak as their new leader, their symbol of institutional continuity, their ceremonial collective voice. I told him gently that they had expected him to be their spokesman and symbol, and this simply angered him further. "I'll resign," he said, "if I can't be myself!" Over time, he learned that leaders can rarely afford the luxury of speaking for themselves alone.

Most leaders become quite aware of the symbolic aspects of their roles and make effective use of them. One of the twentieth-century leaders who did so most skillfully was Gandhi.[12] In the issues he chose to do battle on, in the way he conducted his campaigns, in the jail terms and the fasting, in his manner of dress, he symbolized his people, their desperate need, and their struggle against oppression.

Needless to say leaders do not always function as benign symbols. In the Iran-Contra affair of 1986–87 it became apparent that men bound by their oath of office were lying to the public, lying to the Congress of the United States, and lying to one another. To some Americans they became symbols of all the falsehoods and betrayals committed by a distant and distrusted government.

Representing the Group

In quieter times (we love to imagine that there were quieter times) leaders could perhaps concentrate on their own followers. Today, representing the group in its dealings with others is a substantial leadership task.

It is a truism that all of the human systems (organizations, groups, communities) that make up the society and the world are increasingly interdependent. Virtually all leaders at every level must carry on dealings with systems external to the one in which they themselves are involved—tasks of representing and negotiating, of defending institutional integrity, of public relations. As one moves higher in the ranks of leadership, such chores increase.

It goes without saying that people who have spent their careers in the world of the specialist or within the boundaries of a narrow community (their firm, their profession) are often ill-equipped for such leadership tasks. The young potential leader must learn early to cross boundaries and to know many worlds. The attributes that enable leaders to teach and lead their own constituencies may be wholly ineffective in external dealings. Military leaders who are revered by their troops may be clumsy with civilians. The business leader who is effective within the business culture may be lost in dealing with politicians. A distinctive characteristic of the ablest leaders is that they do not shrink from external representation. They see the long-term needs and goals of their constituency in the broadest context, and they act accordingly. The most capable mayors think not just of the city but of the metropolitan area and the region. Able business leaders are alert to the political climate and to world economic trends.

The most remarkable modern example of a leader carrying out the representative function is Charles DeGaulle. DeGaulle has his detractors, but none can fail to marvel at his performance in successfully representing the once and future France-as-a-great-power at a time when the nation itself was a defeated, demoralized, enemy-occupied land. By his own commanding presence, he kept France's place at the table through the dark days. Years later Jean Monnet wrote:

> It took great strength of character for him, a traditional soldier, to cross the great dividing line of disobedience to orders from

above. He was the only man of his rank with the courage to do so; and in the painful isolation felt by those Frenchmen who had decided to continue the Allied struggle, DeGaulle's rare example was a source of great moral strength."[13]

Renewing

Chapter 12 concerns the task of renewing, so I deal with it very briefly here.

Leaders need not be renewers. They can lead people down old paths, using old slogans, toward old objectives. Sometimes that is appropriate. But the world changes with disconcerting swiftness. Too often the old paths are blocked and the old solutions no longer solve anything. DeGaulle, writing of France's appalling unpreparedness for World War II, said:

> The Army became stuck in a set of ideas which had had their heyday before the end of the First World War. It was all the more inclined that way because its leaders were growing old at their posts, wedded to errors that had once constituted their glory.[14]

Leaders must foster the process of renewal.

So much for the tasks of leadership. The individual with a gift for building a leadership team may successfully delegate one or another of those tasks to other members of the team. One function that cannot be delegated is that of serving as symbol. That the leader is a symbol is a fact, not a matter of choice. The task is to take appropriate account of that reality and to use it well in the service of the group's goals.

Another function that cannot be delegated entirely is the envisioning of goals. Unless the leader has a sense of where the whole enterprise is going and must go, it is not possible to delegate (or carry out personally) the other functions. To have "a sense of where the whole enterprise is going and must go" is, I am inclined to say, the very core and essence of the best leadership.

In a discussion of the tasks of leadership, a colleague of mine said, "I do not see 'enabling' or 'empowering' on the list. Aren't those the central tasks of leadership?" For those unfamiliar with contemporary discussions of leadership, I should explain that reference to *enabling* or *empowering* has become the preferred method of condensing into a single word the widely held conviction that the purpose of leaders is not to dominate nor diminish followers but to strengthen and help them to develop.

But enabling and empowering are not separable tasks. They require a variety of actions on the parts of leaders. For example:

- Sharing information and making it possible for followers to obtain appropriate kinds of education
- Sharing power by devolving initiative and responsibility
- Building the confidence of followers so that they can achieve their own goals through their own efforts
- Removing barriers to the release of individual energy and talent
- Seeking, finding, and husbanding the various kinds of resources that followers need
- Resolving the conflicts that paralyze group action
- Providing organizational arrangements appropriate to group effort

Any attempt to describe a social process as complex as leadership inevitably makes it seem more orderly than it is. Leadership is not tidy. Decisions are made and then revised or reversed. Misunderstandings are frequent, inconsistency inevitable. Achieving a goal may simply make the next goal more urgent: inside every solution are the seeds of new problems. And as Donald Michael has pointed out, most of the time most things are out of hand.[15] No leader enjoys that reality, but every leader knows it.

It would be easy to imagine that the tasks described are items to be handled separately, like nine items on a shopping list, each from a separate store. But the effective leader is always doing several tasks simultaneously. The best antidote to the shopping list conception is to look at the setting in which all the tasks are mingled—the complex interplay between leaders and those "led." That is the subject of the next chapter.

3

THE HEART OF THE MATTER: LEADER–CONSTITUENT INTERACTION

The relationship between leaders and followers varies from one culture to another. This chapter deals chiefly with the interaction as it occurs in the mainstream of American life.

The relationship also varies according to whether the organization or group is in a time of quiescence or crisis, in prosperity or recession, on a steep growth curve or stagnating.

One tends to think of leaders as belonging in one category and followers in quite a separate category. But most of our leaders are followers in other contexts, and followers often perform leaderlike acts. The factory manager may be a leader locally, but a follower in relation to the parent corporation. The college professor may be a leader in academic circles, yet a follower in community affairs.

The Role of Followers

Leaders are almost never as much in charge as they are pictured to be, followers almost never as submissive as one might imagine. That influence and pressure flow both ways is not a recent discovery. The earliest sociologists who wrote on the subject made the point. Max Weber (1864–1920), in discussing charismatic leaders, asserted that such leaders generally appear in times of trouble and that their followers exhibit "a devotion born of distress."[1] In other words, the state of mind of followers is a powerful ingredient in explaining the emergence of the charismatic leader.

Weber's great contemporary, Georg Simmel (1858–1918), was even more explicit, suggesting that followers have about as much influence on their leaders as their leaders have on them.[2] Leaders cannot maintain authority, he wrote, unless followers are prepared to believe in that authority. *In a sense, leadership is conferred by followers.* To say that followers have substantial influence on leaders sounds like the view of someone steeped in the democratic tradition. But Weber and Simmel were writing in pre–World War I Germany; their views were hardly the product of a populist environment.

As I suggested in chapter 1, even monarchs and dictators have discovered that it is costly to take measures that offend the deeply held beliefs of their subjects, and that it is substantially less costly to attain their ends in ways that do not offend. Corporate executives learn comparable lessons today. They learn to operate within the framework of the culture, which is to say within the limits people in the system can accept in terms of their norms, beliefs and expectations. Leaders can go against the grain of the culture, but not without cost.

Contemporary research confirms the two-way character of the relationship. It is this reciprocal aspect that underlies one of the soundest of political maxims: *good constituents tend to produce good leaders.*

There is a striking difference between the situation of political leaders and that of line executives in business or government. In the political process, constituents have a measure of choice—and leaders must compete for approval. In corporate and governmental bureaucracies employees are supposed to accept their superiors in the hierarchy as their leaders. But, of course, quite often they do not. The assumption by line executives that, given their rank and authority, they can lead without being leaders is one reason bureaucracies stagnate. As I pointed out earlier, *executives are given subordinates; they have to earn followers.*

The Masses

Given the well-established and honored role of constituents in our system, it is hard to resurrect the view of "the masses" that held sway throughout most of human history. Aristotle, Machiavelli, Le Maistre, and others contributed to the image of the masses as irrational, undisciplined, easily roused to emotion, prone to violence, needing and wanting to be led. It was widely accepted that any regime reposing power in the people would be inherently unstable and would end in one or another form of iron rule.

The error of the ancient view was to suppose that a society forsaking autocratic leadership had no other choice but to leap into the cauldron of mob rule. The architects of modern democracies saw that a society could move from coercive governance to a middle ground that still maintains the constraints of law and custom without which no society can function. Without such constraints, the ancient worries about instability are relevant.

Our Founding Fathers created a firm constitutional framework that specifies how "We, the people" should choose our representatives. And the institutions within which those representatives function are designed to preserve not only freedom but also balance and order.

Structure and Control

Whatever one may say about the influence of constituents, leaders continue to have a crucial role in the interaction. How should they play that role? It is a question that explodes into a thousand questions. Given our cultural framework, what patterns of leader–constituent interaction are most effective in accomplishing the purposes of the group? Does the group function most effectively when leaders make the decisions without consultation and impose their wills, or when they invite varying degrees of participation in the decision? The tension between the two approaches is nicely illustrated in a story (probably apocryphal) told of Woodrow Wilson when he was president of Princeton University. "How can I democratize this university," he demanded, "if the faculty won't do what I ask?"

Should there be a high degree of structure in the relationship—a sharp differentiation between the roles of leaders and followers, a clear hierarchy of authority with emphasis on detailed assignments and task specifications? Or should the relationship be more informal, less structured, with leaders making the goals clear and then letting constituents help determine the way of proceeding?

Should there be an atmosphere of discipline, constraints, controls—in Navy parlance, a tight ship—or should there be autonomy, individual responsibility and freedom for growth, with the leader in the role of nurturer, supporter, listener and helper?

Should the leader focus on the job to be done—task-oriented as the researchers put it—or should the leader be concerned primarily with the people performing the task, with their needs, their morale, their growth?

More than four decades of objective research have not produced dramatically clear answers to these questions, but they have yielded improved understanding of a set of very complicated relationships.

American industry was puzzled when it became acquainted with the relationship between leaders and followers in Japanese industry in the 1970s when Japan was beginning to outperform us in several industrial sectors. There would have been a lot more puzzlement if two generations of researchers had not enabled us to think in complex and imaginative ways about the leader–follower interaction, and prepared us to understand the alternatives to rigidly structured old-style leadership.[3]

One reason simple answers have not emerged from the research is that there are no simple answers, only complicated answers hedged by conditions and exceptions. Followers do like being treated with consideration, do like to have their say, do like a chance to exercise their own initiative—and participation does increase acceptance of decisions. But there are times when followers welcome rather than reject authority, want prompt and clear decisions from the leader, and want to close ranks around the leader. The ablest and most effective leaders do not hold to a single style; they may be highly supportive in personal relations when that is needed, yet capable of a quick, authoritative decision when the situation requires it.

Some work environments are so rigidly structured that they destroy workers' initiative, while others are so unstructured that the job never gets done. In the latter situation the workers themselves crave a clearer definition of goals, more orderly scheduling, better coordination, more precise assignments, and so on. Disorder is likely to produce demands for a more explicit framework of authority.

Again we must remind ourselves that in all of these matters cultural differences exist. Studies comparing Americans with various European and Asian nationalities have consistently shown a greater inclination of Americans to favor individualism, equality and participation and to exhibit discomfort with hierarchy and status differences.

Two-Way Communication

One generalization that is supported both by research and experience is that effective two-way communication is essential to proper functioning of the leader–follower relationship. It is a point that corporations have emphasized increasingly in recent years. There must be not only easy communication from leaders to constituents but also ample return communication, including dissent. Leaders, to be effective, must pick up the signals coming to them from constituents. And the rule is: If the messages from below say you are doing a flawless job, send back for a more candid assessment.

The huge complex organizations we have fashioned and the sophisticated control systems devised to manage that complexity reduce the amount of face-to-face communication between leaders and led. And we pay a heavy price for the reduction. In interactions involving motivation, trust and loyalty, a message on the computer terminal is not enough. Suggestion boxes are not enough. Employee polls are not enough. Nothing can substitute for a live leader (not necessarily the top leader) listening attentively and responding informally. There is more to face-to-face communication than the verbal component. The leader's style, timing and symbolic acts all carry messages—and demonstrate that messages are being received. Wise leaders are continuously finding ways to say to their constituents, "I hear you." I once headed an agency with over 100,000 employees, and later led an organization with 300,000 members. The effort to deal face to face with as many as possible was exhausting but paid large dividends.

An extremely gifted communicator such as Franklin D. Roosevelt was able to use the electronic media with an effectiveness that approached personal contact. In 1934 I encountered a friend, a construction worker, hurrying home after a hard day's work, and I asked "What's the rush?" He said, "President Roosevelt's fireside chat! I figure if he's willing to take the time to talk to me, the least I can do is be there." The simple earnestness of the reply expressed the hold that FDR had on his followers.

One hypothesis familiar to all who study leadership is that the leader gains by maintaining psychological distance from constituents—limiting access, accentuating status differences, and so on. DeGaulle is often cited as a proponent of this hypothesis. No doubt there are circumstances in which it is valid, but the research evidence is unclear.

Psychoanalytic Interpretations

Obviously any attempt to understand the leader–constituent relationship takes us onto psychological ground, and this may be as good a time as any to comment on psychoanalytic interpretations of leadership.

Much silliness had been perpetrated by shallow diagnoses of leaders based on one or another school of psychoanalysis. One is likely to be put off, for example, by Otto Fenichel's generalization that those who strive the hardest for power and prestige "are unconsciously frightened persons trying to overcome and deny their own anxiety."

Freud himself, when he wrote explicitly about leadership, tended to see it so exclusively through his own theoretical lens that much of the rich complexity of the subject was filtered out. For example, "We know that the great majority of people have a strong need for authority which they can admire, to which they can submit, and which dominates and sometimes even ill-treats them. . . . It is the longing for the father that lives in each of us from childhood days."

Some people no doubt want leadership for the reason suggested by Freud. Others may have no Freudian yearning to be dominated, but find that dependence on a leader absolves them of responsibility. Still others simply believe that things work better when designated people can be put in charge and held accountable.

But it would be a great mistake to reject psychoanalytic ideas, or "psychohistory" in general. Freud's thinking has made important contributions to our understanding of human behavior, and leadership is no exception. There can be no doubt that most of us have, hidden away, memories of the all-powerful, godlike persons who attended us in infancy, and that many of us grow up wanting to find again those comforters and magic helpers.

Many concepts drawn from psychology and psychoanalysis can be useful to the student of leadership. But to apply such notions to known leaders requires not only considerable sophistication in the use of the concepts but a scholar's willingness to master the historical situation in which the leader functioned. In this sense, Erik Erikson's books on Gandhi[4] and on Luther[5] are serious contributions.

The Multilevel Dialogue

In the most memorable conversations, the rational, verbal, conscious elements of the exchange are supplemented by communication at another level—nonrational, nonverbal, and unconscious. Words and sentences, tone of voice, body language, facial expression, timing, unfinished sentences, silences—all contribute to a multilevel dialogue. And so it is in the continuing conversation between leaders and followers.

Any social group, if it is more than a crowd of unrelated strangers, has shared needs, beliefs, aspirations, values, hopes and fears. The group creates norms that tend to control the behavior of its members, and these norms constitute the social order. It is in this context that leaders arise; and it is this context that determines what kinds of leaders emerge and what is expected of them. A loyal constituency is won when people, consciously or unconsciously, judge the leader to be capable of solving their problems and meeting their needs, when the leader is seen as symbolizing their norms, and when their image of the leader (whether or not it corresponds to reality) is congruent with their inner environment of myth and legend.

Effective leaders deal not only with the explicit decisions of the day —to approve a budget, announce a policy, discipline a subordinate—but also with that partly conscious, partly buried world of needs and hopes, ideals and symbols. They serve as models; they symbolize the group's unity and identity; they retell the stories that carry shared meanings. Their exemplary impact is great. There are messages for followers in what leaders pay attention to, in how they deal with critical incidents, in the correspondence between their words and acts, in the ethical tone of their behavior.

Edmund Wilson wrote:

> The poetry of Lincoln has not all been put into his writings. It was acted out in his life. . . . He created himself as a poetic figure, and he thus imposed himself on the nation.
>
> For the molding by Lincoln of American opinion was a matter of style and imagination as well as of moral authority, of cogent argument and obstinate will. . . . When we put ourselves back into the period, we realize that it was not at all inevitable to think of it as Lincoln thought.[6]

Sometimes one particular action taken by a leader speaks so dramatically to the concerns of a constituency that it overshadows the leader's day-to-day performance. In 1919 when Calvin Coolidge was governor of Massachusetts, he took vigorous action again a police strike, saying, "There is no right to strike against the public safety by anybody, anywhere, any time." A number of historians believe that one event took him all the way to the White House.

In 1912 Theodore Roosevelt spoke to a campaign audience for an hour and a half with an assassin's bullet lodged in his chest. Needless to say the incident became a powerful element in the T.R. legend. The same may be said of Ronald Reagan's joking on the way to the operating room after he had been shot.

Truly gifted leaders know not only what constituents need but also what they fear, what they long to be, what they like best about themselves. Woodrow Wilson said, "The ear of the leader must ring with the voices of the people."[7]

To analyze complex problems, leaders must have a capacity for rational problem solving; but they must also have a penetrating intuitive grasp of the needs and moods of followers. The ablest leaders understand, rationally and intuitively, the expectations of people with respect to their leadership. And they are adept at meeting those expectations not only with rational verbal pronouncements but also with symbolic acts, ritual observances, and the like.

The ten weeks between the election and inauguration of a new president rarely bring significant substantive news of programs to come. But it is the time when the president-elect puts together a team—and the release of the names can have an extraordinary symbolic impact. In late 1988, President-elect Bush had mentioned no more than three or four of his probable appointments before the press concluded that his administration would be pragmatic and middle-of-the-road, a marked shift from the heavy ideological cast of his predecessor. Nothing he could have said would have carried a clearer message than the symbolic effect of those early appointments.

Obviously, the two-way communication is enhanced when leaders and constituents share deep cultural ties. The principle was brought home to me vividly some years ago when I boarded a train from Boston to New York and found myself surrounded by a spirited throng of Notre Dame fans enroute to the Notre Dame–Army football game. One after another convivial stranger ("Hi, I'm Pat O'Toole!") urged me to join them in a festive drink. Then a buzz of excitement ran through the car—"He's coming!" And Boston's mayor, James Curley, made his way through the crowd. Curley was for the Irish of his city a symbol of their political triumphs, their memories of struggle, and their traditions as a people. He neither resigned nor lost support when he spent six months of one mayoral term in jail for mail fraud. I had met the mayor on earlier occasions, but in that lively railroad car I had for the first time a moving glimpse of the cultural ties that bound him to his people and them to him.

That leaders and followers share a culture (i.e., share norms and values) enhances communication between the two, but is not an unmixed blessing. When the system is in grave need of renewal, leaders who wear the same blinders as their followers may be of little help in renewing.

Perception and Reality

Leaders develop their styles as they interact with their constituencies. They move toward the style that seems most effective in dealing with the mixture of elements that make up their constituencies.

Conventional wisdom says that there is, on the one hand, the public image of the leader as perceived by followers; and on the other hand, the reality of what the leader truly is. But many researchers agree that how the followers perceive the leader is also reality—and in matters of leadership a more important reality than what the leader is really like. To complicate matters further, it is apparent in the life histories of more than a few great leaders that the real person and the person perceived by followers gradually merged, so that the question "What was the real person like?" became increasingly irrelevant.

Shaper and Shaped

The interaction outlined here, while quite familiar to those who study leadership, is at odds with many conventional notions. People who have not thought much about it are likely to believe that all influence originates with the leader, that the leader is the shaper, never the object of shaping by followers.

Having brought leaders down from that pedestal, one can all too readily fall into the opposite error of supposing that leaders are clay in the hands of followers. Not really. Leaders, because of their significant positions, because of their inevitable symbolic roles, because of their natural persuasive gifts, wield undeniable influence.

I have portrayed a relationship between leaders and constituents in which each is in some measure the shaper, and in some measure the shaped. Obviously the interaction does not always work in balance. Sometimes the leader rides roughshod over the expectations of the people. Sometimes leaders are trapped by their constituents. (Show me a legislator described as "the darling of the liberals" or "the darling of the conservatives," and I'll show you a legislator without options.)

Conflicting Demands

Many years ago Edmund Burke posed a memorable question: Should leaders in a representative form of government be no more than mirrors of their constituents' views, or should they arrive at their own best judgments, taking constituent opinion into account but not being bound by it? Burke himself was repelled by the first alternative because it left no room for the representative's own judgment and conscience. John Adams held a similar view. On one occasion when Adams was proposing unpopular legislation, he urged Congress not to be "palsied by the will of our constituents."

One is bound to admire the political figure who, when great principles are at stake, has the courage to defy his constituency. Sam Houston, hero of the Texas war of independence and one of the most colorful leaders this nation has ever produced, deliberately brought an end to his political career by opposing secession. In an unforgettable warning to his fellow southerners, he said, "Let me tell you what is coming. You may after the sacrifice of countless millions of treasure and hundreds of thousands of precious lives, as a bare possibility, win Southern independence, if God be not against you. But I doubt it."[8]

Admirable, but aside from such fateful moments our system is based on the presumption that political figures are reasonably responsive to their constituents.

Pluralistic Pressures

For years even-handed political scientists pointed out that there is and must always be tension between the two positions described by Burke, and that living, breathing politicians would necessarily move back and forth between the two. But the conditions of contemporary life have made the question itself a bit antiquated. As pointed out earlier, the politician must ask not "What does my constituency want?" but "What do each of my many constituencies want?" The actions that endear the leader to one constituency may anger another. Thus do the forces of a pluralistic society encourage the leader to show different faces to different constituencies or one enigmatic face to all.

One familiar and cynical view of leadership is that leaders do not lead the parade, but find out where it is going and get out ahead of it. For most leaders today, however, the single parade moving on an identifiable path is an anachronism. There are groups of constituents scurrying in every direction.

Beyond that, elected representatives must cope with the participation in the political process today of innumerable highly organized interest groups, many of them capable of bringing great benefit or harm to legislators and, therefore, capable of exerting great pressure on them. So legislators must consider the needs of their multiple constituencies, the demands of powerful interest groups, and finally, one hopes, their own best judgments.

One would like to think that somehow the resulting equation could be worked out in a manner compatible with integrity and sound public policy. But all too many public figures, their judgment befuddled by conflicting pressures or their character eroded by sell-outs, fail the test.

It is foolish to put all the blame on politicians. Each special interest represents a segment of the American people, sometimes a very narrow segment, sometimes very broad. So most of us are in one way or another involved in the multiple pressures that create for our politicians a life of impossible choices. We may properly demand rectitude and deplore lapses of integrity, but we must not pretend we are not implicated.

The moral dilemmas posed by multiple constituencies are not peculiar to politics. For the leader of a private welfare agency, for example, the major constituency is presumably the needy people served, but the rewards for the leader may come from pleasing some other constituency—perhaps the donors, perhaps the agency's governing board.

Trust

There is much to be gained for any leader in winning the trust of constituents. A leader capable of inspiring trust is especially valuable in bringing about collaboration among mutually suspicious elements in the constituency. The trust the contending groups have for such a leader can hold them together until they begin to trust one another.

It is not easy to sort out the ingredients of trust in leadership. I recall the senior partner of a law firm stressing to younger men and women in his firm the importance of client trust. One ambitious young lawyer asked how one went about winning trust, and the senior partner said dryly, "Try being trustworthy."

One of the most important prerequisites for trust in a leader is steadiness. The need for reliability is not only ethically desirable, it is generally a practical necessity. A leader who is unpredictable poses a nerve-wracking problem for followers. They cannot rally around a leader if they do not know where he or she stands. A businessman friend of mine, commenting on his congressman, said, "It isn't that he's crooked, it's just that I can't keep track of him. He's too swift for me—I wish he'd stay in one place."

For leaders seeking to win trust, another requirement is fairness—fairness when the issues are being openly adjudicated, and, equally important, fairness in the backroom. Contending elements seek private access to the leader, and if it is widely believed that such offstage maneuvering works, the system is in a constant turmoil of suspicion. Nothing is more surely stabilizing than confidence that the leader is unshakably fair in private as well as in public.

In public leadership another element in trust is reflected in the question "Is this person one of us—our ethnic group, our social class, our economic level, our religion?" It is not a criterion that philosophers of democracy like to think about, but every observer of politics recognizes it.

A factor that undermines the trust of constituents in their leaders today is the set of practices that someone has described as the engineering of consent. Political managers, through skilled use of the media, convey as reality whatever illusion suits their purposes.

Before condemning the practice, as I intend to do, let us acknowledge that the media illusionists are not introducing an unknown ingredient into the political mix. It is not new for leaders to polish up their image, nor is it new that what followers perceive to be real diverges from reality. Hobbes said that the reputation of power *is* power. Leaders understand. If Merlin of King Arthur's court were to reappear and say to all leaders, "Your followers have many misconceptions about you and I can eliminate all such misconceptions with a wave of my wand," most leaders would consider it a dreadfully risky proposition. They know that many of the misconceptions are to their advantage—perhaps fostered by them. Nor are followers sternly in love with truth. A great many prefer an illusion that comforts them to a reality that breeds anxiety.

What contemporary political media consultants have introduced is not a new art but an old art so highly developed that it changes the very nature of the political process. It works, but like all high-powered advertising that falsifies, it engenders a mixture of short-term acceptance and long-term cynicism. Successful seduction is one thing. Winning trust for a system that repeats endlessly the cycle of seduction and exploitation is something else.

Charismatic Leadership

Max Weber borrowed the term *charisma* from Rudolph Sohm, the church historian, who had in turn borrowed it from St. Paul. As the latter used it, the word referred to gifts or powers that were manifestations of God's grace. Weber used the term somewhat differently. "The term 'charisma' will be applied to a certain quality of an individual by virtue of which he is set apart from other men and treated as endowed with supernatural, superhuman or at least specifically exceptional powers or qualities."[9]

Clearly, Weber did not think of charisma as specifically a manifestation of God's grace. When one reflects on the fact that some profoundly evil people have met Weber's definition, one sees how far Weber took the concept from its original source. Weber emphasized the revolutionary quality of many charismatic leaders, and believed that they are particularly likely to emerge in times of physical, economic, religious or political distress. The truth is that almost any kind of leadership emerges more readily in times of distress, which is to say that it emerges when people need and want a leader.

In contrast to the all-enveloping bureaucracies Weber saw as the model toward which civilized society was moving, the charismatic leader rejects routine. But over time, Weber wrote, such a leader tends to run out of miracles and finds it necessary to organize and routinize to preserve power. Quite aside from the concept of charisma, this latter generalization is on target. The "man on a white horse" does inevitably move from dramatic personal leadership to bureaucratization—not because he runs out of miracles but because the only way to preserve power on a large scale is to organize and institutionalize.

The term *charisma* has not only survived over the many decades since Weber first used it, but has retained a good deal of its original meaning. Yet its usefulness and appropriate definition remain in doubt. Perhaps, if Weber had foreseen how it would catch the public fancy, he would have offered sharper criteria to distinguish charismatic from noncharismatic leaders. As Robert C. Tucker has pointed out, there is no scholarly consensus on the scientific worth or precise application of the term.[10]

Aside from Tucker and several other scholars (e.g., Edward Shils, David Apter), very few students of leadership have made integral use of the concept. In science and scholarship, the most valuable property of a concept is its usefulness to succeeding investigators in their further research and theorizing. Surveying the broad sweep of twentieth-century research and writing on leadership, one would have to say that the concept of the charismatic leader as Weber used the term has failed to meet that standard.

James MacGregor Burns points out quite correctly that the term *charisma* is surrounded by ambiguity and so variously used that "it is impossible to restore the word to analytical duty."[11] Common sense suggests that we drop the historical and theoretical baggage that comes with the word, and accept the fact that it is now part of the popular vocabulary, referring in a more or less uncomplicated way to the magnetism, persuasiveness, or nonrational appeal of certain people. In popular usage, the word is not limited to leaders. Speakers who hold their audiences spellbound, show business celebrities who leave their fans weak-kneed, and almost any variety of magniloquent blowhard may be spoken of as charismatic. St. Paul would find it all quite puzzling.

To the extent that the word *charisma* has any use at all in serious contemporary discussions of leadership, it should probably be confined to leader–constituent relationships in which the leader has an exceptional gift for inspirational, nonrational communication, and the followers' response is characterized by awe, reverence, devotion, or emotional dependence.

Strengthening Followers

If both leaders and constituents are significant actors in the relationship, we must talk not only about failures of leadership but also about failures of followership. There is a vast literature on the failures of leadership—on the abuse of power, injustice, indecisiveness, shortsightedness, and so on. Who will write the essay on individual and collective failures among followers? When it is written the essay will have to cover two matters at some length.

First, there are qualities such as apathy, passivity, cynicism, and habits of spectatorlike noninvolvement that invite the abuse of power by leaders. Bertrand de Jouvenel said, "A society of sheep must in time beget a government of wolves."

Second, there is the inclination of followers in some circumstances to collaborate in their own deception. Given the familiar fact that what people want and need often determines what they see and hear, the collaboration comes easily. But a citizenry that wants to be lied to will have liars as leaders. Have we not tested that generalization at every level of government?

Rather than dwell on the failings, we would do well to focus on how to ensure better performance. Perhaps the most promising trend in our thinking about leadership is the growing conviction that the purposes of the group are best served when the leader helps followers to develop their own initiative, strengthens them in the use of their own judgment, enables them to grow, and to become better contributors. Industrial concerns are experimenting with such an approach because of their hard-won awareness that some matters (for example, quality control, productivity, morale) simply cannot be dealt with unless lower levels of leadership are actively involved. This is a subject to which I shall return.

To the extent that leaders enable followers to develop their own initiative, they are creating something that can survive their own departure. Some individuals who have dazzling powers of personal leadership create dependency in those below them and leave behind a weakened organization staffed by weakened people. Leaders who strengthen their people may create a legacy that will last for a very long time.

* * *

I have already pointed out that the interaction between leaders and constituents or followers does not take place in a vacuum. It is embedded in a historical or cultural context. It has an institutional setting. And these surrounding circumstances substantially affect not only the nature of the interaction but also the leadership attributes that are effective. In the next two chapters we shall look at both contexts and attributes.

4

CONTEXTS

Several questions come up insistently in any discussion of leadership. One of the most popular is "What qualities do leaders have that others do not?" One thinks of the commanding presence of Douglas MacArthur, the eloquence of Martin Luther King, Jr., the vision of Thomas Jefferson, the spiritual force of Mohandas Gandhi, the shrewd statecraft of Elizabeth I.

For many years, those who conducted research on leadership sought to identify universal traits of leaders, but it proved to be a frustrating quest. In 1948 Ralph Stogdill, in an exhaustive survey of the research done up to that date, demonstrated that the studies had simply not succeeded in identifying traits that characterize leaders.[1] What F. E. Fiedler and many others showed in the years following the Stogdill survey is that the attributes which make for effective leadership depend on the situation in which the leader is functioning.[2]

There are no traits that guarantee successful leadership in all situations. The leader of a university faculty may have quite different attributes from the commander of a military attack team. The qualities required of a legislative leader are not those required of a religious leader. This is not to say that the setting or context is everything and the attributes of the indivdual nothing. What produces a good result, as I suggested earlier, is the combination of a particular context and an individual with the appropriate qualities to lead in that context.

In this chapter I seek to show through a number of examples how context and attributes come together to produce leadership performances. In the following chapter I shall focus on attributes.

Contexts and Settings

Haile Selassie of Ethiopia, fighting to defend his country against Italian military aggression, was working in one kind of context. Benito Juarez of Mexico, the full-blooded Indian who set out to modernize a traditional society dominated by the Roman Catholic Church and the military, worked in a wholly different context.

Settings differ in the degree of support they provide for the leader. The infantry lieutenant leading a platoon in combat is supported in innumerable ways. The immediate situation may be hazardous and insecure, but regulations, tradition and group cohesion all support the leader. In contrast, the peasant farmer in a developing country who protests a government action may be totally without institutional support, acting without precedent, lacking any assurance of allies.

Obviously leaders are likely to look best when the context is supportive. But there are stunning examples of leadership in settings that are distinctly unsupportive. When Florence Nightingale arrived in the Crimea on the assignment that made her famous, she faced conditions that would have daunted a lesser figure: on the one hand, a flood of casualties, a totally unacceptable death rate, and scandalously bad provision for the sick and wounded; on the other hand, a military command that bitterly resented the intrusion of a woman into their male world and frustrated her whenever possible. Yet she prevailed.

The Founding of a Nation

Virtually all Americans who have reflected on the nation's history have at one time or another asked themselves what accounted for the emergence in eighteenth-century America of a generation of leaders since unequalled in this country. Much of the answer lies in the context of the times.

In the last four decades of the eighteenth-century the sense of history surrounding the events of the day was intense, the need for leadership urgent and compelling. The key actors in the drama had been handed a shaping role in history and they knew it. In the creation of the new nation, the clay was awaiting the hand of the potter. "These are the hard times in which a genius would wish to live" wrote that remarkable woman, Abigail Adams. "Great necessities call forth great leaders."[3]

The future leaders spent their formative years either in rural areas, in towns, or in what we would now regard as very small cities. In just such intimate settings young leaders are most likely to find their feet and test their abilities.

Given leadership gifts, there was no long, tortuous road to acceptance. Nor had there yet developed the many competing outlets for talent that exist today. Political leadership was one of the few paths to distinction.

Thanks to the intellectual climate in which they were nurtured, the leaders of the day were afflicted with no trace of fatalism. They believed that the locus of responsibility was in them and saw themselves as shapers of the future. And they shared a set of values and philosophical views—the ideas and spirit of what Henry Steele Commager has called "the American Enlightenment."[4]

Although many young people grew up in that historical context, only a few had personal attributes that ensured their emergence as great leaders. I shall mention just one for whom context and personal attributes combined to make history.

More than most of the great figures in American's early days, George Washington was a natural leader in the popular sense of that phrase—a person whose combination of physical presence, vitality, self-possession and strength led others to turn to him. The challenges that called forth those leadership gifts came at two quite separate periods of his life.

In his youth the French and Indian Wars were a vivid reality for Virginians, and the frontier and wilderness were a step away. At the age of 20, Washington became a major in the Virginia militia and led a scouting party into the wilderness. A year or so later he was sent out again, this time in command of two companies. As a result of a victory over the French he was promoted to colonel, and after still another bloody engagement was appointed commander of all the Virginia troops—a considerable achievement for a young man in his mid-twenties.

At age twenty-six, Washington began the second phase of his career, devoting fifteen years to the development and expansion of his plantation. But a greater challenge was looming. He was one of the Virginia legislators who met at the Raleigh Tavern in May 1774 and called for a Continental Congress, and he was one of the delegates when the Congress met in September.

What had been added to Washington's natural leadership qualities as he matured were wisdom and steadiness, a patience and evenhandedness that enabled him to stand above the intense rivalries among other leaders of the new nation. These qualities made him, in James Flexner's phrase, "the indispensable man."[5] The Second Continental Congress, meeting after hostilities had begun at Lexington and Concord, elected him commander in chief of all the colonial forces.

Bureaucracy

Given the role that large-scale organizations—governmental, corporate, or nonprofit—play in contemporary life, considerable interest attaches to their characteristics as a context for leadership. No doubt there are fewer spontaneous leaderlike acts in that context than one might expect in less highly structured settings. Hierarchy, impersonality, an intricate pattern of specialized roles and the extent to which behavior is determined by the position one occupies—all tend to diminish the likelihood of leaderlike action at all levels of organization. But, as students of bureaucracy have found, the formal institutional structure has only a limited capacity to suppress the informal exercise of leadership.

I was once a member of a committee appointed by what was then called the War Department to look at the personnel systems of the military services. After an admiral had spent an hour explaining the promotion system in the navy, a colleague of mine said, "It seems awfully cumbersome and impersonal." The admiral laughed and said, "It would be if it worked according to the book. Perhaps I had better tell you how it actually works." And he then proceeded to describe the informal process by which officers interpreted "the book," developed unwritten procedures, and made it all work. The impersonal bureaucracy turned out to be a very lively scene of personalized leadership.

I return to this subject in chapter 8, Large-Scale Organized Systems.

Legislatures

Among the contexts in which leadership is exercised, none is more interesting than the American legislative body. I have in mind not how legislators lead their constituents but how they rise to leadership of the legislature itself.

As with any formal institution, a legislature is a system that has its own principles of functioning. Idealists are rather scornful of the notion that a new member of the legislature must learn the "rules of the club"; but if new members hope to rise to leadership roles, that is precisely what they must do—as they would in any other institution. They must learn how the system functions, even if it is their intention to beat the system.

As in all other contexts, those who seek to lead in the work of the legislature must understand the needs of their colleagues and be responsive to them. They must know the motives of those whom they would influence, build networks of allies, keep open many channels of information, and interact effectively with all groups relevant to their work. Wilbur Mills, famed as an autocratic chairman of the Ways and Means Committe in the 1960s, and one of the ablest legislators I have ever known, consulted with colleagues meticulously before he took a position.

Where legislative leaders tend to differ from leaders in many other institutions is in their necessary attention to the brokering and negotiating aspects of leadership. The prime task of legislators, of course, is to achieve results that reconcile multiple conflicting interests, and to deal with those vexing circumstances in which equally worthy groups want mutually incompatible things. That requires coalition building and mediating. This honorable and necessary function often requires the skills of a horse trader and the capacity to persuade, cajole, threaten and endear. The leader in this context knows how to reward and punish, how to build networks of obligation, how to amass credits by doing favors and how to call in the credits when needed.

In this fast-moving market environment filled with shrewd manipulators, a high value is placed on trust, keeping commitments, and returning favors punctiliously. Machiavellian principles defeat themselves: unscrupulous members tend to end up isolated. Candor is valued because it enhances predictability, and legislators do not like to be surprised. Throughout thirty-four years in Congress—the last sixteen as Senate majority leader—Mike Mansfield led through his capacity to inspire trust. Character was his stock-in-trade. And so it continued to be for his dozen years as ambassador to Japan.

The Surprise of Harry Truman

It is an old story that unexpected demands sometimes reveal unsuspected strengths; but rarely has the story played itself out more dramatically than in the case of Harry S Truman. The historic context offered the perfect challenge to a potential leader, but could the plain man from Missouri rise to the challenge?

By ordinary measures, he was a success before he became president, rising from a farm background and early failure as a haberdasher to become one of the most respected members of the United States Senate. But that is a long step from historic greatness, and when Roosevelt's death made Truman the nation's chief executive he was, as *The New*

York Times later commented, "without experience, without knowledge, without prestige."

In 1952, the final year of his presidency, he listened as Winston Churchill recalled their first meeting at the Potsdam Conference in the summer of 1945: "I must confess, sir, I held you in very low regard. I loathed your taking the place of Franklin Roosevelt. I misjudged you badly. Since that time, you more than any other man have saved Western civilization."[6]

Jean Monnet put his finger on one of Truman's key attributes, "the ability to decide. . . . He never hesitated in the face of great decisions."[7] Those decisions included the use of the atomic bomb on Japan; initiation of a massive airlift to counter the Soviet blockade of West Berlin; the United States' swift intervention following the Communist invasion of South Korea; and the firing of General Douglas MacArthur. Of course, what was involved was not only decisiveness but also good judgment. If all his moves had turned out badly, we would not be praising his decisiveness.

Interdependence

The very nature of the contemporary world provides certain constraints for leaders. One such constraint is the increasing interdependence of social systems and the unwillingness of sovereign states to acknowledge that reality. But it was in just this frustrating context that the special gifts of Jean Monnet could flower.

The son of a family of brandy makers of Cognac, France, Monnet was involved over a fifty-year period in the most significant international collaborative efforts of his day, and crowned his career with the design and establishment of the European Common Market and the European Community (now known as the European Communities). His vision was broad, and he had a formidable capacity to go to the heart of problems. He was shrewd in enlisting as allies many of the most gifted and powerful individuals of his day, in and out of government.

Monnet seems to have had little or no need for power, glory or status. He did not seek lofty official positions. He had little talent for public presentations of ideas, but in private his lucidity, patient purposefulness and capacity to gain trust made him a formidable advocate and an immensely able negotiator. He understood priorities and focused tenaciously on the most crucial questions. "I am not an optimist," he once wrote. "I am simply persistent. . . . I can wait a long time for the right moment. In Cognac they are good at waiting. It is the only way to make good brandy."[8]

Growing Up With a Revolution

Still another example of how context and personal attributes combine to produce a leadership performance is the case of Indira Gandhi. Family lineage and historical events set the stage for her career. But her personal attributes added dramatic elements.

Her whole life and career were intertwined with India's struggle for independence. Her mother, father, and paternal grandfather were all active in the cause of independence. As a three-year-old she marched her dolls in make-believe demonstrations. One visitor, who arrived at her front door asking for her parents, was told "I'm sorry but mama and papa are in jail." At age twelve she formed a children's organization to smuggle messages past British sentries. After college she became an active member of the Congress party, and on one occasion was imprisoned for more than a year for leading an anti-British demonstration.

When her father Jawaharlal Nehru became the first prime minister of independent India, she became his official hostess and trusted advisor, and at the age of forty-two was elected president of the Congress party. There is some evidence that when the party's old guard selected her as prime minister they believed that she was malleable—a spectacular miscalculation. She proved not only strong-minded but also politically popular. From that point on her career was often stormy, alternating triumphs and troubles, until she was assassinated in 1984. Whatever the merits of her policies, she was never less than formidable as a leader.

Of her leadership, one could say that the historical context provided the opportunity and her family background schooled her for the role, but finally it was her own inner strength that made her a major and controversial figure for over two decades.

Large-Scale Industrial Organization

As modern patterns of large-scale organization came to full flower in the early twentieth century, they provided a new and challenging context for leadership, offering exciting opportunities and considerable hazards. In that new context there emerged two of the most gifted corporate leaders we have ever had, Alfred P. Sloan, Jr., and Theodore Vail.

At the end of World War I, Ford Motor Company dominated the automotive industry. Under Sloan's direction, General Motors Corporation overtook Ford to occupy a commanding lead in the marketplace.

Sloan, who thought about organization in clear conceptual terms, initiated a policy that was often called decentralization but was much more sophisticated than that word implies. He saw that what was needed in a large-scale organization was a combination of strategies that would give a substantial measure of freedom, responsibility and authority to operating managers and at the same time provide a necessary degree of central direction. At the time, it was a highly innovative approach.

Sloan had many of the qualities useful to leaders—brains, vigor, a commanding style, the capacity to win loyalty and much more. But the key to his leadership was that he saw more clearly than any of his contemporaries the possibilities and liabilities of large-scale industrial organization. He saw its potential financial strength and the capacity to dominate markets; but he also saw the potential suppressive effect of large organization on motivation and creativity. The times were ripe for a man who could think imaginatively about the great corporate entities that were being created—and Sloan was the man.

Theodore Vail headed the American Telephone and Telegraph Company from 1907 to 1920. Of the great trusts created in the late nineteenth and early twentieth centuries, AT&T was the only one that survived attack by the trust busters. And its survival was wholly due to Vail's wise leadership.

His approach was spectacularly at odds with the philosophy of capitalists of his day. He embraced regulation: "Regulation should be effective, equitable, acceptable to the public, and final."[9] He advocated the formation of public service commissions, and directed the heads of his affiliated companies to help make the regulatory process effective. "All utilities are dependent . . . upon the public good will and favor."[10]

As Peter Drucker put it, Vail saw that the only way to keep Bell a private company was "to stand for the public interest more forcefully than any public agency could." He saw that "the business of the Bell Company must be anticipation and satisfaction of the service requirements of the public."[11]

Vail's early work as head of the U.S. Post Office's railway mail service showed that he had a keen eye for organization and a talent for management. But his most striking leadership attribute was his largeness of vision. He saw the alternative futures for his company in starkly realistic terms. He understood politics and government policy and comprehended the degree to which government antitrust activity was driven by pressure from a hostile public.

It was not only in regulatory matters that his vision had great consequences. He saw, as few in all of American industry then saw, that scientific and technological research would pay off heavily. Many of his colleagues in the company found it hard to accept his consistently generous support of Bell Laboratories, but he laid the groundwork for its emergence as a research center of extraordinary distinction.

Midlevel Leadership

In earlier chapters I have emphasized that in healthy systems midlevel leadership must function effectively, ensuring that there is vitality throughout the system and not just at the top. Yet so far in this series of examples I have cited only top-level leaders. Let us look at an instance from the upper-middle level.

In this case, the historical moment provided the opportunity. In 1945–1946, the wartime alliance between the Soviet Union and the Western powers dissolved with alarming swiftness. The Cold War was a reality and our policy toward the USSR was unsettled. How were we to understand this surly and threatening ex-ally? What should our policy be? It was the perfect moment for a confident, clear voice to speak up, and the voice came not from the top of our foreign policy apparatus but from an upper-middle-level foreign service officer, far from headquarters. In response to a query from Washington, George Kennan, then charge d'affaires in our embassy in Moscow, filed his legendary "long telegram" offering a lucid and persuasive analysis of the present and future of East-West relations.[12]

Kennan not only influenced his superiors in the State Department and White House, but later had a substantial impact on the informed public through a memorable article signed "X" in the journal *Foreign Affairs*. Though the policy of containment he espoused has been the subject of much controversy, the episode stands as an extraordinary example of leadership through the sheer force of ideas—ideas shaped in a context of action and relevant to future action. It helped that Kennan possessed not only remarkable intellectual and policy gifts but also an exceptional capacity for clear expression.

The Civil Rights Movement

The movement toward racial justice, so agonizingly slow in the half century following the Emancipation Proclamation (1863) and the Fourteenth Amendment (1868), began to develop momentum after the founding of the National Association for the Advancement of Colored People (1910). Both world wars stimulated massive movements of blacks into northern cities. In 1941 President Roosevelt banned racial discrimination in defense industries and later President Truman ordered the desegregation of the armed forces. The Supreme Court's ruling against "separate but equal" schools came in 1954.

Great events were in train. Martin Luther King, Jr., had not set them in motion, but he responded in a more compelling fashion than any of the other black leaders of his time. Now that King is securely established as a commanding historical figure, his contemporaries are loath to remember the rivalries, the controversies and the attacks on him from within the ranks of the movement itself. Some thought he was intoxicated by confrontation and moving too fast. Young black militants, referring to him as "De Lawd," scorned his adherence to nonviolence. This is not to say that he stood alone. He had many able allies, most of whom will never get the credit they deserve.

King had a far broader and deeper philosophical view than most of his contemporaries. He had an eloquence that none could match. And he had unflinching courage. He risked death many times before he was assassinated in 1968.

In their times of greatest intensity, movements are likely to have charismatic leaders, and it is easy for onlookers to believe that the leaders alone are responsible for all that happens. But movement leadership is subject to the general rule that historical performances come from great opportunities greatly met. It does not in any way diminish King's greatness to say that the time was ripe.

5

ATTRIBUTES

One could go on forever examining the diversity of contexts, and the ways in which individuals with attributes appropriate to those contexts rise to greatness. The interplay between context and personal attributes is easy to grasp, and people accept it quite readily. But then they return to their unquenchable curiosity about the characteristics of leaders.

We need not be unresponsive to that curiosity. There is in fact much to be said. The probability is greater than chance that leaders in one situation will be leaders in another situation. So there is no reason why, with appropriate prudence, we should not discuss attributes often associated with one or another kind of leadership. The attributes that follow are not present in every leader. The importance of the attribute to effective leadership varies with the situation. With these cautions—and any others that may occur to the reader—let us proceed.

I have drawn upon the writings of Ralph Stogdill, Bernard Bass,[1] Edwin P. Hollander,[2] and others who have reviewed the extensive body of research in the field. The reader may want to add items to the list or to describe an attribute in terms other than I have used.

1. *Physical Vitality and Stamina.* If one asks people to list the attributes of leaders, they are not likely to mention a high energy level or physical durability. Yet these attributes are essential. Top leaders have stamina and great reserves of vitality. Even the leader of a neighborhood organization is apt to stand far above the average in sheer energy—energy to convene meetings after a hard day's work, to chair long and heated

debates, to represent groups before the city council, and so on. Leaders may suffer from a physical disability (e.g., Franklin D. Roosevelt's poliomyelitis) or episodes of illness (e.g., Eisenhower's heart attack) but they cannot over any significant period of time lack vitality.

Most of Julius Caesar's extraordinary gifts have been commented on but his energy is rarely mentioned. Conquering Gaul and at the same time writing books about it, invading Britain, chasing Pompey across the Adriatic, fighting the political battles of Rome, dallying with Cleopatra and countless less famous ladies—it must have taken energy!

2. *Intelligence and Judgment-in-Action.* There are bright people who lack judgment altogether (which may be the source of the observation that "there's nothing worse than a stupid person with a brilliant mind"). There are able analysts who cannot move from analysis to action. And then there is the failing General Carl Spaatz had in mind when he said of one of his fellow officers in World War II, "He thinks things through very carefuly before he goes off half-cocked." Such people are unlikely to attain leadership.

Some years ago, in conversation with a chief executive officer who had been on the job for six months, I asked his opinion of the second-in-command he had inherited. He said, "He's a superb crisis manager, which is fortunate because his lack of judgment leads to a lot of crises."

Judgment is the ability to combine hard data, questionable data and intuitive guesses to arrive at a conclusion that events prove to be correct. Judgment-in-action includes effective problem solving, the design of strategies, the setting of priorities and intuitive as well as rational judgments. Most important, perhaps, it includes the capacity to appraise the potentialities of coworkers and opponents.

James Madison, standing five feet, four inches tall and weighing about 100 pounds, did not have a commanding presence and was not an effective public speaker. Yet, in his mid-thirties he was one of the most—some say *the* most—important contributor to the design of our political system. He understood how to translate our ideals into a system that worked, and he had the keen political sense and purposefulness to work with others toward a good result.

3. *Willingness (Eagerness) to Accept Responsibilities.* This attribute is the impulse to exercise initiative in social situations, to bear the burden of making the decision, to step forward when no one else will.

On March 5, 1770, a confrontation between British soldiers and a crowd of Bostonians led to the death of five colonists—the so-called Boston Massacre. Fearing popular anger, three lawyers in succession refused to serve as defense counsel. John Adams thought it of great importance that the guilt or innocence of the soldiers be determined by a fair trial. Despite the fact that he was an influential member of the people's party, anything but sympathetic to the Crown, he believed it was his responsibility to accept the defense assignment.

A less dramatic example: When Golda Meir, later prime minister of Israel, was eleven years old and living in Milwaukee, she organized the American Young Sisters Society, a group of schoolgirls who raised funds for children who could not pay the nominal sum charged for textbooks in the Milwaukee public schools.[3] That she should have regarded it as her responsibility spoke of leadership in the bud.

4. *Task Competence*. Researchers on leadership use the phrase to mean the knowledge a leader has of the task at hand. Columbus was not just a man with a burning mission; he said of himself with considerable modesty, "The Lord hath blessed me abundantly with a knowledge of marine affairs."[4] At the other extreme, Winston Churchill's father, Randolph, was appointed chancellor of the exchequer for the most political of reasons. He did not increase his standing when, on being shown a balance sheet, he waved a finger at the decimal points and said, "I could never make out what those damned dots meant."[5]

A more serious example: On a flight to California in my third month as a Cabinet officer, I found myself sitting next to a hard-bitten lobbyist whom I knew well, and I showed him a piece of regulatory legislation to be voted on in Congress that day. We were certain to win and I was elated—but my seat companion cured that. After reading the bill he said: "That's the kind of legislation your opponents love. If they blocked all action on your part they would look bad. Much better to give you this legislation with its vague definition of the practices to be outlawed and its loose enforcement provisions. You'll feel you've won something and they'll know you haven't." I still had a lot to learn.

Obviously the knowledge required varies at different levels of leadership. The lowest levels must have intimate knowledge of the task at hand. Top-level leaders cannot hope to have competence in more than a few of the matters under their jurisdicaiton, but they must have knowledge of the whole system over which they preside, its mission, and the environment in which it functions.

5. *Understanding of Followers/Constituents and Their Needs*. Leaders must understand the various constituencies with whom they work. The late Bear Bryant of the University of Alabama, one of the all-time greats among college football coaches, once said to me, "I know my players better than they know themselves. How else could I get the best out of them?"

6. *Skill in Dealing with People.* This is obviously related to *intelligence and judgment-in-acion*, as well as to *understanding of followers.* At the heart of skill in dealing with people is social perceptiveness—the ability to appraise accurately the readiness or resistance of followers to move in a given direction, to know when dissension or confusion is undermining the group's will to act, to make the most of the motives that are there, and to understand the sensitivities. I once hired a middle manager solely on the basis of high verbal intelligence. His skills with people proved to be virtually nonexistent. He made ill-considered and hasty promises. He was bumptious but not brave, obsequious to superiors, ungracious to peers, and given to nasty altercations with subordinates. It was a lesson for me.

7. *Need to Achieve.* No one who has known leaders or read extensively in the lives of leaders can have missed the evidence of driving pressure to achieve. When Abraham Lincoln was twenty-nine, he addressed the Young Men's Lyceum in Springfield, Illinois. Noting that the field of glory of the Founding Fathers was already harvested, he said: "But new reapers will arise . . . men of ambition and talent will . . . continue to spring up among us." And he made it clear that they would not work on tasks already done. "Towering genius disdains a beaten path. It seeks regions unexplored."[6] Students of Lincoln do not doubt that even then he was dreaming of greatness.

Early in life, John Adams said, "Let Love and Vanity be extinguished and the great Passions of Ambition and Patriotism break out and burn." Ironically, it was almost certainly the love of Abigail that mitigated his deepest insecurities and freed him to pursue the "great Passions."[7]

8. *Capacity to Motivate.* More than any other attribute, this is at the heart of the popular notion of leadership—the capacity to move people to action, to communicate persuasively, to strengthen confidence. Churchill was one of the most spectacular examples of the leader-as-motivator. Communication is, of course, the prime instrument of the leader/motivator, and all leaders take their communicating seriously. One of his closest friends said that Churchill spent a good part of his life rehearsing impromptu speeches. One day his valet, having drawn his master's bath shortly before, heard Churchill's voice booming out from the bathroom. The valet stuck his head in to find out if anything was needed. Churchill, immersed in the bathtub, said "I was not speaking to you, Norman, I was addressing the House of Commons."[8]

9. *Courage, Resolution, Steadiness.* Clearly a leader needs courage—not just bravery of the moment but courage over time, not just

willingness to risk, but to risk again and again, to function well under prolonged stress, to survive defeat and keep going.

Few stories of moral courage are more convincing than that of Anne Hutchinson. The Massachusetts Bay Colony of the 1630s was a stern theocracy, and it was dangerous even for a man to disagree with established church doctrine. Hutchinson not only disagreed, she organized women's discussion groups to explore the areas of disagreement. Put on trial for heresy, she was not given the right to introduce evidence in her own defense, and her defense witnesses were bullied. Excommunicated and banished from the colony, she led her band of followers to Roger Williams's Colony of Rhode Island and then set up her own community. She was a leader.

So was Daniel Webster. Both abolitionists and secessionists were bitterly opposed to the Compromise of 1850, but Senator Webster from the passionately abolitionist state of New Hampshire advocated it and his great seventh of March speech ensured its passage. He knew that he was signing his political death warrant. To friends who tried to hold him back Webster said he had decided "to push my skiff off from the shore alone."[9] The vilification that greeted him was predictable. Horace Mann described him as "A fallen star: Lucifer descending from Heaven."[10] His political career was over, and two years later he died.

As one observer said of leaders, "They *never* give up." It is not possible to overstate the value of steadiness in leadership. Individuals and groups who wish to align themselves with a leader find it hard to do so if the leader shifts position erratically, whether from emotional instability, duplicity or flagging determination. Leaders symbolize many things, among them the capacity of the whole group to stay the course.

10. *Capacity to Win and Hold Trust.* Some leaders have an extraordinary capacity to win trust. General George C. Marshall had the capacity and, as in the case of George Washington, it was a virtually invisible gift. The leader who can win a battle, dazzle an audience or smash electoral opposition has something the journalists and historians can write about. How many have ever written about the bonds of trust that Washington and Marshall forged so quietly?

11. *Capacity to Manage, Decide, Set Priorities.* As British educator Eric Ashby has pointed out, "Indecisiveness is contagious." Leaders must decide. And they must perform from time to time one or another of the traditional tasks of management—formulating goals, setting priorities, framing a course of action, selecting aides, and delegating. Though many leaders are not managers in the conventional sense of the word, they all benefit by having some of the skills of managers. General

William J. Donovan, first head of the Office of Strategic Services in World War II, had about as little interest in managing as any leader I ever knew—but he had the wisdom to surround himself with men who were very gifted managers.

12. *Confidence*. There is a romantic notion that the best leaders do not thrust themselves forward but are sought out. In reality, almost all young leaders nominate themselves—over and over, if necessary. They win recognition through a series of acts of presumption. As Edwin P. Hollander puts it, they have a sense of assurance in exercising positive influence, a confidence that others will react affirmatively.[11] It requires confidence to take the risks that leaders take, and confidence to handle the hostility that leaders must absorb. Acclaim and derision are the rewards of leadership. The laurel is interlaced with poison ivy. In his last letter to Jefferson, George Washington said, "I had no conception . . . that every act of my administration would be tortured . . . in such exaggerated form and indecent terms as could scarcely be applied to a Nero, a notorious defaulter or even a common pickpocket."[12]

13. *Ascendance, Dominance, Assertiveness*. The individuals successful in leadership roles are apt to have a fairly strong impulse to take charge. Their assertiveness does not necessarily conform to the stereotype of the visibly forceful leader—some are quiet and unspectacular—but whatever their outward styles, their impulse is to leave their thumbprints on events. Theodore Roosevelt was possibly the most vividly assertive leader in our history. One contemporary observer said, "Theodore Roosevelt was second only to Niagara Falls as an American phenomenon."[13]

14. *Adaptability, Flexibility of Approach*. It was said of Kemal Atatürk, the greatest figure in modern Turkish history, that he could shift swiftly and without second thought from a failing tactic to another approach, and if that did not work, to still another. Whether the field of action was war or diplomacy or domestic governance, he rarely clung stubbornly to an approach that was not producing results. His goals were stable but his tactics flexible.

One could extend the list of leadership attributes. Available research suggests other important qualities. But the preceding items surely rank among the most important. In any case, the research has demonstrated over and over that we must not think rigidly or mechanically about the attributes of leaders. The attributes required of a leader depend on the kind of leadership being exercised, the context, the nature of followers, and so on.

Illusion and Reality

No doubt even in ancient times people occasionally confused style and substance, choosing as a leader someone who looked the part or talked the part but could not be the part. Most observers would agree that the temptation to be seduced by style has been enhanced by the pervasive force of the media in our lives. To be fair to the media, they can be used to reveal as well as conceal, to enlighten as well as confuse. Clearly they heighten the impact of image, appearance and style as against substance. I touched on the subject earlier but must reemphasize it in this context.

Today the aspirant to political office is likely to seek out quite early the advice of a professional image maker. If funds are available, there begins an elaborate process of information management and behavior modification designed to place before the voting public something other than the real man or woman who seeks the office. *The Washington Post* described how Senator Robert Dole submitted himself to the process as practiced by Dorothy Sarnoff whose firm, Speech Dynamics, specializes in such matters. "He was a wonderful student," said Sarnoff. "We change behavior very, very fast."[14] Susan Peterson, another "media trainer" who has worked with members of Congress says, "Ultimately, if I have done my job right, they will look completely untrained."[15]

Ghostwritten speeches, skillfully produced television spots and ingeniously contrived photo opportunities contribute to a manufactured product. So the public (even the reasonably well-informed public) is deprived of the opportunity so cherished in a free society to exercise its native judgment in choosing the candidate who meets its needs. It knows its needs. But it does not know the candidates—only skillfully manufactured facsimiles thereof. Thus is the very idea of popular sovereignty mocked. We have the right to choose among illusions. And who manufactures the illusions? Not the general run of citizens, we may be sure. The manufacture of illusions is expensive business.

6

POWER

I pointed out earlier that leadership and power are not the same thing. But they interweave at many points. Power is the capacity to ensure the outcomes one wishes and to prevent those one does not wish.

In this country—and in most other democracies—power has such a bad name that many good people persuade themselves they want nothing to do with it. The ethical and spiritual apprehensions are understandable. But one cannot abjure power.

Power as we are now speaking of it—power in the social dimension—is simply the capacity to bring about certain intended consequences in the behavior of others. Parents have power. So do teachers, police officers, supervisors, middle-level executives, all by virtue of their position. Others have power by virtue of intrinsic qualities such as persuasiveness, beauty or leadership gifts.

Generalized power is virtually nonexistent in our pluralistic society. To say that someone "has power" is an incomplete description. Power to do what? Even the most powerful person has power only to accomplish certain specific things. A union leader may have the power to force decisions within an industry, but not the power to prevent an increase in the property tax. The political operators who want to increase the property tax may have power sufficient to that end, but not the power to block an increase in oil prices. There are corporate leaders in our cities whose power reaches to the farthest points on the globe, but who cannot get better refuse collection on the streets where they live. To some extent, this stems from our intention to prevent too much concentration of power in one person, but it is also due to the specialization and complexity of modern life.

Part of the story of power in any society is the reality that many are relatively powerless. Also part of the story are efforts toward empowerment such as the struggles for racial justice and women's rights. Strictly speaking, there should be no citizen who is utterly powerless in our society. Everyone should have a stake in the system.

Leadership and Power

It is necessary to distinguish between leaders and power holders. By definition, leaders always have a measure of power. But many power holders have no trace of leadership. The air traffic controller, the tax assessor, the cop on the beat, the loan officer in a bank, the headwaiter—each has power in some degree, but not necessarily the qualities of leadership. Some power holders—for example, very generous contributors to political campaigns—may be able to run leaders around by the nose, yet themselves have no capacity for leadership.

Although leadership and the exercise of power are distinguishable activities, they overlap and interweave in important ways. Consider a corporate chief executive officer who has the gift for inspiring and motivating people, who has vision, who lifts the spirits of employees with a resulting rise in productivity and quality of product, and a drop in turnover and absenteeism. That is leadership.

But evidence emerges that the company is falling behind in the technology race. One day with the stroke of a pen the CEO increases the funds available to the research division. That is the exercise of power. The stroke of a pen could have been made by an executive with none of the qualities one associates with leadership.

Leaders who hold high rank in organized systems have power stemming from their institutional position, and they do not hesitate to use that power to further their purposes. They may be very persuasive, but they do not live by persuasion alone—rather by persuasion interwoven with the exercise of power. Winston Churchill, Franklin D. Roosevelt, and John F. Kennedy were downright charismatic in the capacity to influence followers; but they also had power and used it regularly.

Leaders differ markedly among themselves in how they use their power. Some employ it to create a climate of coercion and intimidation;

others employ it simply as a useful supplement to their persuasive gifts, and foster a climate of cooperation and willing effort.

The Necessary Exercise of Power

In our democratic society, we make grants of power to people for specified purposes. If for ideological or temperamental reasons they refuse to exercise the power granted, we must turn to others. If you are elected to chair a meeting, and the meeting goes badly because you do not exercise your power as chair, you are a nuisance. The same may be said of mayors, judges, district attorneys and others who do not use the power of their offices appropriately.

When, as Secretary of Health, Education, and Welfare, I was working daily with allies in Congress, I was at first surprised by the enormous differences in their readiness and skill in using what power they had. When I first worked with the chairman of the subcommittee that handled our departmental appropriations I was pessimistic about the future of the relationship. The chairman was Representative John Fogarty of Rhode Island, an able, hard-hitting Irishman who brooked no nonsense from Cabinet members. But I discovered that when I succeeded in persuading that tough-minded politician of the merit of a legislative proposal, I could rest easy. It might fail in the full committee or on the floor of the House, but never for lack of skill on his part. Fogarty used his power effectively in behalf of the measures he believed in. I remember the chairman of another committee who was exceptionally kind and agreeable, a joy to deal with—but he could not or would not wield the power of his chairmanship effectively in behalf of the things he wanted to achieve. I never had an easy moment when my legislation was in his friendly hands.

To say a leader is preoccupied with power is like saying that a tennis player is preoccupied with making shots an opponent cannot return. Of course leaders are preoccupied with power! The significant questions are: What means do they use to gain it? How do they exercise it? To what ends do they exercise it?

When Jane Addams founded Hull House to serve the immigrant poor in the Chicago slums, she created for herself a position of power, but the means and the ends were so admirable that she was universally admired. In contrast, Hitler used treachery and intimidation to achieve power to the end that he might enslave the German people, exterminate Jews, and crush the nations of Europe.

For some power holders, there is no end other than power itself. The sheer pleasure of dominating is the object of the exercise. We have learned neither to admire nor trust such people.

Costs and Benefits

It is possible to think of the exercise of power as a kind of exchange. You want something from me and you have the power to produce in return certain outcomes that I want—or want to avoid. You can give me an A or flunk me. You can promote me to supervisor or reduce me to clerk. You can raise my salary or lower it. You can give or withhold love.

In bureaus where people go to get their licenses renewed or passports issued or Social Security claims validated, everyone has experienced the aggravation of dealing with the minor functionary who savors power.

Power does not need to be exercised to have its effect—as any armed robber can tell you. When I was a Cabinet member, I would listen spellbound as one or another powerful legislator subtly assisted me to the realization that the good will he had shown me in the past and could show me in the future hung precariously on my granting his present request.

The exchange model reminds us that the exercise of power generally involves some cost. I recall an incident in which a well-known senator was fighting and winning a legislative battle of great importance to my associates and myself. At the same time, he was fiercely opposed to a departmental regulation we were about to issue on a quite unrelated matter. He said, in effect, "Quash the regulation or I won't continue fighting your legislative battle." We had no doubt that both of our purposes were worthy, but we could only accomplish one of them. We had the power to issue the regulation—but the cost had become dreadfully high. To achieve one worthy goal we would have to jeopardize another worthy goal, a common experience in the world of action.

In his lively autobiography, *Man of the House*, Tip O'Neill tells of his worries that former Secretary of Defense Robert McNamara would close the Boston Navy Yard. "To get the President's attention, I walked out of a meeting of the Rules Committee just before a vote on a bill . . . the Administration cared about." When he saw Lyndon Johnson a few days later, the president demanded to know why he left the meeting: "What's going on?"

"Mr. President," I said, "I'm spending a lot of my time trying to save the Boston Navy Yard. . . . McNamara keeps threatening to close it."

"Don't you worry about that," said the president. "That Navy Yard will be around as long as I'm in the White House."[1] End of transaction!

Throughout most of human history, leaders have experienced more constraints in the exercise of power than is popularly supposed. Old-style monarchs experienced constraints from the nobility, from the church, from the army, or from the resistant web of custom. Most leaders today are hedged around by constraints—the realities of the external situation, tradition, constitutional limitations, rights and privileges of followers, requirements of teamwork, and the inexorable demands of large-scale organization.

Sources of Power

The sources of power are infinitely varied. Property, position, personal attractiveness, expertness, reason, persuasive gifts, the capacity to motivate—all these and innumerable other sources of power come into play in any normal day of community living. Listen to Heather Lamb, long-distance telephone operator: "There's a real sense of power. I can tell you when you have to stop talking. You have to pay me money."[2] Whatever I control that you want or want to avoid may be a source of power.

The command of one source of power may give access to other sources. Money can buy access to a senator.

Proximity to power is a source of power. With every new administration that settles into Washington comes a new crop of young White House aides who try bravely and gravely to bear up under their new importance. Some prove remarkably able; some do not. But each has the power that derives from proximity to power. As a stable hand carries the scent of the barnyard, the young aide carries the scent of power. Lobbyists, politicians and hostesses sniff the air appreciatively.

Strength

Probably the oldest source of power is the capacity to accomplish physical coercion. It is a source available to the military and to the huskiest kid in the third grade. Mao Tse-tung expressed his appreciation of this source when he said in his little red book, "Every Communist must grasp the truth: political power grows out of the barrel of a gun."[3] The application of force has been an element in the creation of most modern nations.

Most Americans want the exercise of physical power held firmly within the constraints of law and custom. For example, a mother intercepting her three-year-old as he chases his ball into heavy traffic uses gross physical force with the approval of all. But it is no longer permissible, as it once was in the United States, for a husband to beat his wife to bring about compliance.

Custom

The word *custom* does not evoke visions of power. Yet many monarchs and many modern dictators have found their freedom to rule seriously hampered when they sought to move against the grain of tradition.

Custom cannot stand up to machine guns but, as I pointed out earlier, it can raise the cost to the leader of every move that violates its tenets. Most leaders, even well-armed and ruthless ones, tend to accommodate more often than one might expect, and come to see custom as a source of power that they themselves can exploit. I shall have more to say on this subject later.

Organizations and Institutions

Humans create relatively stable patterns of social interaction—communities, states, corporations, armies, churches, universities—to accomplish one or another set of shared purposes. And these human systems are able to confer power on those occupying key roles. The mayor of a city exercises power stemming from organizational position. So do the chief of police and the cop on the beat. Organizational position is probably the most common source of power in the modern world.

During the Russian Revolution and the early days of the USSR, while Lenin and Trotsky were giving spectacular leadership in ideology and revolutionary fervor, Stalin was quietly making himself master of the revolution's organizational base. And that proved to be the decisive source of power. As Khrushchev said, when he was rising in the party hierarchy, "When Stalin says 'Dance,' a wise man dances."[4]

People who have to deal with organizations sometimes come to grief because they fail to understand the way power is distributed throughout the organization. The titular head has one kind of power; heads of operating divisions exercise quite another kind of power; and the lower ranks exercise still another kind. The efforts in the 1960s to reform high school curricula came to naught because of a failure to enlist the conviction and motivation of rank-and-file teachers. They had the power to withhold support.

The most far-flung set of organizational arrangements in any modern society is government. In a democratic society the sovereignty of the people gives power an innocent face, but the reality is there. Every government grant program generates power: favors to give, favors to withhold. Every government licensing procedure generates power in the capacity to grant, deny or delay. Every contracting office generates power. Our federal government is the biggest carrot-and-stick warehouse in the world. No wonder the power junkies gather.

Beliefs

Humans are believing animals. They have religious beliefs. They hold to one or another political doctrine. They have beliefs that supply meaning in their lives, beliefs that tell them how to conduct themselves, beliefs that console. The leader who understands those beliefs and acts in terms of that understanding has tapped a source of power. If the system of ideas is deeply embedded in the culture, it can play a significant role in legitimizing leaders and in validating their acts.

Individuals holding power or seeking it invariably associate themselves with one or another belief system. In Europe for a thousand years monarchs routinely declared their allegiance to the Pope. In Iran Ayatollah Khomeini took power as the spokesman of Allah. Soviet leaders associate themselves with communism, American leaders with democracy.

The alliance between power and beliefs has never been a wholly comfortable one. Those in power are inclined to use the belief system as a convenience, appealing to it when they need it, violating it when they choose. But those who see themselves as custodians of the beliefs are not docile, and the belief system generally ends up being a partial constraint on the exercise of power.

Our constitutional system is based on a set of secular beliefs designed to function as constraints on power. When Franklin D. Roosevelt, seeing his legislative program undermined by Supreme Court decisions, set out to reorganize the Court, he ran head-on into the power of the belief system.

Public Opinion

So much nonsense has been uttered concerning the voice of the people that one approaches the subject cautiously. Even so, it is evident that in our society public opinion is a notable source of power. If leaders have the support of public opinion, their freedom of action is enhanced and obstacles become surmountable. When the support of public opinion is sharply withdrawn, public figures topple, laws become unenforceable and bastions of economic power tremble.

Of course, in matters of governance we want public opinion to be a critically important source of power, and it often is. David Mathews and his associates are engaged in an important effort to ensure that it be a source of wisdom as well as power.[5] They have organized well over one thousand National Issues Forums across the country in which citizens discuss in depth the critical questions of the day.

I have a friend whose favorite political aphorism is "Apathy is rampant, but who cares!" In truth, though, the public is rarely apathetic. Generally speaking, what the critic means by public apathy is a failure on the part of the public to get excited about the critic's issues on the critic's time schedule.

The public speaks every time a pollster asks a question, every time a direct-mail house drops a million letters and gets a 3 percent response (or a .3 percent response), every time a budding politician gets a standing ovation or catcalls, every time a legislator gets bundles of mail on an issue or no mail at all.

Beyond that day-to-day background role, every so often the people act with volcanic force, casting down whole systems of power and raising up new leaders.

The capacity to be persuasive with the public has always been a source of power in democratic societies, but in large contemporary societies it must be linked with the capacity to get one's persuasiveness widely disseminated. So one of the most valid forms of power is the capacity to command the channels of communication.

One still encounters people in powerful positions who take the view that what the public thinks is not one of the hard realities of life. Thus President Nixon, in dealing with Vietnam, was quite realistic about the hard facts of troop strength, weapons, logistics and so on, but unrealistic about the equally hard fact of public rejection of the war. Yet that latter fact determined the outcome. Similarly, in their early clashes with Ralph Nader, the executives of General Motors consistently underestimated the role of public opinion, and paid heavily for their miscalculation.

Such people are becoming a relic of the past. More commonly, people in power today set out to manipulate the flow of information and to shape public opinion in countless cunning ways. The effort to manage the flow of information is not a recent phenomenon. Both Aristotle and Herodotus tell the story of the successful effort by the powerful Athenian Alcmaeonid family to bribe the Delphic Oracle.[6] The episode has a wonderful air of antiquity about it, but the intent to manipulate the flow of information is as modern as today's press release. Some of our contemporary image managers might appropriately burn incense at the shrine of the Alcmaeonidae.

Fifty years ago farsighted people were proposing that every high school offer a course in how to detect all varieties of propaganda. It was much too explosive an idea to be widely adopted, but it's fun to think about.

Symbols

There is a power that derives from custodianship of potent symbols. Presidents vary in their other sources of power, but all presidents have benefited from the power inherent in the symbols of office. Every public relations person serving a president is aware of the symbolic value of the White House, the Oval Office, Air Force One, the presidential seal and the title of commander-in-chief.

Information

Closely related to but not identical with the power of public opinion is the power derived from knowledge, from information. The military services understand this and spend vast amounts of money on intelligence activities. Political candidates understand it and hire their own pollsters. Corporations spend huge sums for research, for information services, for consultants. Science and technology are sources of power.

Lyndon Johnson once said to me, "When the press talks about my successes as Senate majority leader they always emphasize my capacity to persuade, to wheel and deal. Hardly anyone ever mentions that I usually had more and better information than my colleagues." And so he did.

Economic Power

Economic strength is so well understood as a source of power that it requires little discussion here. The rise of Japan to the first rank of world powers on the basis of economic performance is a significant example.

In the heyday of the Industrial Revolution, those who had economic power had almost complete freedom to wield that power—to produce or not produce; to control the purchase, sale and delivery of goods; to render or withhold services; to accumulate and invest capital; and to set prices and wages. But it became apparent that the power inherent in the control of such activities was capable of producing not only great benefits but also great misery—extremes of wealth and poverty, prosperity and starvation, material progress and child labor, technological gains and industrial accidents.

Little by little governments set limits on the capacity of economic power to produce bad consequences. In some nations—the Soviet Union, for one—government took complete control, with disastrous consequences for economic vitality. In the non-Communist industrial countries today, economic and political power are interwoven. In the United States, for example, government controls some of the key levers of economic power and engages in activities that have immense economic impact. At the same time, those who hold economic power in the private sector exert great influence on government.

A familiar feature of economic power is that it is readily translated into other forms of power. The wealthy person can buy symbols of status or can influence public opinion. Money can buy political outcomes.

The Exercise of Power

The unpleasant aura surrounding the idea of power is, of course, well-earned. Woodrow Wilson, a professor of government long before he governed, said,

> "The great stream of freedom . . . is not a clear mountain current such as the fastidious men of chastened thought like to drink from: it is polluted with not a few of the coarse elements of the gross world on its banks; it is heavy with the drainage of a very material universe."[7]

In my high school English classroom there hung at the front of the room a large print of Sir Galahad, and beneath his likeness were inscribed the lines by Tennyson: "My strength is as the strength of ten/Because my heart is pure." Anyone who enters the arena of power armed with integrity alone discovers that the couplet leaves important things unsaid. When Robert LaFollette was seeking the nomination for governor of Wisconsin in 1896, he learned the night before the balloting that the opposition was literally buying delegates away from him with substantial cash offers. He wrote in his autobiography:

> Shortly after midnight Charles F. Pfister came to my headquarters. . . . "LaFollette" he said, "we've got you skinned. We've got enough of your delegates away from you to defeat you." I

told Mr. Pfister that I was able to take care of myself. . . . When the balloting came on the next day, I was beaten.[8]

Eventually, LaFollette became extremely effective in combating such power plays, not by descending to the level of his opponents but by drawing on the power of his devoted constituency, the power of public opinion, and other weapons. He learned, as so many individuals of high purpose have learned, that he had to know his opponents and their sources of power, know when to do battle, and how to make the battleground one of his own choosing. And he learned to use his own power unflinchingly.

It has been my experience that people of lofty motivation are quite capable of learning the hard lessons of action. Saint Teresa of Avila, one of the greatest of Christian mystics, was the founder of the Reformed Carmelite Order, and in that capacity had a highly practical task of institution building to do. As a mystic she lived in a world of visions which she described with unforgettable eloquence. But as a builder of the order she was down to earth, shrewd, diplomatic and purposeful. She had a firm grasp of the political realities of the church. She said, "I'm a great negotiator," and in fact she was.

The leaders of the civil rights movement would never have achieved the historic gains of the 1950s and 60s had they not learned to draw skillfully and tough-mindedly on every source of power available to them—the courts, the legislative process, public opinion, citizens' movements, the media, and so on.

In some environments leadership may depend on an encyclopedic grasp of the complexities and technicalities of procedure. Every veteran remembers a top sergeant who had such total mastery of the "regs" that no fresh-faced lieutenant could possibly cope with him. The skill in itself is not evidence of leadership, but when linked with leadership gifts, it is potent.

A familiar failing of visionaries and of people who live in the realm of ideas and issues is that they are not inclined to soil their hands with the nuts and bolts of organizational functioning. Often there is a snobbish element involved. Some are inclined to believe that the people who work in the subbasements of power and understand the organizational machinery are lesser people. Good leaders do not ignore the machinery. Every leader needs some grasp of how to work the system.

The best work on individual impulses to power has been done by David McClelland and associates.[9] McClelland points out that our young people absorb such a negative view of power that they shy away from leadership roles. I would add that though they may flee the image of power as exemplified by leadership roles, particularly political, many of them become connoisseurs and *aficionados* of power in professional and business fields. But I agree with McClelland, and applaud his conviction that if we are to attract more young people to leadership roles, we must show them the positive aspects of the leader's task.

Perhaps the most familiar aphorism concerning power is Lord Acton's assertion that "power tends to corrupt; absolute power corrupts absolutely." (A mischievous professor has asserted that in the case of university presidents the assertion should be revised to "Power tends to corrupt; the *illusion* of power corrupts absolutely.")

Given the widely shared views concerning the wickedness of power, one is not surprised that Lord Acton's saying is generally quoted without the "tends to," and becomes the flat assertion "Power corrupts." But our society has developed safeguards diminishing the likelihood that power will corrupt except for some individuals some of the time. These latter individuals deserve our sustained attention. The ancient Greeks were not wrong about hubris. And it is no doubt true that some individuals are drawn to power as a moth to the flame. In Washington, D.C., where I lived for many years, the flame burns brightly and singed wings are as common as toothaches.

Even veteran observers are bemused by the overreaching of some who exercise power. It is a source of constant wonder that such an ancient and dreary vice can spring up so freshly. As one who has watched the beginnings of a good many national administrations, I can testify that in the case of some individuals, it takes only a moment for the intoxication of power to take hold. Some famous falls from power have been traceable to overreaching. Senator Joseph McCarthy comes to mind. General MacArthur, after a splendid career in the service of his country, finally overreached. The air traffic controllers overreached.

Power is ethically neutral. It can be used for good purposes or bad. So it is necessary to address ourselves to the moral framework that permits us to judge some purposes as good and others as bad.

7

THE MORAL DIMENSION

We say that we want effective leadership; but Hitler was effective. Criteria beyond effectiveness are needed.

Ultimately we judge our leaders in a framework of values. The framework differs from one culture to the next and from one era to the next. Reflected in the following discussion are the values of this society at this moment in history, as seen through the eyes of one observer.

The Transgressors

Several kinds of leaders clearly transgress our moral standards. First, the fairy-tale image of the bad king is that of the ruler who inflicts cruelty on his own subjects; and one has no difficulty in identifying modern counterparts who terrorize, torture or kill. Idi Amin, who ruled Uganda from 1971 to 1979, killed roughly 100,000 of his subjects, many of whom were first subjected to torture and mutilation. A huge man, six feet, three inches tall, and weighing 230 pounds, he had been a heavyweight boxing champion in his youth. He was so unmeasured in his savagery that he finally alienated all his potential allies and had to flee the country. In the Soviet Union between 1929 and 1933, Stalin introduced measures that resulted in the deaths of 10 to 15 million peasants.[1]

Second, there are leaders who may treat their own followers well but encourage them to do evil things to others. It is in this sense that those who head the Ku Klux Klan transgress. We have seen leaders of both right- and left-wing extremist groups encourage their followers to commit acts of brutality.

Third, there are leaders who may or may not engage in acts of cruelty but who reach for, and use as a source of motivation, our bigotry, our capacity to hate, our desire for revenge, our fear and paranoia, our superstitions. These are emotions and motives whose arousal has proven conspicuously destructive in human history, and the burden of proof is on leaders who think it necessary to evoke them.

Ayatollah Khomeini comes to mind. Hatred and revenge fueled his rise to power and the domestic and international terrorism that followed.

An example of a leader who based his rule on fear and superstition is François "Papa Doc" Duvalier, president of Haiti from 1957 to 1971. His secret police, the Tonton Macoutes, wearing the steel-rimmed dark glasses that were their trademark, made fear a constant presence in Haitian life. As for superstition, Duvalier once had the severed head of a guerrilla leader brought to his palace, announcing that he would use his voodoo powers to extract the plans of the guerrilla forces from the dead man's brain. All of this in a land lying little more than 500 miles off the coast of Florida!

Fourth, there are leaders who diminish their followers, rendering them dependent and childlike, exploiting their unconscious need for the godlike magic helper of their infancy. James Jones of Jonestown worked systematically to obliterate adult judgment and create dependency in his followers. As so often happens in the case of truly evil leadership, something in one's mind—at least in the American mind—does not want to accept the reality of what happened at Jonestown. How many Americans have erased from their memories that just a few years ago in Guyana, 911 people died when the followers of James Jones, most of them from the United States, took their own lives and the lives of their children at the instruction of their leader. Jones systematically deprived his followers of their wills and moved them back toward infancy. He cut them off from the outside world, broke up families, farmed out the children, and fashioned a community where all ties of loyalty ran directly to him as Daddy. Of course his followers, who were after all self-selected (except for the children), did much to collaborate in their victimization.

Finally, there are leaders who destroy the processes that civilized peoples have created over the centuries to preserve freedom, justice and human dignity. I was in Italy the year Mussolini put an end to parliamentary government and launched the Fascist state. Again, one is struck with the failure of observers around the world to be adequately shocked by the out-and-out gangsterism Il Duce employed to gain power.

Adolf Hitler

To top off our brief review of the bad guys, it may be useful to have a somewhat more extended look at Adolf Hitler. Hitler had some qualities that would be counted as strengths in any leader, good or bad—his sheer force of personality, his extraordinary steadiness of purpose over the years, and his genius for organizing and mobilizing. But those strengths were turned to evil ends.

His lust for power was an end it itself. And it was linked to certain obsessive convictions. Believing in the subordination of the individual under an authoritarian regime, he had nothing but contempt for democracy. And he believed that Germans of Aryan descent constituted a master race, the *Herrenvolk*, whose purity was to be preserved at all costs from pollution by the slave races (not only Jews but also all who were not Aryans by his definition). "Virtue lies in blood," he said, and it is impossible to exaggerate the supremacy of this value in his thinking.[2] The good of the *Volk* justified rampant injustice, lies, subjugation, and all the horrors of the Holocaust.

The havoc Hitler wrought stemmed not only from these beliefs but also from his malignant views as to the appropriate methods for pursuing his beliefs. First, he believed that the end justifies the means. All leaders of strong purpose slip into that belief occasionally, some of them habitually, but Hitler was extreme by any standard. Unmeasured violence, the grossest betrayal, the crassest lie—all were justified if they advanced one toward the goal. Before the invasion of Poland he said to his generals, "Close your hearts to pity. Act brutally."[3]

Second, he had contempt for peace and extolled the virtues of heroic war: "Life is preserved only because other living things perish through struggle."[4] And in this struggle, might makes right: "Only force rules. Force is the first law."[5]

Third, as one of the most creative practitioners of the art of propaganda, he embraced total distortion of reality as a legitimate governing device, whether the target was friend or foe. "The masses of the people . . . feel very little shame at being terrorized intellectually and are scarcely conscious of the fact that their freedom as human beings is being impudently abused."[6]

Hitler displayed sinister gifts in the pursuit of his objectives. He had a keen sense of the weaknesses of others—the members of his official family, the German people, his international foes—and he played on those weaknesses with hideous skill, intimidating, bribing, setting opponents against one another, mixing threats and conciliatory gestures.

He understood that most groups and most nations are reluctant to enter into a truly violent exchange, and he knew how to alternate terror with hints of accommodation to heighten that reluctance.

Even more satanic was his capacity to reach for the darker side of human nature, to exploit for his own purposes all the resentment, hatred, paranoia and desire for revenge that lurk in the shadowy corners of the human soul. After World War I those emotions were very much alive in the German people. Theirs was a humiliated nation, in defeat and disarray, suffering inflation, unemployment and social breakdown. Extremist groups had their own private paramilitary forces. Unemployed veterans roamed the streets, tinder for any passing demagogue. Hitler understood every pathological possibility and made the most of it.

Long before his rise to power, he wrote *Mein Kampf*: "What a use could be made of the Treaty of Versailles! . . . How each one of the points of that treaty could be branded in the minds and hearts of the German people until 60 million men and women find their souls aflame with feelings of rage and shame."[7]

Otto Strasser said, "Hitler responds to the vibrations of the human heart with the delicacy of a seismograph . . . enabling him . . . to act as a loudspeaker proclaiming the most secret desires, the least admissible instincts, the sufferings and personal revolts of a whole nation."[8]

This was no ordinary dictator; this was an evil genius. But the evil got out of hand. He was like a mad arsonist, starting with little fires, going on to great conflagrations until he himself was consumed in the firestorm he created.

Examples Close to Home

I have used dramatic examples to illustrate morally unacceptable leadership, so perhaps it had better be said that each of these undesirable behaviors is simply the extreme of a continuum that includes more familiar, close-to-home examples. We have had a good many leaders who have fostered hatred, played on the fears of constituents, or undermined the integrity of government.

And we have had—and still have—leaders whose betrayal of their trust undermines the moral base of our system. Mike Royko, in his biography of former mayor Richard J. Daley of Chicago, describes the corrupt system over which he presided.[9] Federal, state and city tax monies were at the disposal of Daley's Machine. Building projects poured billions into the hands of contractors. Lawyers, banks, engineering firms and countless others received city business, and they paid off with campaign contributions or more immediately with cash kickbacks. Downtown business interests were grateful for the mayor's pouring money into the downtown area and backed him. So did the media.

Still another ingredient was the power to punish—or to overlook. Any city inspector, any official handing out permits or licenses, any law enforcement agency could come down hard on those who did not toe the line or pay up—and could suspend retribution for those who paid. The prostitutes and bookies paid up; the taverns that wanted to stay open paid up.

It is easy to tell ourselves that in all of the situations dealt with in this chapter, the sole source of evil was the leader. But the leader is never a sole causative factor. There is always, *in some measure*, the collaboration of those led. If a leader holds sway by exploiting our greed or our hatreds, the evil is in us too. If a bad leader rules because of our lethargy, we are collaborators. The fault is not in our stars.

Morally Acceptable Leadership

How might one characterize a leader who meets acceptable ethical and moral standards? Such matters are, in some measure, prescribed by the culture, so let us limit ourselves to asking what Americans of our time consider to be acceptable. It is not an easy question to answer. Some Americans despise any and all leaders; other Americans voluntarily join cults in which submersion of individuality and coercion are the rule. Most of us want leaders who are not hungry for power, but some critics say we have created a system in which only the most power-hungry stay the course. We want leaders who serve the common good and at the same time serve our special interests, whatever those may be. We dislike paternalism, but we love father figures. We bemoan the lack of leadership, but we do not treat our leaders very well.

Despite the contradictions, visitors from autocratic societies notice immediately that we do have some rather distinctive ways of thinking about leadership.

Our View of Leadership

Basically, we resist the idea that social caste or class has anything to do with leadership. If we accept leadership from those of hereditary social standing, it is generally despite rather than because of their backgrounds.

Andrew Johnson, who succeeded to the White House when Lincoln was assassinated, was far more entitled to boast of humble origins than most who have done so. But he annoyed many with his gross glorification of the role. "I'm a-goin for to tell you here today; yea, I'm a-goin for to tell you that I'm a plebeian! I glory in it."[10]

We do not conceive of leaders as a group set apart, not in Plato's sense and not in Lenin's. Lenin, in stressing the need for a class of professional revolutionaries to carry through the revolution, exhibited a distrust of the masses worthy of the conservatives of the day. To him the masses were clay to be shaped by the revolutionary cadre.

Relations Between Leaders and Constituents

What should be the relationship between leaders and followers? From the time of our colonial beginnings we have groped toward the appropriate answer to that question. James Flexner, the Pulitzer-Prize-winning biographer of George Washington, described the first encounter between the new commander-in-chief of the Continental Army and his troops in New England: "He quickly discovered that commonly no one gave or obeyed any orders. The militiamen, having elected their officers, expected due subservience to themselves as sovereign voters."[11] Washington straightened that out quickly enough, but we have never ceased to experiment with the relationship.

We do not like to be ordered around. We recognize that much of leading involves the giving of orders, but we prefer persuasion, and where coercion is necessary we circumscribe it in a carefully designed framework of law and custom. Thus arbitrary orders can be issued by an officer in combat or by the parents of a thirteen-year-old boy (which may be another kind of combat), but in each case there are laws and customs that determine the limits and nature of the coercion.

Ideally, of course, one hopes that when it makes sense to issue a flat order, not only the circumstances but also trust and confidence in the leader make compliance a natural act.

We like the leader to play—insofar as possible—a first among equals role. I remember traveling to Michigan with Walter Reuther once and visiting the recreational and adult learning center maintained by the United Auto Workers. I was impressed with the family atmosphere and the good-natured affection and familiarity with which they treated Reuther. I said, "They treat you like a father," and he said instantly, "Older brother!" His reply was not just a bow to the traditional union idea of brotherhood; he made it clear that he rejected the implied deference and paternalism in the word I had chosen.

The leader–constituent relationship is not without tension and conflict. One must not suppose that the ideal consists of leaders and constituents so deferential to one another that nothing happens. The ideal is leadership strong enough to propose clear directions and followers strong enough to criticize and amend—and finally enough community of purpose to resolve disputes and move on.

We believe, with Immanuel Kant, that individuals should be treated as ends in themselves, not as a means to the leader's end, not as objects to be manipulated.

We cannot approve a leader who betrays the common good in the interest of personal aggrandizement or profit. Hitler used people ruthlessly to serve his own purposes; as he approached his final hour, he was quite ready to sacrifice Germany and the German people to preserve his idea of himself and his historic mission.

We expect our leaders to be sensitive to and to serve the basic needs of their constituents. We expect them to have faith in their constituents and a caring concern for them.

Having sketched the portrait of a leader who is responsive and caring, we must not fall into the error of supposing that such a leader must fit the stereotype of the gentle seminar moderator. A gruff and demanding leader may be responsive and caring; a permissive leader may have little interest in the needs of constituents. Miss Butler, who taught English in my high school, was as much a martinet as any Marine Corps officer of my experience. But she was fair, she was consistent, and she obviously cared a great deal whether we learned. The very fact that she expected so much of us was a kind of compliment.

Tasks requiring precision of performance under pressure (a ballet, a football team in midgame, a surgical team in midoperation) can afford to permit little if any creative deviation from the performance that is required and expected. In such situations, leaders are more exigent.

One way of characterizing morally acceptable leaders is to specify what their objectives are with respect to the group and the individuals who make it up. These are the matters on which worthy people differ, so I shall speak for myself—but I believe that the views I express are widely shared. Let the reader judge. Bear in mind that the focus in this chapter is not effectiveness, but performance judged in terms of ethical, moral and social values.

1. The Release of Human Possibilities

Reviewing the enlivening themes that run through our history as a people, one is struck with the depth and continuity of our commitment to the fulfillment of human possibilities. The leaders we have valued the most have reflected that commitment. Woodrow Wilson said, "I believe in democracy because it releases the energy of every human being."

The greatest asset of any society is the talent and energy of its people. Yet no society has ever fully recognized or honored that asset; indeed, most societies have effectively stifled both talent and energy. The release of human possibilities is one of the most basic of social objectives and leadership goals.

Jefferson said, "We hope to avail the nation of those talents which nature has sown as liberally among the poor as the rich, but which perish without use, if not sought for and cultivated."[12]

In times of crises, individuals discover unsuspected strengths and reveal a capacity for bravery, endurance, generosity and loyalty beyond all expectations. An increase in the incidence of crises would not be welcome, but one cannot dismiss the thought of those hidden capabilities. In all of us there are undiscovered gifts, untested strengths. Sometimes capabilities remain hidden simply because the circumstances of life do not evoke them, the challenge never arises, the call never comes. But sometimes the gifts have been buried by early defeats and harsh treatment, or layered over by cynicism, or held inactive by self-doubt. It is a matter of self-interest for every society to remove obstacles to human growth and performance. The battles we wage against physical and mental illness, prejudice, ignorance and poverty are not just exercises in compassion. They are battles for the release of human talent and energy.

In this country we pride ourselves on fostering individual development. But there are no grounds for complacency. The release of human possibilities is at best a half-done task. *There are great untapped reservoirs of human energy and capacity awaiting leaders who can tap them, and societies that deserve them.*

Our concern for the release of human talent and energy must reach beyond the schools and permeate the whole society. It must be reflected in our programs for children whose potentialities may be blighted by crippling illness or severe sensory handicaps or environmental deprivation. It must be reflected in the workplace, in leisure activities, even in retirement planning. What is wanted is an attitude, widely shared throughout the society, toward individual growth, development and learning in the context of our shared values—an attitude that is fiercely impatient with impediments to healthy growth and that never ceases to seek out the undiscovered possibilities in each of us.

2. Individual and Group

Leaders must understand the mutual dependence between individual and group, and must understand what our tradition requires in balancing the two.

Individuals become fully human and find support and identity in the cultural framework supplied by family and community. Sound families and communities provide young persons with security, a sense of belonging, a framework of shared values and a network of caring individuals. But we have seen the collapse of communities, of coherent belief systems, and of opportunities for allegiance and commitment as well as for being needed and responding to need.

We expect that young people, at the same time that they are maturing as individuals responsible for their own actions, will be maturing as responsible members of the community. We foster individual initiative but expect a certain amount of that initiative to be expended on shared purposes.

I shall explore the subject of community more fully in chapter 11.

3. Law, Custom and Belief

I have emphasized the release of energy and talent. But human energy can be turned to evil purposes, and talent has followed some strange banners. Every healthy society we know anything about has created a framework of law and custom to channel talent and energy toward purposes deemed by the society to be acceptable. That was what Hammurabi of Babylon was up to thirty-nine centuries ago when he formulated the legal code that bears his name—and won the gratitude of archaeologists by having it carved in 3,600 lines of cuneiform on a diorite column. (One has the impression that he did not anticipate frequent amendments.)

The ideas a society lives by are embedded not only in written laws but also in custom, in the unwritten norms or standards by which the culture guides the conduct of its members, specifying what is proper and improper, right and wrong. They are embedded in myths, legends and shared symbols; they involve shared assumptions as to the meaning of life and of human history; and they are inseparable from institutions. Among the fundamental values professed in our own society are justice, liberty, equality of opportunity, the dignity of the individual and the sanctity of private religious beliefs.

The power of ideas in guiding human conduct is basic, and those who lead by that power often triumph against forces that are materially more powerful. Confucius, an itinerant teacher, always hoped that one or another of the reigning princes of the day would appoint him to a position of power so that he could put his ideas into effect. It did not happen. But the words of Confucius spread throughout Asia and eventually the world. And who remembers the reigning princes? What heritage was left by those who held great worldly power when Buddha was teaching, or when Isaiah was prophesying or when Jesus spoke by the lakeside?

The contemporary mind recoils from the word *moral*. To many, it recalls religious bigotry, a cold, unforgiving view of human frailty, and a censorious attitude toward all manifestations of sexuality. Such memories are not inaccurate but they constitute a woefully incomplete interpretation of the word *moral*. Morality refers to the standards by which a community judges the rightness or wrongness of conduct in all fields. Our attitudes toward genocide, rape and torture are elements of our morality.

If we look at the array of societies described by historians and anthropologists, we cannot find an instance of a healthy society in which humans have not devised a framework of values, norms of conduct, a moral order. When the community's broad consensus disintegrates or loses its force, the society sickens. People no longer find meaning in their lives. Nothing holds together. In describing such disintegration in Athens after the Peloponnesian Wars, Gilbert Murray introduced the great phrase "the failure of nerve."[13]

Our society has not come to that pass, but signs of disintegration are not hard to discern. In a recent study, a full-time high school drug counselor was asked if she directly approached students she knew to be drug users, and she said, "It's not a problem if there is no effect on the kid's performance. I mean, who are we to say what's right or wrong?"[14]

Despite such adverse symptoms, and despite the disagreements that flow from our pluralism, we still enjoy a considerable measure of agreement. It is not clear and sharp, but it is there and it prevails a great deal of the time.

Look at a more or less average American community. In the dimension of values, what you see is very imperfect by the standards we ourselves set, very imperfect when tested against our highminded professions of national virtue. You find crime, tax evasion, greed, hypocrisy, immorality and all the other reliable signs of human habitation. But it is not yet a jungle nor a wasteland nor a place of moral anarchy. Most of our citizens are law-abiding and most of our communities reasonably orderly. And that would not be possible if there did not exist, despite our pluralism, a healthy measure of agreement on some fundamentals.

We must hope for leaders who will work with us to defend those fundamentals and to regain lost ground, enriching our commitment to freedom, to justice, to equality of opportunity, to the dignity and worth of the individual, and to the sanctity of our private religious beliefs. In large measure those commitments are embedded in our laws. Our history as a people is richly instructive on our faithfulness and faithlessness concerning these commitments.

We must hope, too, that our leaders will help us keep alive values that are not so easy to embed in laws—our feeling about individual moral responsibility, about caring for others, about honor and integrity, about tolerance and mutual respect, and about individual fulfillment within a framework of values.

A special word must be said about tolerance as a value. If we are to be serious about values, we must be equally serious about tolerance, and adamant about the limits to which one can impose one's own values on others.

We have difficulty—the old human difficulty—in honoring in our behavior the values we profess. That has not changed in human history. And we seem to have particular difficulty with the ideal of brotherhood. We can no longer afford to indulge without constraint the ancient human impulse to hate and fear strangers—those not of our tribe, not of our religion, not like us.

Normally we expect leaders to function within the framework of law and custom and the agreed-on purposes and values of the system over which they preside. But room must be left for dissent. The arena of values is the scene of conflict—and should be. Carrie Chapman Catt and her predecessors, fighting the battles that led to the Nineteenth Amendment giving women the vote, were closing an intolerable gap between our professed values and accepted practice.

Dissenters have rights. They also have obligations. We ask that they pursue their objectives within the law, and that they set forth the rational and moral basis for their dissent. Martin Luther King, Jr., was a model of the principled dissenter. He placed before the American people the religious and philosophical basis for his dissent—and in time, a very large segment of the public came to believe that he had made his case.

Regeneration of Values. The truth is that disintegration of the value framework is always going on—but so are regenerative processes. Some people see little hope that such processes can be effective, believing that we have lost the capacity to generate a new vision. A still gloomier view is that we may have lost the capacity to *tolerate* a new vision. The debunking reflex is powerful today. We are sick of past hypocrisies. We have seen the fine words of morality used as a screen for greed, for bigotry, for power seeking. Granted. But to let that estrange us from all attempts to regenerate the moral framework would be petulant and self-defeating.

Creating value systems is something that the human species does. "It's our thing" as the recently popular saying goes, and without that irrepressible impulse civilization would not have survived. Destroy every vestige of law and morality, demolish every community, level the temples of justice, erase even the memory of custom, and one would see—in the midst of chaos, savagery and pillage—an awesome sight: the sight of men and women, bereft of all guiding memory, beginning to forge anew the rudiments of order and justice and law, acting out of the mysterious community-building impulse of the species.

4. Individual Initiative and Responsibility

Given our ideals of individual responsibility, our leaders have an obligation to encourage the active involvement of constituents or followers in pursuit of group goals. In political matters, a passive constituency invites the abuse of power. In corporations or bureaucracies, workers passively awaiting orders ensure inertness and sluggishness in the organization's functioning. The devolution of initiative and responsibility is a requirement of vitality, both for organizations and for the society as a whole.

In the course of developing the ideas that found expression in *Self-Renewal*, I had a number of conversations with Alfred Sloan, the legendary figure who built General Motors into an industrial giant. I was concerned with the growth, decay and renewal of individuals, organizations and civilizations, and found that Sloan had lively ideas on the suppressive effects of large organizations on individual initiative. On one occasion he said, "I worry about the General Motors executives scattered around the country whom I have never met. . . . I want to keep them awake and thinking about what they can contribute to the future of General Motors. And the only way to do that is to push some decisions in their direction." One could hardly state more succinctly the problem of ensuring that individuals in large organizations keep a sense of personal involvement.

Most people in most organizations most of the time are more stale than they know, more bored than they care to admit. All too often it is because they have not been encouraged to use their own initiative and powers of decision. And if they are not expected to use their decision-making powers, they are off the hook of responsibility. That is the damaging element.

Unrelenting autocracy down the chain of command undermines initiative. It says by implication that your responsibility is not to identify problems beyond those implicit in your orders, not to think about solutions. Wait for the next order! If something goes wrong that is not strictly within the scope of your orders, you need not worry about it. The disclaimer in the Navy used to be "It didn't happen on my watch." Followers who are passively awaiting orders have lost much of their capacity to be of help.

It is a loss we cannot afford. It is in the very nature of large-scale organization that its only hope of vitality is the willingness of a great many people scattered throughout the organization to take the initiative in performing leaderlike acts, in identifying problems at their levels and solving them. Without that, the organization becomes another of those sodden, inert, nonadaptive bureaucracies that are the bane of modern corporate and governmental life—rigid, unimaginative, and totally unequipped to deal with a swiftly changing environment.

On one of my field trips as Secretary of Health, Education, and Welfare, I fell into conversation with a middle-aged professional, quite low-ranking in the organization, who worked on one of our programs at the grass roots. He told me he had informed his bureau chief in Washington that the latest regulation governing his program was seriously defective and that he was adopting a variant procedure. Later that day I mentioned the conversation to our regional director and he said, "I listened to his argument, and he's right. The regulation will have to be amended."

Was my dissenting friend a leader? He had four people under his direction and was about as far down in the hierarchy as he could be. But he certainly was not a conventional follower; at the very least he was a contributor, and in truth, he was sharing the leadership task.

We need leaders who can bring alive in individuals all down the line that kind of capacity to share the leadership task. When the system in question is not a corporation or agency but the society itself, such sharing of leadership tasks results in a more responsive and responsible political system. It ensures that the true needs of people are perceived by grass-roots leaders near at hand. Some needs are met locally, others communicated up the line for action at a higher level.

That requires leaders who can delegate responsibility, who consult and listen, who respect human possibilities, who help us to grow and to remove obstacles to our own effective functioning. Lyman Bryson said, "A democratic way of doing anything is a way that best keeps and develops the intrinsic powers of men and women."[15]

Leadership is necessarily concerned with group activity. But leaders who fail to leave a place for individual creativity are doing the group no favor. Every leader should ponder the words of Caryl Haskins, one of our most respected scientific leaders: "It is the gifted unorthodox individual in the laboratory or the study or the walk by the river at twilight who has always brought us, and must continue to bring to us, all the basic resources by which we live."[16]

8

LARGE-SCALE ORGANIZED SYSTEMS

So far in our discussion, despite an occasional acknowledgment of historical and cultural context, we have given little attention to the fact that today's world is characterized by vast and interdependent organized systems. In the next four chapters we examine those systems.

If one calls to mind ancient images of leadership—Moses leading the Israelites out of Egypt, Leonidas leading the Spartans in the defense of Thermopylae—and then reflects on the kind of leadership required to get anything done today, one might wonder whether the same word should be used for such spectacularly different activities. I am for keeping the word, even though the changes have been extraordinary.

The first thing that strikes one as characteristic of contemporary leadership is the necessity for the leader to work with and through extremely complex organizations and institutions—corporations, government agencies at all levels, the courts, the media of communication, and so on. Leaders must understand not only the intricate organizational patterns of their own segment but also the workings of neighboring segments. Business leaders must understand how our political system works. Political leaders must understand our economic system.

The leaders who succeed in making large and complex systems work may not achieve fame. Although their success is noted by those in the particular field in which they function, generally they do not achieve the "figure against the sky" visibility that they might have gained as individual performers. Some hire public relations people to pump them up and occasionally it works, but it is not a natural outcome.

Steven Muller, president of Johns Hopkins University and one of the wisest, most effective leaders in higher education today, points out how difficult it is to play a highly visible role nationally and still do justice to leadership of a great contemporary university with its size, complexity, huge investments in research, and so on. "We . . . are builders. Our task is to help to remodel our institutions for tomorrow."[1] If we want our complicated world to work, we had better revise our conception of leaders to make room for the Steven Mullers.

Large-Scale Organization

Many years ago, Max Weber, the great German sociologist, provided the first authoritative description of the bureaucratic form of organization that has dominated both governmental and corporate life throughout the twentieth century.[2] He pointed out that it was more efficient than the preindustrial modes it displaced, but warned that ultimately society might not like the "iron cage" it was constructing for itself. Not many people heard the warning. The division of labor, the specialization, and the rational allocation of functions characteristic of bureaucracy lent themselves to modern purposes, and the industrial societies proceeded hell-bent down that road.

One factor that blinded us to the difficulties that lay ahead was our belief that the word *bureaucracy* applied only to government agencies; we did not see that the problems were present in all large organizations, corporate as well as governmental.

A New Trend in Industry

There were some who looked at large-scale organization with a more perceiving and prophetic eye.[3] Alfred P. Sloan of General Motors recognized early that as systems increase in size and complexity, thought must be given to dispersing leadership and management functions throughout the system.

But most corporate leaders were not listening. They were against bureaucratic centralization by government, but embraced it unthinkingly in their own companies.

In the 1970s American industry was shaken to its foundations by the emergence of Japan as an immensely effective competitor, and we set out to examine the organizational practices behind Japan's phenomenal performance. The reexamination soon broadened to include every aspect of our own organizational functioning. And other segments of the society beyond industry began to reexamine their own practices. It is quite likely that historians will see the last half of the twentieth century as a time when we undertook a revolutionary reevaluation of large-scale organization and the sources of organizational vitality.

Problems of Large Organizations

We have come to recognize that the sheer size of an organization can create grave problems for the leader interested in vitality, creativity and renewal. We cannot escape the necessity for large-scale systems of organized human endeavor. A complex society—to say nothing of a complex world—requires such systems; but we now know that we can design them so that they do not suffer the worst ailments of size. There are ways of making them flexible and adaptive. There are ways of breaking them up into smaller subsystems.

All large-scale systems develop certain characteristic failings, some of which are destructive of organizational vitality. Largeness leads top executives to create huge headquarters staffs to monitor and analyze. Substructures proliferate, an elaborate organization chart emerges, and obsessive attempts to coordinate follow. Creative leaders work to reduce complexity, slim down central staff, eliminate excessive layering, and create units of manageable size.

In large organizations the chain of command becomes excessively long. Decisions are slowed and adventurous moves blocked by too many screening points and multiple sign-offs. As one production executive put it, "If I can get an idea past my boss and his boss and the financial vice-president and the general counsel, it's probably too feeble an idea to change anything."

The industrial community has in recent years expended great effort to accomplish the deeper involvement of workers in their jobs—through job redesign, autonomous working groups, schemes for feedback on performance, and various ways of providing recognition for work well done. Since sheer size creates problems in the organizational environment, some corporations have worked to counter the trend toward larger units. The chief executive officer of Hewlett-Packard Company, John Young, was recently rated as the most admired leader in the high-tech industries. He says, "Having small divisions is not the only way to organize a company, but having organizations that people can run like a small business is highly motivational. . . . Keeping that spirit of entrepreneurship is very important to us."[4]

Recognizing that the impersonality (some say dehumanization) of large-scale organization leaves many people feeling anonymous, powerless, and without a sense of their relationship to the whole, effective leaders create a climate that encourages two-way communication, participation, and a sense of belonging. They pay attention to people. They eliminate conditions that suppress individuality.

The goal is to give the individual employee and the lower levels of supervisors and district managers the conviction that their voices are heard, their participation welcomed. Everyone recognizes that autocratic practices work against this. Not everyone recognizes that depersonalization of the society may be a greater enemy than autocracy. My boss may be autocratic, but if he gets sore when I make a suggestion, at least I know he heard me. When a sense of impersonality pervades an organization, the conviction spreads that any suggestion I make will surely be lost in the complex processes of the organization.

The Turf Syndrome

Everyone who has worked in a large organization has memories of one or another zealous bureaucratic infighter. In the late 1940s, when I was serving as consultant to a large government agency, I had my first opportunity to observe over a considerable period a prime example of the species. Too timid to lead, too vain to follow, his game was turf defense. He was a master of the hidden move and the small betrayal. He understood with a surgeon's precision the vulnerabilities of his colleagues, and he masked calculated unresponsiveness in a thousand innocent guises. As a young observer eager to understand bureaucracy, I found him an open textbook.

Predictable characteristics of large-scale organization include a complex division of labor, specialization, fixed roles, and careful definitions of rank and status. Equally predictable are the proliferation of defined subsystems, increasingly rigid boundaries between subsystems and emergence of the turf syndrome. Rivalry and conflict develop, and effective internal communication is diminished. Referring to conflicts among his chief lieutenants, Henry Ford II once told me, "I try to remind them that the enemy is not the guy across the hall. It's the guys out there selling Chevys or Hondas."

All of this hampers adaptability, creativity and renewal. The organization most likely to renew itself enjoys good internal communication among its diverse elements. Effective leaders tear down rigid internal walls and bureaucratic enclaves, counter segmental loyalties through the creation of working groups that cut across boundaries, and foster informal exchange throughout the organization.

The Informal Organization

As everyone knows, the formal channels of communication and influence as defined by the organization chart do not constitute a complete description of what goes on. There are complex patterns of communication and influence that are generally spoken of as the *informal organization*. Because it is not one coherent system, it might be more accurate to speak of *informal groups* and *informal networks*.

Call them what you will, they are essential to the functioning of the system. They carry the bulk of communication relating to the organization's internal politics. They are the haunts of gossips and grumblers, sycophants and saboteurs, but they are also favored instruments of the natural leaders and power brokers scattered throughout every organization. Flexible and disrespectful of boundaries, the informal networks can serve the purposes of leaders shrewd enough to use them.

Communication

Communication is at the very heart of the leader-follower or leader-constituent relationship. The greater the size and complexity of the systems, the harder it is to ensure the kinds of two-way communication necessary to effective functioning.

Communication Downward

Our political system assumes that constituents are adequately informed to make sound judgments. But those who exercise political power generally find it much to their short-term advantage to withhold certain kinds of information. It is not a tendency that can be remedied once and for all. Citizens face the certainty of a never-ending battle to obtain necessary information. And top leaders must recognize that even if they themselves favor a free flow of information, many at the second, third, and fourth levels will act to block, filter or distort the downward flow.

The problem is not peculiar to the political system. It exists in all large, organized systems. A high-ranking air force general once said to me, "The intentions of the chief of staff get reinterpreted as they pass down through each level. The colonels who really run this place [the Pentagon] make the final interpretation, and it may bear little resemblance to the original."

Communication Upward

Middle- and upper-level executives should recognize that they are dependent on information that has been filtered, analyzed, abstracted, sorted and condensed by other segments of the organization. It is hard for them to stay in touch with unprocessed reality. Every official must periodically step outside the executive cocoon and experience the basic realities that the system is presumably designed to deal with.

Every organization has its frontline activities—selling, fighting, healing, teaching—and its bureaucratic or executive-level activities. Both are important, but the frontline activities take place far from the executive's swivel chair. The frontline people who wrestle with action problems every day know a lot more than anyone ever asks them.

The layers of middle and upper management can be a formidable filter against creative ideas generated below; and there have been many attempts to create alternative opportunities for communication upward, such as the suggestion box and the inspector general. But there is probably no substitute for creating a culture—a set of attitudes, customs and habits throughout the organization—that favors easy two-way communication, in and out of channels, among all layers of the organization. Two key messages should be implicit in such a culture: (1) "You will know what's going on," and (2) "Your voice will be heard."

Lateral Communication

In any large-scale organization, over time each of the component parts tends to create its own distinctive culture and to establish boundaries that are less permeable than one might wish. Enlightened executives work continuously to correct such insularity—through cross-boundary transfers of personnel, cross-boundary working groups, and reorganization.

In communities there are fewer bureaucratic boundaries, yet the problem of lateral communication among different segments (ethnic, occupational, socioeconomic) is just as real. People live in different worlds and are out of touch with one another in essential matters.

The Media

The means at our disposal for communicating with other human beings are unimaginably greater than ever before. But the needs that drive people to communicate seem limitless, so that the flow of messages expands as rapidly as the opportunities. Result: hubbub.

So despite the wonders of modern communication, the leader with a serious message has a problem. It is a big, noisy society. The leader has to compete with popular entertainment, skillfully crafted commercial messages, the drama and violence of the news, and so on.

Another problem is that though the means of bombarding people with messages seem to expand without limit, the capacity of individuals to receive and absorb messages seems to remain about the same. Result: overload.

So it is immensely frustrating for serious contemporary leaders to try to get their messages across. Constituents not only suffer from overload, but they also have notoriously short attention spans. And their alertness or deafness is influenced by the fashions or anxieties of the moment. During the oil shortage of the 1970s even fairly dull stories on alternate sources of energy commanded attention. A half dozen years later, a genuinely exciting story on the subject drew editorial ho-hums.

The most effective means of gaining access to the media is to spend money, and the impact of that simple fact on the political process has been profound. Politicians scramble for dollars because they simply must have them to compete in the television era—and in the process they tend to become accountable to donors rather than constituents.

It is easy to indict the media. But for anyone who has observed the devastating consequences of a controlled press, the bottom line is clear. Throughout our history our free press has made an overwhelmingly positive contribution.

Dorothea Dix's successful nineteenth-century campaign to reform the treatment of the mentally ill would never have resulted in effective legislation without the collaboration of the press in every state in which she worked. The Pure Food and Drug Act of 1906 owed almost everything to Upton Sinclair's exposure of the meatpacking industry in *The Jungle*, and the dissemination of his revelations through the press. And in more recent times, exposure of the Watergate scandals was a triumph of effective journalism.

Dispersion

Conflicting Impulses

In the history of this country there has been a tug-of-war between two conflicting intentions. One is to disperse power, to create pluralistic arrangements, to design systems in which initiative and responsibility are widely shared. Our Founding Fathers expressed that intention in the separation of powers, the reservation of powers to the states, and other features of our political system. The intention is vividly reflected in our private sector today; both its profit and nonprofit segments exhibit extraordinary diversity and dispersion of initiative.

The other intention is to centralize in the name of efficiency, coherence and order. Among the Founding Fathers, Alexander Hamilton symbolized the impulse.

Conflict between the two approaches is ancient and at the same time quite contemporary. The corporate headquarters in New York City tries to decide how much freedom to give the branch manager in Tucson, Arizona. The parent in Tallahassee, Florida, worries that the federal government is trying to control the schools. Both are expressions of the same crucial question for any social system: to what extent are power and initiative to be dispersed throughout the system? The answer arrived at will profoundly affect patterns of leadership.

The impulse to centralize, latent or manifest in all societies always, gained strength in our society in the late nineteenth and early twentieth centuries. Far-flung organized systems are nothing new; the Roman Empire was such a system. But technological advances, particularly in transportation and communication, have made central control possible to a degree never before envisaged. Caesar did not have to arrange a teleconference with the Roman Senate before his raid on Britain.

Our Preference for Dispersion

Compared with other western democracies, the United States has leaned toward dispersion—and we think with good reasons. Dispersion ranks second only to the rule of law as a means of domesticating power and ensuring liberty.

Beyond that, dispersion suits our style. We believe that a society should be vital in all its parts and not just at the center; that ideas, initiative and creativity should flow both ways between the center and the periphery. We believe that social controls should not emanate solely from the top but also out of the community, neighborhood, family—and not least out of self-discipline. We believe that individuals throughout the system should have a keen sense of responsibility—not just for their own behavior but for the larger good.

Allocation of Functions

Top managers in large systems, seeking to govern the behavior of people they will never see face to face, create a dense thicket of rules and regulations. But excessive central rule-making leads to overstandardization—too many rules over too wide a territory.

In every large national organization, the truly effective local manager solves many problems by bending the rules. Not long ago the local manager for a famous national corporation pointed out to me the inappropriateness of the latest edict from headquarters. "I don't really blame them," he said. "What do they know about conditions here in San Francisco? I just do a little judicious reinterpreting and it all works out." Top-level decision making on certain matters is absolutely essential, but most matters can be settled far below the top, many at the grass roots.

When Don Peterson was elected president of Ford Motor Company in 1980, the corporation was sustaining huge losses and the quality of its product was distressingly low. In 1986—by this time Peterson was the chief executive officer—Ford's earnings exceeded those of General Motors for the first time in sixty years, and it was producing the most reliable American-made cars. Peterson says that the company pushes decision making "as far down in the organization as we think we possibly can, on the very sound principle that the farther down you get, the closer you're getting to where there's true knowledge about the issues."[5]

In 1988–89 I served on the National Commission on the Public Service, chaired by Paul Volcker, former chairman of the Federal Reserve Board. In its final report the commission came out strongly for devolution of initiative and responsibility within the vast federal establishment.

To pose the issue as a choice between centralization and decentralization is misleading. An ill-conceived decentralizing can be disastrous. Some functions and decisions are best made at the periphery of the system, some at the center. It is a matter of allocating functions to the appropriate level.

State and Local Government

In examining the dispersion of initiative and responsibility in our own society, one is bound to consider the role of state and local government. Given the pluralistic tradition with which this nation began, one might suppose that state and local governments would have flourished from the beginning, but the record is poor. There have been brilliant exceptions, to be sure. Wisconsin in the days of LaFollette exhibited great vigor. Pittsburgh, under the beneficent team leadership of Richard King Mellon and Mayor David Lawrence, set a remarkable standard for urban leadership. One could mention other shining examples, but for most of our history state and local governments have not been an effective countervailing force to the centralizing trends in American life.

Then in the 1960s, there began a slow but unmistakable reassertion of vitality at state and local levels. The Supreme Court's reapportionment decisions—*Baker* v. *Carr* (1962) and *Reynolds* v. *Sims* (1964)—broke the grip of rural constituencies and opened the way to a wave of state legislative reform. During the same period, both state and city administrations grew stronger as they found themselves charged with administering very large federal grants.

The valuable strengthening of state and local government should not lead, as some ideologues would have it, to a withering away of the federal government. This huge and complex society cannot do without a vigorous and effective federal government. What is wanted is the optimum balance of federal, state and local initiative on each particular issue. The civil rights advances of 1954–1968 would never have occurred without action at the federal level.

Motivation and Initiative

As I suggested in the preceding chapter, to maintain a high level of motivation it is essential that the largest possible number of individuals within the system feel that they share ownership of the problem (to use the currently popular phrase), and that they themselves are part of the solution. One of the root difficulties of large-scale organization is that those far from the top are insufficiently motivated. Daniel Yankelovich reports that fewer than 25 percent of workers today say that they work at full potential, and about 60 percent believe they do not work as hard as they once did.[6] Roughly 75 percent say they could be significantly more effective than they are now.

The large-scale organization must ask a great deal of its lower-level people. It needs their local knowledge, their initiative, their problem-solving skills, their intimate grasp of realities on the firing line. Unfortunately, some supervisors do not welcome eager subordinates. In a recent cartoon the boss said, "Of course you're worth more than you're getting, Dobbins. Why don't you let up a bit?"

The same considerations apply when we ask how the whole society can be made to function effectively. A great many individuals down through the system must take action at their level, reweaving connections between warring subsystems and proposing redesign of malfunctioning processes. If it were not for this wide dispersal of leadership, our kind of society could not function.

There is bound to be a certain trade-off between the need to push initiative and autonomy out to the constituent parts of the organization and the need for the cohesion that every system must have in some degree. And in seeking a solution, executives will find that a widely shared understanding of the organization's goals and values will do much to ensure cohesiveness even when the various parts of the organization are given considerable autonomy.

The Leader's Advantage

Just about everything in large-scale organization seems to militate against leadership. All the intricate processes slow the leader down. Innumerable system manipulators push their particular agendas and block the leader's initiatives in untraceable ways. Cyert and March point out that an organization is generally a coalition of individuals and groups with diverse goals, engaged in continuous bargaining for power.[7] Elective officials have multiple constituencies that further complicate leadership.

But no matter how numerous the frustrations, leaders have advantages. They have a centrality that heightens their capacity to make strategic moves. Unless they have foolishly isolated themselves, they are privy to more kinds of information than anyone else in the organization. They have many ways of granting or withholding favors and almost invariably have veto power over many decisions within the organization.

The leader generally has the power to set the agenda. I have known a number of mayors who essentially had no more power than any other member of the city council, but had the right to set the council's agenda. That, plus shrewd use of access to the media, enabled them to lead very effectively.

Leaders have the capacity to mobilize lower-level leaders within the system and to reach out to potential allies at all levels. With respect to most of the initiatives the leader wishes to take, there will be numbers of individuals down through the organization who are wholehearted allies, and the leader can often activate them regardless of intervening resistance in the chain of command. Leaders can turn on green lights throughout the organization with a minimum expenditure of energy.

Bennis and Nanus say that a major task of leadership is the management of attention.[8] The symbolic role of leaders, coupled with their privileges as the prime source of official information, gives them voice and visibility.

9

FRAGMENTATION AND THE COMMON GOOD

The world is made up of many national systems, each claiming sovereignty. And each nation has its subsystems. We speak of the American system in the singular, but in fact it is made up of many systems. The framers designed a federal government consisting of three independent branches, and the Tenth Amendment, with its explicit reservation of powers to the states, laid the basis for the complex relationships of federal, state and local government today.

The United States outstrips all other nations in the size and autonomy of its nongovernmental sector. Both profit and nonprofit segments of the nongovernmental sector have many dealings with government, but both recognize that their vitality depends in part on their success in holding themselves free—within the law—of any central bureaucratic definitions of goals.

The nonprofit segment of the private sector is uniquely American in its diversity and strength. It exists elsewhere but its richness and scope in this country are a source of surprise to visitors from abroad. It includes many diverse religious groups; cultural institutions such as symphonies, ballets, museums; private schools and colleges; philanthropic foundations; hospitals and social agencies; youth organizations; unions and professional associations; and innumerable organizations pursuing one or another social objective—civil rights, voter education, accountable government, conservation, and the like.

Terminology can mislead us in our references to such organizations. They are *in* the private sector, and this is important because it gives them a freedom they might not otherwise have. But many of them are in an important sense *public* institutions, crucial parts of our public life.

Leadership Pyramids

Our leadership mirrors the condition of the whole society. It is not tightly knit; at best it is loosely knit, at worst completely unravelled. It is a mystery that it works at all. We have many leadership pyramids. The leaders in the various pyramids do not all know each other—or want to. Often they are in conflict. Such conflict is generally played down by writers who prefer to believe that the society is governed by a more or less monolithic power elite. There is no clear pecking order among leadership groups. Business interests are dominant with respect to certain issues, farmers with respect to other issues, and so on. There is no fixed national power structure. To be sure, there is often a fixed power structure at the community level, sometimes the city-hall gang, sometimes a network of powerful families, sometimes a dominant industrial concern.

The Power of Organized Groups

In the past forty years there has been tremendous growth in the number and diversity of organized groups seeking to influence public policy. There are literally thousands of organized business groups, and they are often in conflict among themselves. There are many labor groups, again often at odds with one another. The professions have their own organized groups, some of which have become immensely powerful. There are agricultural groups, maritime interests, groups representing institutions such as hospitals and community colleges.

In the majority of these groups, the element of cohesion is supplied by a common economic activity or interest. Of quite a different order are the movements—most notable in the case of women's rights and civil rights—that seek to redress injustices they have suffered at the hands of society.

Most of the groups that contend with one another have legitimate concerns; some of them have concerns that are, by any standard, urgent. But as more and more of them learn how to organize for effective action and how to slug it out in the adversary mode, what started as healthy competition develops destructive aspects.

The organized groups have their lobbying organizations in Washington and in the state capitals, and have gained command of substantial chunks of power generally thought to reside in government. In the process they have not made big government easier to live with, and they have neither halted nor disciplined the growth of government. They have established beachheads in Congress and in agencies of the executive branch; their representatives are placed on advisory councils, their trusted friends appointed to key agency posts, their purposes written into statutes.

In the process, the boundary line between government and interests outside of government becomes badly blurred. There are several notable consequences. One is that the normal chain of command is bypassed. A Cabinet officer may be powerless to disrupt what political scientists have called "the iron triangle," the collaboration of his or her own bureau chiefs with outside lobbying groups and with the congressional servants of those outside groups.

A president has even greater difficulty in dealing with the countless organized groups, which is one of the reasons that each new president, after a few weeks in office, begins to wonder whether the buttons on his desk are wired to anything.

James Madison spoke quite explicitly about "the mischiefs of faction." But our situation today is more complex and difficult than any we have known before.

War of the Parts Against the Whole

How many times have we seen a major American city struggling with devastating problems while every possible solution is blocked by one or another powerful commercial or political or union interest? Each has achieved veto power over a piece of any possible solution, and no one has the power to solve the problem. Thus, in an oddly self-destructive conflict, the parts wage war against the whole.

The war of the parts against the whole is the central problem of pluralism today. We are moving toward a society so intricately organized that the working of the whole system may be halted if one part stops functioning. Thus our capacity to frustrate one another through noncooperation has increased dramatically. The part can hold the whole system up for ransom. Anyone who has lived through a transit strike in a major city can testify to the resulting chaos.

Grievances Unlimited

Because all groups cannot prevail, one encounters in group after group an undercurrent of grievance. Each is convinced of the rightness of its aims and the centrality of its role. Why then does it not prevail?

Mark Twain said, "There isn't a parallel of latitude but thinks it would have been the equator if it had had its rights." Each group concludes that the importance of its contribution is unappreciated, and that it is being pushed around by undeserving others. Each has nagging doubts about the integrity of other elements in the society.

The grievances of business people, labor, and farmers are familiar. It is not widely recognized that virtually every group has comparable grievances—schoolteachers, police, truckers; the list is endless. Each group in its own way feels victimized. A physician friend of mine said, "We want to serve the society, but it's hard to serve when you're under constant attack." Civil servants feel they are mocked and denied the respect that is their due. A sheetmetal worker with a comfortable income and a pleasant suburban home told a journalist, "I frankly think nobody in the whole society gives a damn whether folks like me live or die. We're not poor so we get no sympathy, and we're not rich so we have no power."

People who think of themselves as victims are in no mood to collaborate with others to shape a constructive future. They are more likely to be accusatory and intransigent. Any suggestion that a particular group curb its self-interest for the common good is seen as a hostile effort to undermine its position.

Each group, believing itself to be engaged in a lonely fight for survival, develops a kind of collective paranoia and irrationality. Several years ago angry farmers drove their tractors down the avenues of Washington. On another occasion, independent truckers blocked the highways around the capital. In a southern city recently, members of the fire department refused to respond to alarms. One would hardly guess that all have a stake in the common good.

"But," says a scientist friend of mine, "we scientists contribute to the common good just by existing." Business people express comparable sentiments, and so does every other element in the society. A union leader says, "When we improve the lot of the workers, that *is* the public good." They believe in the value of their roles for the good of the whole society, and we can accept that kind of healthy self-affirmation. But when battle lines are drawn and tensions rise, the good of the whole society disappears from view in the clash of segmental purposes.

The Common Good

As long as we accept the idea of pluralism (and we cannot abandon it), we let ourselves in for the consequences. There is an ancient adage among British sailors that the only sure cure for seasickness is to sit on the shady side of an old brick church in the country.

But a society in which pluralism is not undergirded by some shared values and held together by some measure of mutual trust simply cannot survive. *Pluralism that reflects no commitments whatever to the common good is pluralism gone berserk.*

A primary task of our dispersed leadership is to achieve a workable level of unity within the society. It is well to specify a workable level because the last thing we want is unqualified or oppressive unity. Our freedom, our pluralism, our dispersion of power all invite healthy conflict as various groups and individuals pursue their diverse purposes. The reconciling of such divergent purposes is one of the tasks of the leader.

It is built into the nature of human systems that what is good for (or thought to be good for) one or another of the diverse segments or individuals within the group is not necessarily good for the group (community, tribe, nation) as a whole. Garrett Hardin, in his famous essay "The Tragedy of the Commons," pointed out that sometimes when each member of a community acts to maximize his or her short-term self-interest, the long-term consequence may be the destruction of values or purposes that the group held in common and did not, in fact, wish to destroy.[1]

One encounters from time to time a clever debater who undertakes to prove that any such idea as the public interest or the common good is a delusion, a will-o'-the-wisp, and that everything boils down to someone's special interest. If it is a delusion, it has a long history—twenty-five centuries at the very least. If it were impossible for citizens to agree on *anything* that could be defined as the public interest—if there were no common ground of *any* sort—then there could be no Constitution, no criminal code, and no way of living together peaceably from day to day.

There are various terms for the values or purposes held jointly by the group: *the common good . . . the common weal . . . the public interest.* It is not a difficult notion to grasp. But the next step—determining in a particular situation what the common good actually is—turns out to be very difficult indeed. Does one listen to farmers who want more money for their crops, or consumers who want lower food prices at the market? Does one listen to residents who want to preserve the tranquil rural character of their town, or to business interests that see economic growth as the overriding goal? In our society we resolve such questions partly through the free market and partly through our representative institutions. If the free market is working as it should, which happens fairly often, and if our representative institutions are working as they should, which also happens fairly often, they move toward some approximation of the common good—not perfect, but better than the outcome in those societies that lack a free market or representative institutions.

At the same time we acknowledge the right of any and every citizen, wise or foolish, to assert that the outcome is a travesty of the common good. The framers of our Constitution knew that majorities do not always define the common good. One recalls the two little boys who excitedly told their mother that their younger brother had fallen in the lake. "We applied artificial respiration," they said, "but he kept jumping up and running away." Their majority solution was apparently not acceptable.

The One-Segment Leader

Unfortunately, a high proportion of leaders in all segments of our society today—business, labor, the professions, and so on—are rewarded for single-minded pursuit of the interests of their group. They are rewarded for doing battle, not for compromising. It might be useful to devise another set of standards by which to judge them. Suppose that leaders who refused to reach out beyond their own groups came to be regarded as distinctly inferior to the leaders who accepted larger responsibilities, who without forgetting the goals of their own groups also worked with others to resolve conflicts and serve the larger good. Would that not move us at least a few steps along the road to coherence as a society?

Implications for Leaders

In an isolated, monolithic system the authority stemming from the leader's hierarchical position is a potent weapon, always there, even if the leader chooses to use it with a light hand. But in a tumultuous, swiftly changing environment, in a world of multiple, colliding systems, the hierarchical position of leaders within their own system is of limited value, because some of the most critically important tasks require lateral leadership—boundary-crossing leadership—involving groups over whom they have no control. They must exercise leaderlike influence beyond the system over which they preside. They must do what they can to lead without authority.

Within the executive branch, the president of the United States can act with hierarchical authority, but every president must deal with powerful and resistant external systems—the Congress, the media, countless highly organized interest groups, and foreign governments. Fortunately, the president can get help. Washington is awash with men and women who make profitable and interesting careers out of their capacity to deal effectively with Congress, the media, and all the other elements with which the president must contend. But even with all the available help, President Carter never mastered congressional relations, and President Johnson never dealt effectively with the media.

If one is engaged in administering, it makes a great deal of difference whether the people one is seeking to influence are subordinate, superordinate, or on the same level. Leadership overrides such distinctions. It moves in any direction it can. The best university presidents lead their boards of trustees even though the boards are above them in authority.

The best of our ambassadors abroad are classic examples of leaders who must make their impact felt in ways that are often at odds with the conventional image of the leader-constituent relationship. The ambassador is the president's personal representative. Within his or her jurisdiction, the ambassador is chief diplomat, chief bureaucrat and chief politician. With respect to the community of United States agencies and citizens in the host country, the ambassador is mayor, chaplain and a source of help in time of trouble. Beyond that, an effective ambassador finds and exploits opportunities to play a discreetly leaderlike role with respect to both the government and the populace of the host country. And the ablest ambassadors undertake significant leadership efforts with respect to their superiors in Washington.

Coping with Multiple Systems

Leaders unwilling to seek mutually workable arrangements with systems external to their own are not serving the long-term interests of their constituents. A corporate leader must not only maintain internal unity but must also find a way of living harmoniously with the systems that impinge on the corporation—every level of government, consumer groups, the general public, and so on. A recent army study, in describing the competencies of a four-star general, states: "Persuasive skills are required . . . in negotiations with Congressional committees, in managing interdependence with allied leaders, in international networking, in coping with local political leaders."[2]

Dwight D. Eisenhower, whose World War II performance as chief of the Allied forces revealed an extraordinary gift for the handling of interdependent systems, said "I'll tell you what leadership is: It's *persuasion* . . . and *conciliation* . . . and *education* . . . and *patience*."[3]

When I was appointed Secretary of Health, Education, and Welfare, perhaps the biggest challenge facing the department was the initial enforcement of the Civil Rights Act of 1964—and Eisenhower's formulation was closely applicable to our situation. The first task we faced was to cope with the complexities of the department itself and the rest of the federal government since the enforcement effort involved several agencies. Dealings with Congress were continuous and often heated, with senators and representatives from southern states accusing us of exceeding our authority. It was necessary to pay the closest attention to the decisions of the courts on civil rights so that we could shape a policy consistent with judicial interpretations and thus not be thrown into disarray by unexpected court judgments.

Relations with government at the state level were continuous and sometimes stormy. We received many visits from southern governors, not in a spirit of cordiality. Our dealings with local officials, particularly school superintendents and principals, were difficult and delicate. From the private sector, civil rights organizations were regular visitors, always pressing for tougher and speedier action. And the media were ever present.

It was a struggle. But I had the good fortune to have a superb team, effective legislation, a supportive public mood, and above all, the steadfast support of President Lyndon B. Johnson.

Such luck is rare. Bruce Murray, professor at the California Institute of Technology and former director of the Jet Propulsion Laboratory, describes how, when high-level leadership failed, America's space program was devastated by the conflicting purposes of special interests.[4] After the powerful support of presidents Kennedy and Johnson and the inspired entrepreneurial guidance of James Webb, coherent leadership gradually fell apart, and the first golden age of America in space ended in confusion, in cross purposes, and eventually in searing tragedy.

Make no mistake about it, our beloved pluralism places special burdens on leadership. As I shall point out in the next chapter, the task for leaders is not just to work across boundaries to achieve the goals of their own particular system. Despite differing objectives, all must help our communities and our nation to survive and flourish.

10

THE KNITTING TOGETHER

Government and the Private Sector

The reconciling of conflicting interests that cannot be reconciled in the marketplace or elsewhere is not an unfamiliar or inappropriate task for our governmental institutions. The judicial branch pursues the task full time through the resolving of disputes. The other two branches come at it in more varied ways but their efforts, when they are functioning properly, are often attempts to reconcile the larger objective of the common good with the immediate reality of special interests.

Unfortunately, all too rarely have any of the special interests shown the slightest concern for the health of the political process. All too often they have been satisifed with incompetent, disorganized, or even corrupt government, provided that they could influence it. But a weak and corrupt government that sells out to one interest group will sell out to a rival group just as readily. The old wisecrack, "He's very reliable: if you buy him he stays bought," doesn't apply. What one buys from a corrupt government is preference until a higher bidder shows up. Once, as a member of the board of directors of a corporation, I commented to one of the executives on the weakness of the regulatory body under which our industry operated. He said, "We like it that way." Six months later he was furious when the regulators, under political pressure, showed shameless favoritism to one of our competitors.

Every organized interest should encourage the effective and equitable functioning of government. This does not mean more or bigger government. It might mean less government. Our political and governmental processes, functioning at their best, are designed not to impose arbitrary solutions but to preside over the peaceable competition of conflicting interests, and to reconcile those interests within the framework of our shared purposes. We cannot afford to continue our neglect of commonweal priorities.

But government cannot do it all. In what Harlan Cleveland describes as a "nobody in charge" system, everyone had better be partly responsible for the good of the whole. It is essential that leaders from business, labor, the minority communities and so on address themselves to community issues. If we want to preserve the kind of society we have—a society in which a high proportion of the talent, resources and institutional strengths lie outside government—we must find ways of mobilizing those assets in behalf of the community when occasion requires. The only alternative would be for the nation to build into government at all levels the full capability of dealing with any and all crises and problems. Then business, the universities and all the other segments of the private sector could pursue their specialized missions with unruffled calm. For them, the alarm bell would never ring. But that would be a very different kind of society.

It has been a long time since a planter named Washington, a printer named Franklin, a lawyer named Jefferson, a banker named Morris and others of various occupations made themselves experts in statecraft in order to address their shared problems. On occasions since then—particularly World War II and the immediate postwar period—we have seen that the spirit is recoverable, but we are far from that spirit today.

Networking

A few years ago one rarely heard *network* used as a verb, but the usage has spread because it describes an increasingly necessary function: the process of creating or maintaining a pattern of informal linkages among individuals or institutions. In a swiftly changing environment, established and formal linkages may no longer serve, or may have been disrupted. New and flexible interconnections become necessary.

If each segment of our national life is to find a way of flourishing that is compatible with—even contributes to—the flourishing of other segments, the first step is to create communication among the diverse elements. And to this end key people throughout each system must establish networks of informal give and take with people in neighboring systems. Obviously the same process is relevant in international systems.

Many a group bent on achieving one or another goal in the larger society has failed because it could not bring itself to enlist allies outside its own field. Businesspeople talk to businesspeople in terms that persuade businesspeople. The same is true of labor. Many a liberal or conservative group has failed because its members made little effort to communicate with those who did not share their views. We have all experienced the joy of talking "plain common sense" with those who share our illusions!

Sometimes, of course, leaders are willing to deal constructively with other systems but have a fatal ignorance of the people with whom they must deal. They know the people in their own organizations, their own cultures, so to speak, but how well do they know those outside? Legislators! Journalists! And so on.

In my first appearance at a congressional hearing, I didn't know any more about legislators than I did about armadillos, and it showed. I struck out over and over during that interminable session. In the years when Bob Feller had the most dazzling fast ball in the major leagues, Bucky Harris undertook to prepare a rookie who was coming up to bat for the first time against Feller. He said, "Go up and hit what you see. If you don't see anything come on back." That was my problem. I didn't see where the questions were leading until it was too late. Now, after years of dealing with legislators, I recognize how ignorant I was.

The higher one rises as a leader, the more certain it is that one has to deal with the media. The old saying is, "Never argue with people who buy ink by the barrel." Perhaps one should not argue with them, but one had better understand them.

A good many top executives go through their whole careers without ever understanding journalists as human beings. Journalists have been exposed to every form of guile and humbug. It is their business to detect duplicity and dissembling. They all live with the frustration of not getting stories they know are there. And at least for some of them, the more powerful one is, the more one stirs the natural predator in them. A leader had better understand them, had better understand legislators, had better understand all the groups that may help or hinder the leader's work.

Leaders must build outside networks of allies in the many other segments of society whose cooperation is required for a significant result. Wise chief executives place in key positions throughout their organizations individuals who are networkers by inclination. They establish informal cross-boundary working groups. They devise assignments that send their most promising young executives out into the world; for example, for a year's internship in government or an assignment in a foreign country.

Conflict Resolution

We are a combative species. Our seemingly limitless capacity for contention has left no possible cause of dispute untested—mistrust between families, tribes, nations; economic and political differences; racial, religious and class tensions. The tribe that lives on the plains feuds with the tribe that lives in the hills. Neighbor clashes with neighbor. The field office resents headquarters.

Sooner or later every leader must face the task of dealing with conflict. The sounds of bickering are part of the necessary noisiness of a free society; but we are beginning to see that beyond a certain point, adversary action, confrontation and nonnegotiable demands may be counterproductive. If our leaders in all the various fields—business, labor, agriculture, the professions and so on—are concerned, as they must be, with holding the society together, they have no choice but to learn the arts of preventing, defusing and resolving conflict at every level. In a world characterized by multiple, interacting systems, substantial rewards flow to leaders who have mastered the bargaining arts.

That a conflict should rage openly and damage the joint enterprise is not the only bad outcome. It can go underground, remain unresolved, and do even more damage. Bringing unacknowledged conflicts to the surface is part of the leader's task.

Obviously, external conflict offers appealing opportunities to leaders vicious enough to exploit them. Hitler said, "The art of leadership consists of consolidating the attention of the people against a single adversary."[1] We cannot tolerate those who foster external disputes in the hope of diminishing internal conflict.

Of course, every leader finds that he or she must occasionally engage in combat in a justifiable cause. Indeed the fortitude to engage in necessary combat is essential to leadership. Sometimes a wrong cannot be righted without precipitating conflict. But we should send a clear message to our leaders that we do not intend to reward them when they foster conflict for their own aggrandizement.

In the past half century a great deal has been learned about the resolving of disputes, and leaders should familiarize themselves with it.

Leaders experienced in dispute resolution bring their influence to bear on both sides to scale down irrational demands and provocations. They foster the transition from a cross fire of accusations to a collaborative search for solutions. They look for the underlying sources of misunderstanding: breakdowns in communication, differing perceptions of the facts, insensitivity of each side to the other's legitimate needs, and so on. One goal is to give each side the possibility of compromising without losing face. Brian Urquhart, former United Nations undersecretary general, says, "Don't ask either party to commit suicide. Provide a graceful way out."[2]

Leaders open many channels of communication between opponents and create many kinds of interchange, letting each side have its say and requiring that each listen. They recognize the inevitability of—but seek to reduce—the counterproductive forms of communication, such as lies and posturing before third parties.

Leaders experienced in resolving conflicts seek among the tangle of interests held by the adversaries those interests that constitute common ground and may be pursued to mutual advantage. They generate alternative possible solutions.

I recall one instance in my Cabinet days in which a Senate committee chairman and I were in grim and (we thought) hopeless disagreement on a proposed piece of legislation. The draft of the bill prepared by the senator's staff was unacceptable to me and the version prepared by my staff was unacceptable to the senator. Both sides were digging in for a test of strength when the late Wilbur Cohen, undersecretary of the department, took a hand. Cohen, a wonderfully gifted negotiator, studied both drafts and proposed a number of changes in language that brought the two versions closer together without offending either side. Then with patient good humor, he proposed a variety of alternative solutions ingeniously drafted to fall between the two entrenched positions. Slowly, almost imperceptibly, we began to see a way of agreeing—and eventually solved our problem. Elliot Richardson said of Wilbur Cohen's negotiating skills, "He led you to join him in being resourceful about ways of resolving the dispute."[3]

The considerable knowledge we now have about techniques of conflict resolution should be taught in every high school and college in the land.

Coalition Building

Closely related to conflict resolution is the art of coalition building. Where dispute resolution typically involves two sides seeking to deal with one or more key points of disagreement, coalition building usually involves multiple parties with a welter of differing interests seeking ground for collaborative action. Dispute resolution envisions a reasonably early terminal point; coalition building generally envisions a long-term relationship. The parties to a coalition may disagree on many things and still work together provided their leaders find and foster a few important shared goals.

In 1967, when the urban riots were producing a frightening level of violence throughout the country, an extraordinary group of the nation's top leaders from the private sector came together to form the National Urban Coalition. Its purpose was to get at and remedy the racism, poverty and other grave ailments that afflicted our great cities. There were businesspeople such as Henry Ford and David Rockefeller, union leaders such as George Meany and Walter Reuther, mayors such as Richard J. Daley and John Lindsay, minority group leaders such as Whitney Young and Bayard Rustin, together with educators, clergy and others. Needless to say, the items of potential disagreement within the group were virtually limitless. My task as chairman was to hold them to their few shared purposes.

Coalition builders seek to formulate goals and values that lift all participants out of their separate preoccupations by gaining their commitment to larger objectives. It was not only the skilled conceptual work of Madison, Hamilton and others that finally forged thirteen former colonies into a nation. It was also the vision of something in the future, the destiny of a new nation, that lifted them out of their parochialisms and moved them toward union.

The other major task in coalition building is to establish trust among the participants in the coalition. It has been my experience that contending parties may agree on the facts, even see possible paths to agreement, but harbor such distrust of one another's motives that agreement cannot be achieved. Coalition requires that all parties develop habits of candor, that they hold posturing and game-playing to a minimum, that they be forthright not only about their real interests, needs and goals but also about their fears and suspicions. Such objectives are furthered not only through formal discussion but also through informal communication under congenial circumstances.

Leaders of a coalition must ensure that each member of the coalition becomes fully acquainted with the constituencies of the others around the table—what they want, what they fear, and what assumptions (or misconceptions) they hold concerning the subject at hand. Sometimes what seems irrational in the member at the bargaining table becomes wholly understandable if one knows the concerns of the member's constituents. And only through such knowledge can the group find what the late Carl Holman, a distinguished civil rights leader, called "convergence issues"—the common ground on which collaboration can go forward.

Often the process of coalition building fails to get started because there is no suitable convenor, or because those who could play the convenor role decline to do so. The convenor must be perceived by potential members of the coalition as neutral and trustworthy, but need not be seen as powerful; indeed, powerlessness has its uses. When a number of nations came together in the early 1950s to form the European Coal and Steel Community, the only source of power was their intention to work together. In the ensuing years a crucial role was played by lesser powers such as Belgium and the Netherlands, at least in part because they did not arouse fears of domination.

Many committees are, in fact, coalitions. Any member of a legislative body who is seeking action on a proposal engages in coalition building. In a corporation the group of division heads who meet weekly to deal with companywide issues are in some respects a coalition—and sometimes a rather fractious one. The Joint Chiefs of Staff are in important respects a coalition, not without its tensions. When General William J. ("Wild Bill") Donovan appeared before the Joint Chiefs to report on the work of the Office of Strategic Services in 1942, one of the chiefs asked him to explain the term *psychological warfare*. Donovan is said to have responded "It's what you fellows practice on each other."[4]

Networks of Responsibility

If our pluralistic system is to regain any measure of cohesion, leaders from various segments are going to have to come together in what I have called *networks of responsibility* to appraise and seek to resolve the larger problems of their community, region, nation or world. The mayor cannot turn a city into a community through sheer personal leadership skills. The fabric of community must be woven by many groups—municipal agencies, civic organizations, businesses, unions, schools, churches, neighborhood organizations, the community foundation, community college and so on. Leaders from all segments, at all economic levels, must have formed networks that permit continuous collaboration among government, business and the nonprofit sector, identifying issues and moving toward consensus. Such networks do not flourish in the contemporary climate if they resemble the old exclusionary Establishments. There must be access and openness to participation.

The National Urban Coalition tried to create, in the major cities of the country, local coalitions composed of all segments of the community (in other words, networks of responsibility) but the idea took root in only a few places. As recently as 1986 a study undertaken at the request of Chicago's business and civic leaders concluded among other things that

- Effective public–private interaction in Chicago is extraordinarily difficult because key participants do not understand or respect each other.
- Public officials and business executives perceive each other as unwilling and unable to establish ongoing communication, with the give-and-take that it implies.
- There is no sustained forum for effective interaction between the public and private sectors in Chicago.[5]

Minneapolis–St. Paul and a few other metropolitan centers have demonstrated that leaders from diverse segments of the community can, in fact, collaborate effectively. Sometimes the networks form very swiftly in time of crisis. When New York City faced fiscal disaster in the mid-seventies, bankers, city officials, union leaders, real estate people and many others joined hands to save the city.

Instead of being sporadic responses to crisis, such networks must become a standard way of doing business. A network of responsibility does not need to have any official standing—in fact it may be better off without it. By avoiding such formalities, it remains free to approach the broadest problems of the city (or the nation) and its future freely and flexibly.

There are, however, some requirements. First, such a network must include every significant segment of the community. Second, those who participate must be respected members of the segment from which they come, though it is not necessary—perhaps not even desirable—that they be official representatives of their segments of the community.

It would be foolish to suppose that such networks can dissolve the real conflicts among powerful segmental interests within the community. The promise of the network is simply that segmental leaders may pursue more productively the hard tasks of mutual accommodation, and look more broadly at the largest questions of the community's future. The role of leaders in the process can hardly be exaggerated.

Impact on Elected Officials

If leaders in all segments were to develop through such collaboration a habit of concern for the common good, top political leaders would surely find their work greatly facilitated. The mayor would find that, in addition to all the multiple special interests, there was a *constituency for the whole*. So would governors, senators, representatives and the president. I suspect that no other event would so quickly restore the attractiveness of public life.

Politics

These tasks do not evoke the conventional image of the heroic leader. I have even used the unheroic word *compromise*. But leadership has always involved politics and never more so than today. The political process generally involves taking into account the needs or demands (some of them mutually conflicting) of diverse constituencies, weighing the realities of power, calculating consequences, negotiating, and bargaining. An absolute dictator could dispense with much of that. In a land without law, brute force would have its way. We reject both dictator and lawless force, and ask politicians functioning in the framework of our representative institutions to accomplish the mediating and brokering necessary to reconcile diverse views.

When I think of the usefulness of politicians, I sometimes call to mind Congressman M. He was from a one-party district, the product of an entrenched political machine, a modest man, a survivor. An occasion arose in which environmentalists were furious at an amendment proposed by industry that would have weakened legislation they were seeking. Congressman M brought the two sides together and hammered out a compromise that was publicly praised by both sides. It may take heroes to challenge systems, and leaders to change systems, but systems that function successfully from day to day do so because ordinary men and women perform their appointed tasks well. Congressman M was performing with skill one of the unsung tasks of the politician.

Politics has its fraudulent side, as does business, education, religion and all else. But it also has its good and necessary side, and it is curious that a process so essential to a pluralistic society should be so widely scorned. One reason the average citizen has grave doubts about politics is that decisions one would expect to be simple become immensely complicated when multiple interests are at stake. That is as it should be—but the citizen longs for simplicity. When "Mr. Smith Goes to Washington" he seems to cut through all the complexity and to show how simple it can be when common sense and integrity prevail. But that is the wonderful world of cinema.

With just a bit of exaggeration, one might say that the lay person's notion of high-level decision making is a simple one-act drama. The leader sits alone on a bare and silent stage. Two aides enter. One states the argument for choosing path A, the other for choosing path B. The lay person is strongly inclined to believe that one of the paths must be clearly right, the other clearly wrong. Black or white. The good versus the bad. The leader chooses.

Ring down the curtain on that charade, and lift the curtain on the real world of the functioning leader. The stage is crowded; there is not just one leader but several and they clearly have differing views. Everyone is talking at once and portions of the audience continually surge up onto the stage. And there is a large clock on the wall that ticks off the minutes like hammer blows. Before the clock strikes noon, a great many decisions must be made. And on virtually none of them is there a virtuous path A or wicked path B. Indeed there rarely are just two sides or two parties to the dispute. There is relatively little black and white, mostly shades of gray.

Sometimes a leader cannot do one good thing without endangering another good thing. Often short-term considerations are at war with long-term consequences. Sometimes a leader chooses a bad path A because path B is worse. Often it becomes clear that some intermediate compromise is the way to go. Sometimes there is no alternative to a dangerous path A, and the only issue is damage control. And the tyrant is the clock on the wall. A few of the decisions can be put off, but most demand attention now—and in any case the afternoon schedule is equally crowded.

In one instance the decision is on the merits of the alternatives; in another on the relative trust the leader has in the proponents of the alternatives (or relative indebtedness to the proponents). The leader knows that information is incomplete, knows that mistakes will be made, knows that hostility will be aroused. The clock ticks on.

Institutional Politics

Politics is a part of the life of every institution, be it corporation, school, church or union. The process does not always have the tumultuous quality just described but it is rarely tidy. As in the public arena, the connotations of the word *politics* are decidedly negative. To say of one's organization "We don't have any politics around here" is considered by some to be a high compliment. But it is almost certainly untrue. Even the most worthy ends are generally pursued through political activities—to reconcile conflicting parties, to sort out many purposes in search of a common purpose, to mobilize a group in pursuit of shared goals—or simply to keep peace in the family.

One of the reasons institutional politics has a bad name is that the word is popularly used to cover a variety of unattractive circumstances that transform an office into a piranha pool. When people say, "There's too much politics in this place," they are generally referring to manipulation, mistrust and hidden agendas; or to envy, unseemly rivalry and self-promotion; or to favoritism and hidden alliances. Strictly speaking, all of these are organizational ailments—chiefly failures of honesty, integrity and loyalty—that may exist quite independently of politics.

All that we have been discussing—the fragmentation, the drifting away from shared purposes, the breakdown of communication—may be seen from another angle as the collapse of community. So we had better have a look at the concept and reality of community.

11

COMMUNITY

In some measure, what we think of as a failure of leadership on the contemporary scene may be traceable to a breakdown in the sense of community.

The Uprooted, Oscar Handlin's great book on the nineteenth-century immigrants to America, contains a moving account of the European peasant villages from which so many began the long journey.[1]

Handlin wrote of the unchanging, intimately known physical setting—the road, the brook, fields and trees, the small cluster of houses, the smithy, the mill, the church, the burial ground. He described the seamless web of family, fellow villagers, land, religion, occupations, rights and duties. It was a world characterized by coherence and continuity, allegiance and the experience of being needed.

The breakdown of community is not a uniquely modern phenomenon. No doubt it occurred in the world of antiquity when the interaction of tribal cultures in an ancient city shook the faith of the tribesman, or when the tales of traders from distant places planted seeds of questioning in parochial minds.

But those were occasional happenings. With the Renaissance, the breakdown of communities began to be a common experience, not yet devastating, but common. By the time Emile Durkheim wrote his classic *Le Suicide* in 1897, the diagnosis was clear.[2] He spoke in the most lucid terms of the breakdown of traditional belief systems and social groups. And in our time we continue to see the weakening and collapse of communities of obligation and commitment.

The disintegration of communities and the loss of a sense of community are clearly detrimental to the accomplishment of group purpose. As I pointed out earlier, it is in communities that individuals develop identity and a sense of belonging. It is in communities that values are generated and regenerated. With the disintegration of communities comes disintegration of shared values—and leadership of the sort we seek and respect is made very much more difficult. I say "leadership of the sort we seek and respect" because there are demagogues, some of them quite evil—Hitler is the prototype—who feed on social disintegration.

If leaders cannot find in their constituencies any base of shared values, principled leadership becomes nearly impossible. Leaders are community builders because they have to be. Cicero, in his essay "De Re Publica," wrote: "A people is not just any collection of human beings brought together in any sort of way but an assemblage of people . . . associated in an agreement with respect to justice and a partnership for the common good."

There is another reason that leaders benefit from social coherence. In our system, leaders expect of constituents or followers or lower-level leaders a great deal of participation and sharing of leadership tasks. Social disintegration diminishes the possibility of participation.

The impact of such disintegration on value systems is clear. In a healthy society the process of value generation goes on continuously in stable, face-to-face groups such as family, neighborhood and community. One must include school, church and workplace if they are, in fact, communities. Some are; some are not.

The community teaches. If it is healthy and coherent, the community imparts a coherent value system. If it is fragmented or sterile or degenerate, lessons are taught anyway—but not lessons that heal and strengthen. It is community and culture that hold the individual in a framework of values; when the framework disintegrates, individual value systems disintegrate.

We have seen all the disorders of men and women torn loose from a context of community and of shared values. Individuals often experience a loss of meaning, a sense of powerlessness. They lose the conviction that they can influence the events of their lives or the life of the community (noncommunity) in which they live. Some of the consequences are dealt with in the psychiatrist's office, some in the system of criminal justice. Drugs and alcohol claim their share.

In recent years we have been puzzled by a steady parade of intelligent, successful Americans who have destroyed their own careers through amoral or criminal acts—from ambitious public servants to greedy Wall Street figures. Gifted and richly rewarded, they overreached and brought themselves crashing down. A common assumption is that for a price (money, power, fame, sensual pleasure) they betrayed their standards. The other possibility is that they did not have any standards to betray, that they were among the many contemporary individuals who had roots in no set of values, or have torn loose from their roots. A society afflicted with the disintegration of family and community will inevitably feed such gifted transgressors into the stream of our national life.

A great many of our contemporaries, left without moorings by the disintegration of group norms and torn from any context of shared obligations, have gotten drunk on self. We value the individual. We value individuality. Self-reliance, self-discipline, self-help are honored in our scheme of things. But we cannot respect the crazy celebration of self that one sees today.

Intellectuals of the 1960s cried "Life is absurd." Life is indeed absurd when the web of community meaning is shredded, when belief systems are shattered, when there remains no embracing framework of values. Daniel Bell charges that in modernist culture "there are no sacred groves that cannot be trespassed upon or even trampled down."[3]

The Traditional Community

So where do we go from here? Stories of the traditional communities of nineteenth-century America or Europe evoke nostalgia, but we can never bring them back, and if we could they would prove hopelessly anachronistic.

The traditional community was relatively homogenous. We live with heterogeneity and must design communities to handle it.

The traditional community experienced virtually no change from one decade to the next, and resented the little that it did experience. We must design communities that can survive change and, when necessary, seek change.

The traditional community commonly demanded a high degree of conformity. Our communities must be pluralistic and adaptive, fostering individual freedom and responsibility within a framework of group obligation.

The traditional community was often unwelcoming to strangers, all too ready to reduce its communication with the external world. Hard realities require that present-day communities be in continuous touch with the outside world, and our system of values requires that they be inclusive.

The traditional community could boast generations of history and continuity. Few communities today can hope to enjoy any such heritage. They must continuously rebuild their shared culture, must consciously foster the norms and values that ensure their continued integrity.

The traditional community was typically small—and no doubt a sense of community thrives on smallness. But the organized systems in which most of us live out our lives are not small. Large cities, large corporations, even large schools and churches, must create smaller subsystems in which affiliation and loyalty are realities and the sense of belonging can flourish.

In short, much as we cherish the thought of the traditional community, we have to build anew, seeking to reincarnate some of the cherished values of the old communities in forms appropriate to contemporary social organization.

Ingredients of Community

A glance at the contemporary scene reveals diverse kinds of communities. Most familiar to us are territorially bounded communities such as towns, suburbs and neighborhoods.

For centuries, however, there have also been dispersed communities. The eighteenth-century Jesuit missionary, Eusebio Kino, traveling alone through northern Mexico and through territory that is now Arizona, exploring, mapping, helping the Indians to diversify their agriculture, celebrating the Mass alone in the desert, never doubted that he was an integral part of the dispersed Jesuit community. Our Foreign Service, in its times of high morale, has been a dispersed community.

If a sense of community is to exist today, it will have to be nurtured in many diverse settings. One of the difficulties in creating a sense of community today is the sheer heterogeneity of almost any population one deals with. Gone forever, except in a few out-of-the-mainstream localities, is the community in which a stable set of shared values rests on the even more stable bedrock of a single religious denomination, a single ethnic identity, and an unchallenged tradition. *Today we live with many faiths. We must nurture a framework of shared secular values (justice, respect for the individual, tolerance and so on) while leaving people free to honor diverse deeper faiths that undergird those values.*

Having visited innumerable schools, I concluded years ago that some were communities in the best sense of the word, while others were simply geographical locations where students gathered to perform specified tasks. Later the same diversity struck me with respect to congregations. And workplaces. And cities. What attributes made the difference? In seeking to answer that question, I was driven to think analytically about the ingredients of community.[4] The following list of ingredients is arguable. Consider it provisional, on the way to something better. The important thing at this stage is to get past the generalized idea of community to an understanding of what conditions make it real.

1. *Wholeness Incorporating Diversity*. A community is obviously less of a community if fragmentation or divisiveness exists—and if the rifts are deep, it is no community at all. Schools in which faculty and students carry on a kind of trench warfare, congregations divided into cliques, cities in which people of diverse ethnic origins form mutually hostile groups—these are obviously not healthy communities.

We expect and want diversity, and there is dissension in the best of communities. But vital communities face and resolve differences. Some cities have created special boards to deal with disputes between groups of citizens. Others have interracial councils or have made provisions for citizens from one segment of the community to know and work with citizens from other segments.

2. *A Shared Culture*. The possibility of wholeness is considerably enhanced if the community has a shared culture, that is, shared norms and values. If the community is lucky (and fewer and fewer are) it has a shared history and tradition. It has its symbols of group identity and its story, which it retells often. Social cohesion is advanced if the group's norms and values are explicit. Values that are never expressed are apt to be taken for granted and not adequately conveyed to young people and newcomers. The well-functioning community provides many opportunities to express values in relevant action.

A healthy community affirms itself and builds morale through ceremonies that honor the symbols of shared identity and enable members to rededicate themselves to shared goals. This does not mean that they suppress internal criticism or deny their flaws. The community that cannot tolerate disagreement fails to meet the earlier criterion, "wholeness incorporating diversity."

3. *Good Internal Communication*. Members of a well-functioning community communicate freely with one another. There must be occasions when members gather; there must be provision for forums, and organizations willing to serve as meeting grounds. People have to believe that they can have their say. Each segment of the community must understand what the other segments need and want.

In cities much of the communication is through the media, and all civic leaders and institutions must urge the media toward responsible coverage. But it is a mistake to depend on the media alone. Civic leaders should create an information sharing network among a wide variety of institutions and organizations. Maximum use should be made of institutions that can serve as neutral convenors; for example, community foundations, community colleges, universities and churches. Leaders must combat "we–they" barriers that impede the free flow of communication within their membership.

4. *Caring, Trust, and Teamwork.* A good community nurtures its members and fosters an atmosphere of trust. Members deal with one another humanely, respect one another, and value the integrity of each person. They both protect and give a measure of autonomy to the individual. Everyone is included.

Such attitudes make it possible to work together on necessary common tasks. Undergirding the teamwork is an awareness by all that they need one another and must pool their talent, energy and resources. There is a feeling that when the team wins everybody wins.

It is necessary to add that a community can be too tightly knit, suppressing dissent and constraining the creativity of its members.

5. *Group Maintenance and Government.* A functioning community has institutional provisions for group maintenance or governing. In a corporation it is the board of directors, management and the chain of command. In a college it is the trustees, administration, faculty council and student government. In a town or city it is not only the formal governing mechanisms but also the nongovernmental leadership exercised through various private sector institutions.

6. *Participation and the Sharing of Leadership Tasks.* The healthy community encourages individual involvement in the pursuit of shared purposes. In cities, voter registration and voter turn-out are key indices. Cities can get significant nongovernmental participation through hearings, advisory boards and citizen commissions. Strong neighborhood groups are useful. A wide range of nonprofit civic groups and institutions can play a role.

It is not uncommon in our towns and cities today that the groups most involved in the affairs of the community all come from one or two segments of the community. All segments must participate.

Whether in a city or an organization, the possibility of effective participation is considerably increased if everyone is kept informed, and if individuals feel that they have a say. We must never forget that our conception of community involves the participation of mature and responsible individuals. We don't want community bought at the price of the individual's mindless submission to the group. *The good community finds a productive balance between individuality and group obligation.*

Everyone need not participate actively with respect to any given community. We must guard the *right* to participate while recognizing that some will choose not to do so. Individuals expending enormous energies holding their families together may be thankfully passive members of their church congregation. The individual who is an activist in the workplace community may be a passive member of the neighborhood association.

7. *Development of Young People.* The opportunities for individual growth are numerous and varied for all members. And the mature members ensure that the young grow up with a sense of obligation to the community. Beginning in elementary and high school, boys and girls should learn to take some responsibility for the well-being of any group they are in—a seemingly small step but without doubt the first step toward responsible community participation. And for that matter, the first step in leadership development. On the playing field and in group activities in and out of school, teamwork can be learned. Through volunteer and intern experiences outside of school they learn how the adult world works and have the experience of serving their society. Every organization serving the community should find ways of involving young people.

8. *Links with the Outside World.* There is always a certain tension between the need for the community to draw boundaries to protect its integrity on the one hand, and the need to have fruitful links with the larger communities of which it is a part. The school, for example, must be in some respects a haven for its students, capable of shutting out some of the most destructive aspects of city life, but it can maintain itself as a strong institution only through extensive community relations and intelligent dealing with the school district and the state. A city must relate to its metropolitan area, the state, the nation and the world.

Skill in the building and rebuilding of community is not just another of the innumerable requirements of contemporary leadership. It is one of the highest and most essential skills a leader can command.

Leadership Skills

I have touched on a considerable variety of leadership skills throughout this book. Which particular skills are required to deal with the fragmented world I have described in the last three chapters? Which skills are needed for an interdependent world where, as Jeff Luke puts it, *managing interconnectedness* is the basic task?[5]

Obviously, we need leaders who have some acquaintance with systems other than their own with which they must work. The day of the hard-shelled military leader who never bothered to understand civilians is over, as is the day of the hard-nosed business executive who never bothered to understand government, and the day of the leader who never bothered to think internationally.

Without proposing a definitive list, the following five skills seem to me to be critically important:

- *Agreement Building*. Leaders must have skills in conflict resolution, in mediation, in compromise, in coalition building. The capacity to build trust is essential to these actvities, as are judgment and the political skills to deal with multiple consituencies.
- *Networking*. In a swiftly changing environment established linkages among institutions may no longer serve or may have been disrupted. Leaders must be skilled in creating or recreating the linkages necessary to get things done.
- *Exercising Nonjurisdictional Power*. In an earlier day, corporate leaders or government agency heads settled most matters through internal decisions; and they had the power to do so—power inherent in their institutional positions. The new leaders, dealing endlessly and on many fronts with groups over whom they have no jurisdiction, find that often the power of their institutional position simply is not decisive. They must know how to exercise the other legitimate forms of power—the power of the media and of public opinion, the power of ideas, the power that accrues to those who understand how various systems work, and so on.
- *Institution Building*. With problems so much more complex than they used to be, the leader's untutored good judgment no longer suffices. Even highly educated judgment no longer suffices. So, as I pointed out earlier, we construct systems, build problem-solving capability into them, and then choose leaders who can preside over the systems. Institutionalizing the leaders' tasks enhances continuity and predictability. As a general rule, we no longer want leaders to spend time coping with specific problems. Micromanagement is not the function of leaders. The task of leaders is to have a sense of where the whole system should be going and to institutionalize the problem solving that will get it there. The pace of change is such that leaders find themselves constantly rebuilding to meet altered circumstances.
- *Flexibility*. A year or so ago, I met with a group of Silicon Valley

venture capitalists to hear their views on the kind of leader/manager it takes to run the start-up companies in which they invest. At the end of the meeting I offered them a comparison. A few years earlier the officers of one of the biggest corporations in the world asked me to spend two days with their board, and I had the impression of immensely able officers piloting a huge ocean liner—a liner that set a steady course and held to it through the roughest seas. Now, as I listened to my Silicon Valley friends describe what it takes to lead one of their fast-moving companies, the image that sprang to mind was of someone steering a kayak through the perilous white water of the Salmon River. Flexibility is essential.

RENEWING

Fragmentation, the loss of shared values, and the difficulty of reconciling antagonistic forces are not the only organizational problems the leader must deal with today. Leaders discover that the great systems over which they preside require continuous renewal. Organizations and societies age. Historians tell of the decline of Greece and Rome. Business journals recount the growth and decay of commercial enterprises.

It is not a question of excellence. A society that has reached heights of excellence may already be caught in the rigidities that will bring it down. An institution may hold itself to the highest standards and yet already be doomed by the complacency that foreshadows decline.

Motivation tends to run down. Values decay. The problems of today go unsolved while people mumble the slogans of yesterday. Group loyalties block self-examination. One sees organizations whose structure and processes were designed to solve problems that no longer exist. If regenerative forces are not at work, the end is predictable.

The processes involved in the rise and fall of human institutions are universal. But the cycle of birth, maturity and death is not inexorable in organizations and societies as it is in living things. Renewal is possible, and an organization or society may go through a number of waves of decay and renewal before its story ends.

Historically, most leaders have accepted and have worked within the structure of existing systems. Aside from disasters of nature such as famines and plagues, change was brought about chiefly by conquest or migration. Other sorts of change were relatively slow, and a powerful system (such as the Ottoman Empire) might survive centuries of decay before its final collapse.

Not so today. The pace of change is swift. Institutions that have lost their capacity to adapt pay a heavy price. Yet the impulse of most leaders is much the same as it was a thousand years ago: accept the system as it is and lead it.

That is rarely possible any longer. Continuous renewal is necessary. Leaders must understand how and why human systems age, and must know how the processes of renewal may be set in motion. The purposes are always the same:

- To renew and reinterpret values that have been encrusted with hypocrisy, corroded by cynicism or simply abandoned; and to generate new values when needed.
- To liberate energies that have been imprisoned by outmoded procedures and habits of thought.
- To reenergize forgotten goals or to generate new goals appropriate to new circumstances.
- To achieve, through science and other modes of exploration, new understandings leading to new solutions.
- To foster the release of human possibilities, through education and lifelong growth.

Much of this is implied in the valuable distinction made by James MacGregor Burns between transactional and transformational leadership.[1] Transactional leadership accepts and works within the structure as it is. Transformational leadership renews.

Organizations—Young and Old

The effective contemporary leader lives with the idea of renewal. Before examining the duties of leaders in that dimension, let me offer a quick sketch of some more or less typical changes that occur in a human system (organization, corporation or society) as it moves from infancy to maturity. At each stage something is gained and something lost.

The earliest stage in the life of an organization is very likely to be all motion and commotion. On the good side, there is great flexibility, high motivation, a willingness to try new things, and the capacity to respond quickly. The downside is that almost nothing gets done in an orderly way: budgeting procedures may be haphazard, record-keeping may be a harum-scarum thing, and central files nonexistent. It's great fun if disaster doesn't strike. In the case of societies, consider the frontier community before the advent of law and order. Life was adventruous and unsafe. It was not a world of elaborate manners or oppressive procedures. Simplicity and direct action were ruling characteristics.

By contrast, a mature organization is generally quite orderly. It knows where it is going. It has its budgeting well in hand, its procedures clearly defined. But it is burdened with rules; it has a pecking order; it exhibits the turf syndrome. Instead of bold pathfinding, there is patient advance along established routes.

After I visited one new organization recently, I told a friend it reminded me of eight small boys chasing a chipmunk: lots of noise and confusion, scrambling in every direction, a lot of wasted energy—but great flexibility and unlimited motivation!

At the other extreme, there are mature organizations that remind one of a powerful locomotive steaming down the line: everything functioning predictably, energy being efficiently transformed into forward motion, but no learning, no innovation, no possibility of going anywhere except where the tracks lead.

In this matter sensible leaders want to eat their cake and have it too: to keep the zest and flexibility characteristic of youth, but without the disorder, and to benefit by the orderliness of maturity without the rigidity. Leaders who hope to accomplish that have to understand the maturing process and to comprehend why gains in maturity so often tend to be accompanied by constricting disadvantages.

The Process of Maturing

All great performance involves improving the ways one achieves the result—better methods, better means to the goal. But means tend to triumph over ends. Form triumphs over spirit. People become prisoners of their procedures. The means and methods were originally designed to achieve some specific end, but when circumstances change and new means are called for, it turns out that the old ones have become sacrosanct; the means have become ends in themselves—no longer effective perhaps, but enshrined. People forget what they set out to do. It happens all the time. So the the mature organization ends up with a web of customs, procedures, written and unwritten rules that is extremely hard to cut through.

Frontier societies and organizations in early stages of development tend to be simple, fluid, and uncompartmentalized; and this puts pressure on the individual to be versatile. Thus the "universal man" has most commonly appeared in young and relatively unstructured societies, or early in an era. Recall the versatility of our Founding Fathers.

In later stages, societies and organizations develop a complex division of labor and extensive compartmentalization, which presses the individual to specialize. To the extent that this diminishes versatility, it lessens the capacity of the organization to renew itself.

Organizations are created by their founders to serve vibrant, living purposes. But all too often the founding purposes fade and what finally get served are the purposes of institutional self-enhancement. It happens in hospitals to the detriment of patients, in schools to the detriment of students, in business to the detriment of shareholders and customers, and in government to the detriment of taxpayers. It is rarely the result of evil intent: It happens because means triumph over ends, form triumphs over spirit, and the turf syndrome conquers all.

Continuity and Change

Leaders must understand the interweaving of continuity and change. Particularly important to a society's continuity are its long-term purposes and values. Those purposes and values also evolve in the long run; but by being relatively durable, they enable a society to absorb change without losing its distinctive character and style. Purposes and values do much to determine the direction of change. They ensure that a society is not buffeted in all directions by every wind that blows.

Failure to understand the interweaving of continuity and change is not the only mistake we make. We are an impatient people. We want everything done now, and are tempted to believe that one ought to be able to analyze a particular social need, come up with a neatly blueprinted solution, and put it into effect with no missteps and no broken crockery. As Nelson Polsby has pointed out in his thoughtful book, *Political Innovation in America*, social innovation is not the work of a day. It is not, as he puts it, "a task for those who need quick gratification."[2]

Social problem solving is not only slow, it is untidy. Purposeful social change occurs through a long and disorderly process of trial and error not unlike that of an infant learning to walk. The infant tries, fails, has partial successes, learns, bumps its nose, cries, and tries again. It has many failures before it succeeds. That is why Harlan Cleveland says that "planning is improvisation on a sense of direction."[3] No plan for social or institutional improvement can be put into effect without innumerable in-course corrections.

Innovation is sometimes dramatized as a powerfully disruptive force that shatters the status quo. And sometimes it is. But undue emphasis on its disruptive character can be misleading. Historically, the status quo in human societies primitive or civilized, has been upset not by innovation but by failure of food supply, disease, the hostility of neighboring societies, competition from superior technologies, and inner decay. In such cases, innovation may increase chances of survival. Ironically, the fact that the innovator may come in the role of savior does not necessarily ensure acceptance by those who cherish the status quo. Like children, they may fear the doctor more than the disease. One of the tasks of a leader is to help the group achieve the sense of security and freedom from fear that enables it to risk renewal.

The image of innovation shattering a serene status quo is particularly inappropriate in the modern world. Given the tumultuous sweep of technological and social change, there is no serenity to shatter. The solutions of today will be out of date tomorrow; the system in equilibrium today will be thrown out of balance tomorrow.

Of course, all change is not good change. A society (or organization) must court the kinds of change that enrich and strengthen it rather than the kinds that fragment and destroy it. The person who works for social change must not be assumed to be a believer in Utopia and human perfectibility. Change will occur. We must cope. Leaders should understand the point made by Francis Bacon 350 years ago. "He who will not apply new remedies must expect new evils; for time is the greatest innovator."[4]

The Trance of Nonrenewal

The problems of the aging organization are systemic. It is not a question of healthy systems whose leaders happen to lack creativity. If we could pump creativity into the leaders, they would still be faced with the reality of systemic stagnation. Organizational arrangements designed to deal with old realities must be redesigned. Individuals who are functioning far below their potential must be awakened.

In some systems that have gone too long without renewal, people understand that change is needed and are restless. This was spectacularly true of Turkey when Kemal Atatürk, one of the great renewers of modern times, was a young officer. Long before World War I he had joined the Young Turks who sought a constitutional government for the decaying 600-year-old Ottoman Empire. After the war he drove out the various foreign powers threatening Turkey's autonomy, created the Turkish Republic, and then, as president, launched an extraordinary series of reforms. He disestablished Islam as the state religion; abolished old codes subordinating women; substituted the Roman alphabet for the Arabic; instituted a new civil and penal code; abolished the traditional—mainly religious—educational system, and established secular schools.

Such far-reaching changes would have been quite impossible had there not been an influential body of Turks who were ready for change. Humiliated by defeat in war, alienated by the decay of the sultanate and acutely conscious of their country's backwardness, they were eager to put the past behind them.

Such readiness for change is not common. In most systems (societies, corporations, whatever) needing renewal, people are satisfied with things as they are, and the leaders are satisifed, too. It is as though the system were asleep under a magic spell. A feature of the trance of nonrenewal is that individuals can look straight at a flaw in the system and not see it as a flaw. Although the organization that is gravely in need of renewal may show many signs of its threatened condition, the signs cannot be seen by those who are under the spell.

But the spell can be broken. Disaster is a spellbreaker, but sometimes the system gets destroyed in the process.

Steps Toward Renewal

What can leaders do? They cannot hope to relax every rigidity and change every fixed habit in the system over which they preside—and they should not even if they could. But there are broad measures that may be taken to enhance the possibility of renewal.

The Release of Talent and Energy

Leaders must give thought to how human talent and energy are handled in the systems over which they preside. The quality of the educational system has much to do with the society's capacity for renewal. In organizations, the conern for human resources starts with recruitment and involves the selective movement of people in and out of the organization. Many an organization has gone downhill because good people drift away, just as many a country town has lost vitality from the continued emigration of its most energetic young people.

If they are concerned for renewal, both recruiters and those concerned with leadership development must have an eye out for the maverick quality that enables young potential leaders to escape the bondage of "what is" and point the way toward "what might be." Call it what you will—imagination, originality, an independent mind and spirit, a capacity to cast new light on old ideas. Sometimes such individuals make a poor showing because their very independence may mean they do not fare well on conventional scoreboards. The highest marks of approval go to those whose performance and cast of mind fit the requirements of the system. That is the way the system affirms itself. Unfortunately, those who have fitted themselves assiduously to the system often cannot save the system.

Nothing is more vital to the renewal of an organization than the arrangements by which able people are nurtured and moved into positions where they can make their greatest contribution. In an organization this requires a concern for the growth of the individual that extends from early training through executive development. Given the importance of the process, one might expect organizations to provide special rewards for those executives who are "people developers," but it rarely happens. An organization rewards managers for producing, for marketing, for staying within budget, for running a tight ship, but rarely rewards them for developing people.

If a leader has the will to develop people, there is no great mystery in how to do it. Experts have written extensively on the subject: Bring them in on decisions. Delegate. Feed them responsibility. Stretch them. And change their assignments periodically.

Reassignment

Reassignment is one of the most promising—and most neglected—strategies for developing the talent and releasing the energy within an organization. As I pointed out earlier, young people benefit by periodic shifts to tasks that pose new challenges, hone new skills, and broaden their experience. This is particularly important for young potential leaders who need exposure to many constituencies and must end up as generalists; but organizations should consider adopting the practice for a substantial percentage of its people as a means of preventing staleness.

A well-designed system of personnel rotation yields high dividends not only in the growth of the individual but also in organizational fluidity. Free movement of personnel throughout the organization reduces barriers to internal communication, diminishes hostility between divisions, and ensures a freer flow of information and ideas. It contributes to the versatility of the individual and the fluidity of the organization.

Motivation

Obviously, for the leader who is concerned with renewal, there is hardly any subject more important than motivation. In an aging organization or society people have generally lost sight of the goals they once had, and are deeply preoccupied with the procedures and routines of the present. Only if they regain a concern for goals toward which they are prepared to strive with energy can they break out of the prison they have built for themselves. It requires effort to break the bonds of habit and entrenched procedures.

Any organization planning for a major renewal must bring into key positions individuals who have a gift for motivating and are themselves highly motivated. Unfortunately, in the upper ranks of any organization needing renewal there are individuals who are too jaded and cynical to help in the necessary transition. But if the organization has been in need of a shake-up for some time, there are no doubt a good many people down through the ranks who constitute a hidden constituency for renewal. The sooner the leadership team establishes contact with them the better.

Pluralism, Alternatives, Dissent

As I suggested in an earlier chapter, leaders concerned for renewal encourage a measure of diversity and dissent. Dissent is not comfortable, but generally it is simply the proposing of alternatives—and a system that is not continuously examining alternatives is not likely to evolve creatively.

Leaders must seek to ensure that the systems over which they preside are hospitable environments for creative men and women, for those whom Harold Leavitt speaks of as "the pathfinders."[5] Leaders conscious of the need for renewal create a climate favorable to problem solving, risk taking and experimentation. They create the seedbeds for new solutions. The ever-renewing organization (or society) is not one which is convinced that it enjoys eternal youth. It knows that it is forever growing old and must do something about it. It knows that it is always producing deadwood, and must for that reason attend to its seedbeds. The seedlings are new ideas and new ways of doing things.

Free societies have clear advantages in the task of continuous renewal. A totalitarian regime coming to power on the heels of a revolution may be well fitted to accomplish one great burst of change. But in the long run, its spurt of energy dies out and is replaced by deadly rigidity. As the Soviet Union has demonstrated in recent years, the only way to escape that grip of death is to introduce a greater measure of freedom.

The private sector is the chief seedbed and greenhouse of our pluralism. Its most prominent and widely celebrated participants are involved directly in the economic functions of the society—businesspeople, farmers, union members and the like. But there is a new awareness today of the importance of the private sector's nonprofit segment. In their future as free entities, the profit and nonprofit segments of the private sector are tied to one another. Much of the funding and volunteering for nonprofit institutions is provided by business, labor and the professions. The profit and nonprofit segments of the private sector, taken together, account for much, indeed most, of the innovation that occurs in our society.

Touch the Earth

As we have seen, leaders sometimes give more weight to procedures and routines than they do to their original purpose. The subordination of original purpose is made easier if the key decision makers have positioned themselves at some distance from reality. As I pointed out earlier, top decision makers generally depend on information that has been filtered through many layers of subordinates. As Secretary of Health, Education, and Welfare, in thousands of hours spent on health programs, I rarely saw a patient. In thousands of hours devoted to education programs, I rarely saw a student. I almost never saw a child on welfare. Having commented in *Self-Renewal* some years earlier that every general should go to the front lines, I made conscientious efforts to do the equivalent, but such was the departmental grapevine that when I did visit a clinic or school everything was scrubbed up and everyone was rehearsed.[6] But leaders have to try. First-hand contact with reality reminds them of their original purposes.

Internal and External Communication

If an organization is to remain vital, it must have easy, open, fluid communication among all its parts. Aging organizations create rigid internal walls that block free communication. The point has been dealt with extensively in books on management. The leader's task is to restore open communication.

The aging organization also tends to reduce communication with the outside world. It hears less, and the increasingly dogmatic convictions it entertains serve to filter what it does hear. This is unfortunate because messages from outside can be a stimulus to renewal. From outside comes word of emerging competitive pressures, of adverse reactions, of alternative solutions. The leader's task is to open the doors and windows.

I once believed that it might be possible to design an ever-renewing organization, one that would never run down, never lose its vitality. It would provide for dissent, it would institutionalize the devil's advocate, it would provide the seedbeds for new ideas and solutions. It would never cease learning and developing. But after many years, I concluded that human beings are much too firmly wedded to the status quo to let anyone get away with such a scheme. They will discount the devil's advocate. They will silence the dissenter by outright punishment, or more commonly through the blandishments of good fellowship. They will root out the seedbeds.

So, for many organizations faced with the need for renewal, salvation can come only from outside. Only from outside can one be sure of disinterested criticism, astringent appraisal, the rude question. Only from outside can one expect judgments untainted by the loyalty and camaraderie of insiders, undistorted by the comfortable assumptions held within the walls.

How can such appraisals be made possible? I dream of the time when organizations are so conscious of the need for renewal that there will be institutionalized arrangements for outside evaluation—as traditional as the outside auditor. Another way to increase the impact of the external world is recruitment from outside into the middle and upper ranks of the system.

Science

In the broadest terms, research and development in science and technology must certainly be listed among the most significant and far-reaching measures that a society can take to ensure renewal. They bring about change, and help us to cope with change. How much a nation spends on nonmilitary research and development is one measure of its concern for continuous renewal.

The Visible Future

Of the popularly expressed requirements for leadership, one of the most common is that leaders have vision, which can mean a variety of things: that they think longer-term; that they see where their system fits in a larger context; that they can describe the outlines of a possible future that lifts and moves people; or that they actually discern, in the clutter and confusion of the present, the elements that determine what is to come.

Many readers will remember the notice that is said to have appeared in a British provincial newspaper: "The annual meeting of the Suffolk Soothsaying Society has been postponed due to unforeseen circumstances." Leaders have to do better than that.

For leaders, timing is immensely important. Wise leaders sharpen their sense of things to come. They are sensitive to the currents of change and to emerging trends. It does not work if they come to the task with a set of fixed ideas that they try to impose on events. It works only if they let their minds be open and keep a sense of the movement of things. I am not suggesting that they sway with every breeze that blows; but they had better know which way the wind is blowing and whether it is a zephyr or a gale. In 1968 a number of prominent political figures bet their futures on the proposition that the spirit of the 1960s was the wave of the future, and they lost their bet.

The saying in university departments of economics is that there are many prophets without honor, few without honoraria. Critics say that it is the economists who have exemplified over and over the hazards of prophecy, but in fact, some economists make quite a good living peering only a short distance into the future.

There is such a thing as "the visible future." The seedlings of twenty-first-century life are sprouting all around us if we have the wit to identify them.

Most significant changes are preceded by a long train of premonitory events. Sometimes the events are readily observable. The number and in rough terms the ethnic compositions of the nation's high school graduates in the year 2000 can be approximately foretold because they are alive today. Sometimes the premonitory events are harder to sort out. For example, I believe that twenty-five years from now people will look back on our present day-care practices as primitive, and I have no doubt that the precursors of twenty-first-century practice in this field are out there today for those shrewd enough to identify them.

In short, with respect to some things, the future announces itself from afar. But most people are not listening. The noisy clatter of the present drowns out the tentative sounds of things to come. The sound of the new does not fit old perceptual patterns and goes unnoticed by most people.

And of the few who do perceive something coming, most lack the energy, initiative, courage or will to do anything about it. Leaders who have the wit to perceive and the courage to act will be credited with a gift for prophecy that they do not necessarily have.

Reorganization

Leaders turn to reorganization to remedy many of the ailments of corporate or governmental bureaucracies. One special purpose of reorganization in connection with renewal is to change the constellation of key players. It isn't "the old ways of doing things" that block renewal; it is the people whose shared assumptions and habits hold the old ways in place. Knitted together in a web of human relationships, they block dissonant information from outside and reinforce in-house delusions. Sometimes the only way to cut through is to break the pattern of relationships; and that, in fact, is the hidden agenda of many reorganizations.

I was once director of a company in which the chief executive officer was having difficulty persuading a part of the company—call it division A—to overhaul its antiquated ways of doing things. The division chief, with under-the-table backing from a member of the board of directors, resisted every proposal of top management. The CEO's patience finally ran out. He proposed and the board approved a reorganization that merged the troublesome division into another division of the company. In the process, the CEO ensured that the identity and coherence of division A as an organizational entity simply vanished. Before the merger it had held fortresslike possession of the top two floors of a building; after the merger it was scattered through four different buildings. The division chief and the key members of his old staff were situated far from one another. All of the CEO's intentions with respect to renewal were quickly accomplished.

The Leader's Need for Renewal

There is no doubt that leaders can play a significant role in the renewal of institutions and societies. But suppose that the leader is in need of personal renewal. Sometimes the appropriate course is separation. H. G. Wells said, "Leaders should lead as far as they can and then vanish. Their ashes should not choke the fire they have lit." But often renewal is quite possible without separation. Let me describe some of the hazards that lead to a need for renewal.

Successful leaders, particularly political leaders, have in common with novelists and film makers that they tend to establish durable understandings with their constituencies. In effect, the constituents (or readers, film fans) give their support conditional on the leader (or novelist, film star) delivering the same unvaried performance. The distinguished film director Fred Zinnemann refers to the understanding as a kind of contract. Over time, the contract may inhibit the growth and change so necessary for personal renewal.

Another hazard is boredom. Too many times around the track. Too few new challenges. Too many nasty problems recurring on schedule. The essayist Logan Pearsall Smith said that boredom can rise to the level of a mystical experience, and I have known middle-level executives who rank with the great mystics of all time. It is a well-padded boredom, to be sure, with all the perquisites of the executive suite; but leaders in that condition suffer a clear loss in capacity to lead. The dry gravel of boredom does not kindle fires, nor does it make for renewal.

Still another problem for leaders is surrender. Some years ago I was startled to hear a Cabinet member say that he had simply given up on one of the major bureaus under his jurisdiction. He said (and I'm quoting from memory), "They're too good at blocking my efforts to change them. To do what needs to be done would take years and eat up energy I can spend on winnable battles."

There is no doubt that a certain number of top executives have, in the secrecy of their minds, closed the books on one or another portion of their responsibilities. Worse yet are the instances in which leaders give up not on just a small piece of their territory but in effect on the whole thing. They may still look like leaders and occupy leadership posts but they have essentially surrendered and stay on as custodians. Implausible? Not at all. There are not many undefeated people around.

Stress

Stress may seriously affect leaders and inhibit their capacity to provide renewing leadership. One source of stress is hostile criticism, and all leaders are targets.

A second source of strain—the invasion of privacy—is particularly severe for public leaders. Newspaper readers came to know the most intimate details of Ronald Reagan's prostate gland and, if present trends continue, may learn more than perhaps they should know about the glandular functioning of all political candidates.

A third source of stress is work overload and all that goes with it—fatigue, loss of sleep, the encroachment on time normally spent with family and friends, lack of leisure to read and reflect.

A fourth source of strain not often mentioned is the combat that goes with top leadership. Defeat can be costly. Everyone who has lived around top leaders knows individuals who have never recovered from a severe electoral defeat or a disastrous business setback. All leaders carry bruises, balanced or not by the bruises that they have given others. What is worth our attention are the cases in which the consequences are disabling.

Alcoholism is one such consequence. When I was serving in President Johnson's Cabinet, I had to testify on various occasions before a distinguished committee chairman who took solace in alcohol. I will not entertain the possibility that he fortified himself particularly for my appearances. It was an unnerving experience. For a time Franklin Pierce had something of a drinking problem. He had served as a brigadier general in the Mexican War, and it was said of him, justly or unjustly, that he was the hero of many a well-fought bottle. Wilbur Mills, former chairman of the Ways and Means Committee and one of the ablest, most dedicated legislators of his day, brought his great career to a sad and spectacular end under the influence of alcohol.

Much more common are the leaders who show no outward signs of trouble and exhibit no visibly neurotic behavior, but are nonetheless disabled. Bitterness, paranoia and self-pity are among the most common afflictions. Paranoia is particularly difficult to deal with in elective officials because there really are people out to get them. One recalls what is said to be the world's shortest play: The opposition political leader, fleeing from his homeland through the mountains, encounters a mountaineer and says, "I'm fleeing from tyranny. Will you help me? There is a price on my head." The mountaineer asks, "How much?"

How Leaders Handle Stress

Lord Moran once wrote, "Men of good will saddled with the fate of others need great courage to be idle when only rest can clear their fuddled wits."[7] In fact, they are lucky if rest is all they need; good sense dictates attention to the full range of fitness measures—diet, sleep, exercise, relaxation techniques, reduction in substance abuse, and so on.

Leaders have widely diverse notions as to what constitutes rest. One fairly constant ingredient is retreat or solitude. Montaigne said of his home, "I endeavor to free this corner from the public storm, as I do another corner in my soul."[8] Unfortunately, for most leaders home is not far enough from the clamor. Distance helps.

A few seek nothing more than isolation and inactivity, but most have some favored environment or pastime—a beach to walk on, a stream to fish in. Having talked with a great many leaders on these matters, I am struck by the fact that most of their solutions can be summed up in a brief line of advice: "Do something nonverbal." Music, nature, sensory enjoyment, work with one's hands, gardening, sports—so goes the list. Contrary to the popular connotation of the word *rest*, energetic, even arduous activity is not ruled out. But with the exception of light reading, the rational, verbal functions of the organism are rarely mentioned as stress-relievers.

Another approach to stress reduction is to ask what haven the leader has from the world of combat and dog-eat-dog striving. Is there a shelter where solace is assured and performance is not the price of admission? One thinks of family, a circle of loved ones, religion. The leader learns that deference is not friendship, acclaim is not love. In Shakespeare's *Richard II*, the king says, "I live with bread like you, taste grief, need friends." A wise Frenchman defined celebrity as the dubious honor of being known by those who know you not.

The leader needs a circle of associates who are willing to be both supportive and critical. Pity the leader who is caught between unloving critics and uncritical lovers. Leaders need reassurance, but just as important they need advisors who tell them the truth, gently but candidly.

Finally the best remedy or preventive for the stress of leadership is probably a healthy perspective on life. No leader can function for long without making mistakes and suffering defeats. As Joe Louis said, "Everyone's got to figure to get beat sometime." The question is not "Did you take a fall?" but "Did you get up and continue?" The best have resilience. They do not overemphasize either their successes or their failures. They take criticism and grow. They know that life has a lot of chapters. James Michener once said, "I like challenge. I don't mind defeat. I don't gloat over victories. I want to stay in the ballgame."[9]

Renewers of the Culture

In discussing the collaborative efforts of leaders and constituents toward shared goals, we rarely mention the role of what anthropologists call the culture: the body of custom, ideas, assumptions, and institutional patterns transmitted from one generation to the next. Yet the culture is an immensely powerful element in determining how the group sees its needs and moves to meet those needs. It provides both constraints and opportunities with respect to the ways in which leadership can be exercised.

It may be, then, that we had better examine the role of those rare, seminal human beings who change the culture. The truly great cultural changes in human history are rarely attributable to individuals, but individuals play key roles. In the emergence of monotheism, for example, Moses was surely the most central figure of whom we have extensive knowledge. As Aaron Wildavsky has shown, Moses was a farsighted leader.[10] What he aimed at was not just law but institutions for the transmission of law.

Similarly, in the fifth century B.C. a number of Greeks were moving toward a new rationality, but Socrates stands preeminent as the one who said to all who would listen: You have a mind capable of reasoning; use it! In an age that was still slumbering in the long night of superstition and ignorance he was, to borrow a phrase from Freud, "one of those who disturbed the sleep of the world."[11]

In the years immediately preceding 1530 the canon of the cathedral at Frauenburg in East Prussia was a most extraordinary man named Nicholas Copernicus. His canonical duties did not seem to have weighed heavily on him, because he also practiced medicine. Neither canonical law nor medicine but his earlier work on mathematics and astronomy led to his conclusion that the earth revolves daily on its axis and moves in yearly orbit around a stationary sun—a view that sent tidal waves of alarm and excitement through religious, philosophical, and scientific circles for the next century.

Moses is generally thought of as a leader, but neither Socrates nor Copernicus is placed in that category. I have no desire to stretch the concept of leader beyond the point of usefulness, and would be inclined to use the term *renewer* for Socrates and Copernicus.

Talent and Energy

The consideration leaders must never forget is that the key to renewal is the release of human energy and talent. Society can do much to ensure that release; and the most important thing it can do is to remove obstacles to individual fulfillment. That means doing away with the inequalities imposed on some of our citizens by prejudice, poverty and other handicaps. And it means continuous and effective education and career counseling to help young people achieve the promise that is in them. It means opportunity for lifelong growth. The benefits accrue not only to the individual but to the society. The renewing society must be continuously refreshed by a stream of talent from all segments or strata.

The formal educational system is critically important, but concern for the release of individual potentialities requires far more than attention to schooling. It requires that all of our institutional life be designed to further the great result. Every corporation should have a philosophy of individual growth and renewal built into its personnel and career development practices. Every union, church, club, and professional firm, should make provision for the growth of its members. It is not enough to set aside funds for an educational program. What may be needed most is a way of treating individuals that provides them with the challenges that produce growth.

Is it not obvious that human talent and energy are crucial to the flourishing of any society? Surprisingly, it is not at all obvious. We have all seen those gleaming projections of the society of the future that feature an endless array of technological marvels and never mention human talent and energy. It is as though the technology invented itself.

Looking at the impressive physical structures that humans create—great cities, for example—one can gain the impression that there is a lot more to civilization than the humans who make it up. But there isn't. A little maybe, but not a lot. The dance doesn't exist without the dancer.

I believe that all detailed attempts to design the society of the future are no more than smoke blown into the high winds of change. Obviously, we must have our minds amply stocked with contingent plans, estimates of better and worse paths to travel, visions of what could be or might be or ought to be. But blueprints of the future there can never be. To prepare for the swift transitions ahead, our surest assets are highly motivated men and women with a sense of what is important for the human future. The surest guarantors of our future are individuals and the ideas they have in their heads, including the values, intellectual, moral, and social, that they convey to young people coming along. Fortunately, that is an immensely significant resource.

What is needed is an attitude, widely shared throughout the society, toward individual growth, through development and learning in the context of our shared values—an attitude that sees learning as lifelong, that never ceases to seek out the undiscovered possibilities in each of us.

SHARING LEADERSHIP TASKS

I have pointed out that in our society the functions of leadership are widely dispersed, that is, widely shared. Some believe the functions should be so broadly and evenly distributed throughout the group that the very concept of leadership disappears. This view is rarely stated so explicitly, but it has deep roots in American populism and deserves attention.

Are Leaders Necessary?

Let us begin with a look at modes of social functioning without leaders. Leaderlessness crops up in various guises.

Preliterate and Traditional Societies

Anthropologists have described a good many preliterate tribes in which leaders in our sense of the word did not exist. These were coherent, relatively stable cultures in which tribal tradition and universally shared values exerted a powerful influence. Each member knew what he or she must do—and most of the time did it. Custom governed—coercively.

Historians give similar reports of static traditional societies. Robert A. Nisbet has written, "Leadership . . . was so subtly and so delicately interwoven into the fabric of kinship, guild, class and church that the conscious problem of leadership hardly existed."[1] The more securely the group's norms and values are internalized in its members, the less need there is for explicit leadership.

The Market

Much of the time the forces of the market provide a significant example of social functioning without leadership. Producers want higher prices for their goods and consumers want lower prices in the stores. We expect the market to decide, and much of the time it does, quite efficiently with little administrative overhead or bureaucracy. But market forces left untrammeled do not always produce outcomes acceptable to the society or to groups within the society. Hence innumerable interventions such as regulation by government and monopolistic practices by commercial firms.

Sometimes institutions are simply the sum of the historical accidents that have befallen them. Like sand dunes, they are shaped by influences but not by purposes. Or to put the matter more accurately, like our sprawling and ugly metropolitan centers, they are the unintended consequences of many unrelated influences and purposes. Leadership may be virtually absent.

A great many social outcomes—perhaps most—are not the consequence of action by leaders at any level, nor of the people's wishes, but of action by nonleaders who are in positions to exercise power. This is not conspiracy theory, which asserts that there is an unseen but coherent group wielding power. There is no such group. Power flows in thousands of streams.

Bureaucracies

Occasionally one encounters agencies of government that seem to function virtually without leadership, either at the top or down through the executive levels. To the extent that such agencies succeed in functioning at all, the binding role is played by a durable web of written and unwritten rules, a sacrosanct organization chart, and documents that establish the mission of the agency. But the lack of dynamism in such leaderless agencies is legendary. They find it difficult to cope with change, difficult to energize the people within them, and virtually impossible to renew themselves as organizations.

Of course, absence of top leadership does not mean that an agency is leaderless. What at first appears to be a lack of leaders often turns out to be minimum leadership at the very top with leadership networks functioning quietly but effectively at second and third levels. Such second- and third-level leadership, if long entrenched, may be capable of paralyzing a newly appointed top executive.

Both the strengths and limitations of second-level leaders were illustrated by a major university that some years ago suffered an extended period without top leadership. The second- and third-level leadership—deans, department chairs, and leading professors—created an informal but effective coalition to keep the institution on a steady course. It worked so well one was tempted to say that top leadership was unnecessary; and of course, university faculties find that an easy thought to bear. But difficulties emerged. For example, the "locked arms" strategy for maintaining stability made it virtually impossible to deal with a seriously deteriorating department. A live-and-let-live, no-one-rock-the-boat compact was part of the deal. Beyond that, because each of the second- and third-level leaders was chiefly preoccupied with his or her own bailiwick, little thought was given to long-term plans for the university as a whole.

Measurement of Public Opinion

There are those who believe that the systematic measurement of public opinion might be an effective substitute for leadership. Television communication can be so designed that the viewer can press a button on the set and send a signal back to the studio. The possibility presents itself that "the people" could sit in their living rooms—with fingers on the buttons—and govern by voting on issues and candidates. Why not? In the days when I was stumping the country urging that citizens be more alert and active in public affairs, that question was put to me a number of times by earnest young people.

The answer is that nothing in our experience with plebiscitary democracy gives us reason to believe that it would work. Everything we know about the formulation of sound public policy says that it involves a great deal of untidy debate and many-leveled give and take between voters and their representatives. Trust plays a part. Not just opinion but the intensity of opinion affects the result. The proposed button on the television set bypasses the complex processes by which conflicts are resolved and consensus achieved.

In contrast, Daniel Yankelovich offers wise and penetrating thoughts on how the measurement of public opinion can be linked to education and public debate to achieve a deeper understanding of issues.[2]

Hostility to the Idea of Leadership

Finally, there are those who have an active distaste for the very idea of leadership. From the beginning of our national life, a certain number of Americans have been deeply suspicious of hierarchy and inclined to interpret the ideal of equality as casting a moral shadow over all superordinate-subordinate relations.

Some are so zealously committed to participatory forms that they see no room for leaders. Benjamin Barber says, "Complete self-government by an active citizenry would leave no room for leaders or followers."[3] Barber, who favors extension (necessarily with modifications) of the town meeting approach to governance, quotes with approval the remark of Jean-Jacques Rousseau: "The instant a people allows itself to be represented it loses its freedom." So much for Congress!

There is much that is valuable in Barber's discussion of what he calls direct democracy, but he does not solve the problems of scale involved in applying the town meeting model to huge cities and a vast nation.

The Need for Leaders

There is no doubt that we tend to overemphasize the part played by leaders, as in Emerson's saying that an institution is the lengthened shadow of one man. It is sometimes true. But an institution is more likely to be the lengthened shadow of many men and women interacting in complex ways in a particular historical context.

In short, one can accept a diminished emphasis on the role of leader. But to imagine that the society can be run without leaders ignores several difficulties.

The first is that many people *want* leaders. An undetermined percentage, behaving as Freud would have predicted, want a parent-figure, a savior, someone to depend on and revere and follow. And even people who would regard such yearnings as infantile may wish in times of trouble that their concerns and the concerns of their fellows could be focused and symbolized by some individual who is a leader *and accountable*.

A second difficulty is that whether or not people want leaders, there are circumstances in which they appear to need leaders to perform functions the group cannot perform for itself. The Bible touches on the concept of leader as servant (e.g., Luke 22:25–27) and Robert K. Greenleaf has written an essay, "The Servant as Leader."[4] The same notion is evident when we speak of our government leaders as public servants. It would be incorrect to say that the servant concept is prominent in popular thinking about leadership. Yet even in pragmatic and worldly terms, there is a sense in which groups do need the *services* of a leader.

Douglas McGregor, an industrial psychologist, was famous for his belief that followers should be given maximum opportunity to exercise their own initiatives. But after he had done a tour of duty as a college president, he wrote:

> I believed . . . that a leader could operate successfully as a kind of adviser to his organization. . . . I couldn't have been more wrong. . . . I finally began to realize that a major function of the top executive to take on his own shoulders the responsibility for resolving the uncertainties that are always involved in important decisions. . . . He must also absorb the displeasure, and sometimes severe hostility, of those who would have taken a different course.[5]

A third difficulty is posed by the hazards of peer pressure. People hostile to the idea of leadership tend to assume that coercion always comes from above. But in fact, the group or factions within any group, acting in horizontal relationships, are very powerful sources of coercion, often more relentless than any leader. Objective studies of peer group pressures confirm the point. Those of us who have chaired committees, commissions and boards count it as one of our familiar duties to rescue individual members who have been put down, shut up or intimidated by the group or a strong faction within the group.

The final issue is the most serious. Power lodges somewhere. When "the people" take power away from an individual or group they dislike, they may inadvertently empower those they like even less. In a leaderless system, where will power lodge?

The least attractive outcome is that by doing away with (or seriously weakening) visible leaders, one may leave the game to unseen manipulators of power. There is a French saying, "Be sure you want the consequences of what you want." We have plenty of invisible power holders in our society pulling the puppet strings. For leaders, invisibility is not an option. In our zeal to prevent the abuse of power we are inclined to make leaders the targets of our hostility, diminishing their stature and stripping them of power. *But leaders, provided we have effective means of holding them accountable, can serve as checks on the unseen players. When accountable leaders are stripped of power, the people lose power.*

For most of our ventures we need able and vigorous leaders. Let us choose them with care, hold them accountable, demand that they be responsive. But let us not destroy their effectiveness.

Constituents

Most of the endlessly debated questions about leadership are ancient, but there is one that has a distinctly modern ring: *How can we define the role of leaders in the way that most effectively releases the creative energies of followers in the pursuit of shared purposes?* The concept of sharing leadership tasks responds to that question. To explore the concept we have to examine several aspects of the role of constituents. The oldest mode of sharing leadership tasks in our kind of society is voting. So let us start with voters.

The best research and the largest body of data on constituents in this country has to do with the voters in national elections.[6] In responding to the initiatives and propositions that appear on the ballot, voters share directly in the shaping of public policy. In choosing among candidates they share somewhat indirectly.

On the whole the research on voters injects a sobering note of reality into idealistic notions of an informed national electorate. Political issues and events are not high on the voters' list of priorities, ranking well below such matters as their economic well-being, their health and their aspirations for their children.[7]

Only about one-quarter of the adult public watches the evening television news. Only about one citizen in ten is an activist (e.g., active in political campaigns, writing to public officials).

Unfortunately there has been a steady decline in voter turnout. Though voters are not impressively well-informed on issues, they have definite ideas about fair play, about the use and abuse of authority, about race, religion and certain moral values. They are much less trusting of their national government than they were in the 1950s, and have much less faith in politicians.

Any elected official can tell you in detail what the folks back home want, but it is apt to be a listing of those items pressed by organized groups: jobs, better wages, higher prices for crops, reduced taxes, and so on. They are less likely to talk about (though they may understand very well) various needs and wishes that do not relate to legislation. People want to believe that their lives have meaning. They want reassurance. And they want their leaders to reaffirm the pieties. No cynicism, no irreverence. Leaders may part company with voters on this or that policy issue, but it is a reckless leader who violates the people's cultural norms (even norms that the people themselves are hypocritical about).

The point has been made in earlier chapters that the behavior and attributes required of a leader are contingent on the situation. And so it is with followers. Members of a group fearing outside attack may make demands on a leader quite different from the demands of a group that is secure and prosperous. A group torn by internal strife makes still different demands.

Hidden Constituencies

A leader has a known and visible constituency. Leaders with imagination and experience know that they also have hidden constituents—potential allies not necessarily known to them but waiting to be awakened or, if awakened, waiting to be called. The proportion of known to unknown constituents varies from one situation to the next. When I founded Common Cause, a citizens' movement for accountable government, virtually all of our potential constituency was hidden. We did not even know whether it existed. The only way to find out was to announce the launching of a national movement with all possible fanfare, and then pray. If no one had shown up it would have been a highly visible nosedive—a possibility I reflected on apprehensively. Fortunately, postal workers were soon hauling mailbags off the elevator and the movement attracted 100,000 members in the first twenty-three weeks, another 100,000 in the year that followed.

Sometimes potential constituents remain more hidden than they need be because of our tendency to categorize, stereotype, and label groups of people. We say "Labor will be for it . . . the conservatives will oppose it," and so on. But in real life, groups are not monolithic; they contain diverse elements, some of which may be hidden constituencies for leaders imaginative enough to seek them out. For example, Nixon and his political advisors discerned by the late 1960s that the labor movement, hitherto solidly Democratic, contained a hidden constituency of voters who though economic liberals were social conservatives.

If one is trying to accomplish something substantial in the world of affairs, one encounters sooner or later big, resistant bureaucracies that seem absolutely immovable. Leaders accustomed to the search for hidden constituencies are not discouraged. The bureaucracies are intimidating but not immovable. It is their business to look monolithic but they are not. A new chief executive officer brought in from outside to revive a sluggish corporation can easily gain the impression from the executives reporting to him that the whole organization has its heels dug in against change. The leader who is willing to test that proposition will find that down through the ranks are many potential allies who have been waiting a long time for signs of life at the top.

When Common Cause undertook to accomplish certain reforms in the state legislatures in the early 1970s, some of our state organizations were inclined to approach the task in a highly adversarial frame of mind. Like troops laying siege to a walled city, they entrenched themselves outside and prepared to lob mortar shells over the walls. Those with more experience had to persuade them that they should seek and find allies within the walls. It may not be true militarily, but in the normal struggles of institutional life one always has friends in the garrison. And that fact has strong implications for the tactics one employs. Why storm the fortress until one learns whether allies inside will open the gates? Robert Colodzin tells the story of the fire chief who admonished, "Before you bust through a door with your axe, try the knob!" Common Cause eventually found important allies in every state legislature.

Marketing specialists are quite ingenious at sniffing out hidden constituencies. So are politicians. Almost all other categories of leaders are woefully unimaginative about it.

Just as we categorize and stereotype groups, we categorize people. We are all too quick to say that an individual is for us or against us. But people are not monolithic either; they are bundles of motives, some of them in conflict. Somewhere in there may be motives that the leader can appeal to. Experienced leaders do not linger long over the question of whether an individual is for or against their proposals. Recognizing that the person has many and varied motives, they ask themselves to which of those motives they should appeal.

Participation

Participation takes many forms. The first duties of citizens are not of a sophisticated political nature. Those duties are to look after one another in the family circle, get themselves educated and equipped to support themselves, obey the law, pay their taxes, and rear their children as responsible members of the community. These are authentic forms of participation, though they are rarely mentioned in discussions of the subject.

Each one of us teaches—good lessons or bad—through our actions.

We influence our children, influence those who love or admire us, influence those who work for us, perhaps even influence strangers. If the lessons we teach are lessons that strengthen the community, that give heart to others, that lead others toward the light, it would be foolish not to count them as significant forms of participation.

In our society, we believe that everyone should have the chance to be heard. But one encounters considerable variation around that norm. The extent to which the individual's view is heard, or having been heard, is taken into account depends on:

· *The Nature of the Group*. Is it a combat patrol or a faculty meeting? A business organization or a political caucus? Within limits, the culture accepts different standards of participation for different groups.

· *The Nature of the Situation*. Is there an emergency or an intense competitive situation? The culture accepts diminished group participation in some such situations. In the tense moments of surgery, the chief surgeon does not expect extensive debate among members of the surgical team. When the quarterback calls a play he does not expect team debate.

· *The Predilections of the Leader*. The culture allows leeway for differences among leaders provided they remain within acceptable limits.

The word *participation* has been used in recent decades chiefly to denote political involvement, as in the phrase *participatory democracy*. But it is not wise to allow a valuable word to be so arbitrarily narrowed. Parents who serve on the school board are participating. So is the senior citizen who serves as a volunteer in a hospice for the terminally ill. So is the college student who serves as a volunteer tutor for disadvantaged children. All are making their constructive contribution to the life of the community—taking part, participating. The voluntary sector of our society offers endless opportunities for such involvement.

In the discussions that follows, I focus on citizen action in the political realm. In the political arena we ask that citizens follow public affairs intelligently and vote. Beyond that many people give no time to political responsibilities, some because they are unmotivated, others because they have deep commitments in directions other than public affairs (e.g., to their families, their jobs, their churches).

Others—many others—choose to go farther, participating in the politically active sense of the word. For citizens to take part actively in the workings of their society is not only good democratic doctrine, it is essential to the renewal of the society. Communication upward from grass roots to higher levels of decision making regenerates the society.

Citizens' Organizations

It is my belief, widely shared today, that leaders should have a nurturing relationship to their constituency, should empower their followers, should enable group members to achieve goals of the members' own choosing. But I do not believe that constituencies should sit around waiting for such nice things to happen. They must speak up. And in order to do so effectively they must consider the usefulness of affiliation with one or another citizens' group. To speak out is one thing, to be listened to is quite another. Our fondness for individualism draws us to the lone crusader, but most successful citizen action is group action. Fortunately, thanks to the measureless fertility of our society in spawning voluntary groups, there is an organization to suit virtually every interest and every shade of opinion.

Citizen action is not always wise, nor does its success always produce desirable outcomes. In my youth there occurred one of the most dramatic examples of effective citizen action this nation has ever seen. Two groups, the Anti-Saloon League and the Woman's Christian Temperance Union, steamrollered Congress into passing the Volstead Act over President Wilson's veto, and the result was one of the more foolish chapters in our history—the Prohibition Era.

Despite such negative instances, the history of citizens' movements is overwhelmingly positive. When I was young, women were not allowed to vote, and child labor was a grim reality in many states. That women were finally given the vote nationally in 1920, 144 years after the Declaration of Independence, owed everything to organized action by citizens, chiefly women, beginning with the Seneca Falls convention in 1848 and culminating in the work of Carrie Chapman Catt and her associates after World War I. The story is the same for child labor legislation—success after literally generations of citizen advocacy.

The establishment of our first national park (Yellowstone) in 1872 and other government actions on conservation were preceded by years of advocacy by citizens, including John Muir, George Catlin, William Bartram, James Audobon, Ralph Waldo Emerson and Henry Thoreau. Despite such a precedent and the vigorous advocacy of President Theodore Roosevelt, the movement languished and had to wait until the mid-twentieth century for a new burst of life. As late as 1960 the organized environmental movement could not have numbered more than a few hundred thousand Americans. But they acted with such vigor that they placed environmental concerns firmly on the national agenda.

When I signed the regulations under the Clean Air Act of 1965, there was still a question of how much public support there would be for the measure. We had yet to learn that environmental pollution was an authentically popular cause. By 1988 the presidential candidates were vying with one another in their professed devotion to environmentalism.

The abolition of slavery, laws governing industrial safety, pure food and drug legislation—all were preceded by intense and effective citizen efforts.

There is enormous value to grass-roots organizations in which citizens can work with their neighbors under leadership that is drawn from their own ranks, and can see with their own eyes the launching of a citizen's effort and the local outcome of the effort.

One of the interesting developments of the past two decades is the emergence in low-income areas of grass-roots community organizations that work on housing, economic development, job training, day care and the like. Some community development organizations finance and operate shopping centers, industrial parks and even small factories. The Ford Foundation, which has played a key role in fostering such organizations, has issued a report by Neal R. Peirce and Carol Steinach that provides a brief, informative tour of the field.[8]

One of the most remarkable of the community development organizations is Mississippi Action for Community Education (MACE) which, together with its sister organization, the Delta Foundation, covers fourteen counties in the Delta, one of the most impoverished rural regions in the nation. Illiteracy, inadequate health care, unemployment, substandard housing, and lack of sewer and water systems plague the area. MACE, a membership-based organization, engages in an extraordinary variety of activities including job training, housing projects, education reform, leadership development, voter registration, and public health activities. It operates a revolving loan fund and provides technical assistance for small entrepreneurs, builds housing for the elderly and the handicapped, supports farm cooperatives and community-owned supermarkets, and owns several small factories (e.g., one that makes jeans for J.C. Penney Company, Calvin Klein, and Jordache; another that makes nationally distributed Chico-San Rice Cakes).

Larry Farmer, president of MACE, says, "Jobs, income, decent living conditions—providing these should not really entail genius. They just require determination and the belief that it can be done."[9]

Sharing Leadership Tasks

Forty years ago Kenneth Benne and Paul Sheats saw the leadership role "in terms of functions to be performed within a group in helping the group to grow and to work productively." They pointed out that groups may operate with various degrees of diffusion of leadership functions among members or with concentration of such functions in one member or a few members.[10]

Alex Bavelas expressed somewhat similar thoughts in 1960[11] and more recently Edgar H. Schein, in his valuable book, *Organizational Psychology*, wrote:

> Leadership is best thought of as a function within the organization. . . . It can be distributed among the members of a group . . . and is not automatically vested in . . . whoever has formal authority. Good leadership and good membership, therefore, blend into each other . . . in an effective organization. It is just as much the task of a member to help the group reach its goals as it is the task of the formal leader.[12]

It is interesting to reflect on why such a significant insight, expressed so clearly by authoritative voices a generation apart, has been so neglected in contemporary leadership literature. Leadership is rarely discussed as a set of functions, and virtually never as functions that might be diffused among the group. Yet those are the realities. In this book I have used the term *tasks* instead of functions, but the tasks are functions.

The democratic impulse—the desire of people to have a hand in the affairs of their community or state—emerged some twenty-five centuries ago. At first it focused on participation in choosing those who made the community's decisions, and participation in the decisions themselves. It was the deciding function that mattered most, and the focus was on government.

Today, for proponents of participatory or populist democracy such as Benjamin Barber, the focus is still on the deciding function as it relates to governing, and the preferred mode is for citizens to decide after face-to-face discussion of issues in town-meeting-like forums. That is a worthy focus, but the authors quoted earlier in this section clearly have something broader in mind, and so do I. The leadership tasks involved in keeping a community going are richly varied and extend far beyond the deciding function. We must find a way of thinking which reflects that variety, and the concept of sharing leadership tasks does just that.

The Leadership Team

One manifestation of sharing is the leadership team, the few individuals who work closely with the leader. Most of the conversation and writing about leadership deals with The Leader, splendidly alone. But even a cursory glance at the real world reveals that most leadership involves a number of individuals acting in a team relationship. Teams have leaders, of course, and most ventures fare better if one person is in charge, but not as a solo performer, not as a giant surrounded by pygmies.

Team leadership enhances the possibility that different styles of leadership—and different skills—can be brought to bear simultaneously. If the leader is a visionary with little talent for practical steps, a team member who is a naturally gifted agenda setter can provide priceless support. The important thing is not that the leader cover all bases but that the team collectively do so.

The best leader is one who ensures that the appropriate talent and skill are built into the team. Every president since Truman has admired the spunky, plain-spoken man from Missouri. I suspect it appeals to them that a man so battered by criticism while in office could be so well treated by history, but I have not known one of them who, in praising Truman, mentions one of his greatest qualities—his gift for surrounding himself with individuals of exceptional ability.

John F. Kennedy had the ability to draw talent to him, and to establish alliances that pulled the best performance out of his multiple aides and advisors. He quickly established ties with the most diverse types—seasoned political operators, nonpolitical academics, military people, civil servants, and so on.

One cannot expect much from a leader mired in chores that should have been left to well-chosen teammates. But recruiting team members of high caliber is not necessarily the first impulse of individuals who hold power. All too often they recruit individuals who have as their prime qualities an unswerving loyalty to the boss and no power base of their own that would make insubordination feasible. When those criteria prevail, what might have been a leadership team becomes, all too often, a ruling clique or circle of sycophants.

Such a clique tends to increase the leader's isolation, and to withhold the loyal but candid criticism so necessary to individuals in positions of power. Even more serious, such a clique generally neglects one of the prime tasks of the team: to activate widening circles of supplementary leadership. Such an extended network reaching out from the leadership center carries messages both ways. It can be equally effective in letting the intentions of leadership be known or in tapping a broad range of advice and advocacy.

A curious but familiar phenomenon is the leader who does not form a team; that is, one who may hire able subordinates but never creates the trust and sense of mutual dependence that characterize a team. Two years ago one of the nation's top CEOs was fired. He was bright, he had some spectacular ideas, and finally he made some big mistakes. Shortly after the event, I found myself traveling with one of his board of directors, and I asked how the man's closest advisors could have let him make such errors. My friend said, "He confided in no one. That was the problem. He went over the cliff all by himself."

I have seen it happen, and the stupidity of it always surprises me. Someone said that the difference between genius and stupidity is that genius has its limits. Leaders at every level can have access to sound and honest counselors if they want them.

How Sharing Occurs

The sharing of leadership tasks extends far beyond the leadership team. Indeed, it can extend down through all levels and out to the farthest limits of the system.

On any athletic team that is falling behind in a contest, there are always a few individuals who undertake on their own to prevent a drop in morale by building the confidence of their teammates. They are sharing the leadership task of motivating.

When a group is internally divided, there are always a few who, acting in a wholly unofficial capacity, try to heal the rift. They are sharing the leadership task of unifying.

When an organization is clinging to outmoded ways that no longer get results, there are always a few clearheaded, courageous individuals who speak out for change. They are sharing the leadership task of renewing.

In the mid-1960s Erik Jonsson, mayor of Dallas, invited a large number of citizens to play active roles in helping to set goals for their city, and many hundreds accepted the invitation.

The citizens of a town in New York State believed that their streets were left unplowed too long after heavy snowfalls. Town officials pointed defensively to the citizens' frequent demands to keep the budget down. Tempers flared. One citizen—an engineer by profession—took leader-like action. He calculated (1) the amounts of equipment and personnel that would be required to meet various standards of promptness and thoroughness in clearing the streets and (2) the costs the taxpayers would incur in meeting each of various standards. Presenting the results, he simply put the question: "How much do we want to pay for how much service and convenience?" The heat went out of the discussion, and a sensible compromise was reached. It was an example of a citizen sharing a leadership task.

The sharing of leadership tasks by group members is not a dream of something that might be made to happen; it is something that is already happening, has no doubt always happened—and could be made to happen on a larger scale.

Advantages of Sharing Leadership Tasks

I made the point in chapter 8 that the only hope for vitality in large-scale organization is the willingness of a great many people scattered throughout the organization to take the initiative in identifying problems and solving them. Without that, the organization becomes another of those sodden, inert, nonadaptive bureaucracies that are the bane of modern corporate and government life—rigid, unimaginative, and fatally unequipped to deal with a swiftly changing environment.

The taking of responsibility is at the heart of leadership. To the extent that leadership tasks are shared, responsibility is shared.

The wider sharing of leadership tasks could sharply lower the barriers to leadership. For every person now leading, there are many more who could share leadership tasks, testing their skills, enjoying the lift of spirit that comes with assuming responsibility, and putting their feet on the lower rungs of a ladder that rises to higher leadership responsibilities. Many who lack the self-assurance to think of themselves as leaders would find within themselves the confidence to test the lower rungs of the ladder. Others who now feel excluded, or shut out from the possibility of leadership, would find that the entry points were numerous and welcoming.

Accountability

The sharing of leadership tasks offers challenging opportunities to citizens, but citizens have another and sterner duty. They must hold leaders to account. Some who exercise power can be trusted to be adequately self-critical and disciplined; but it is a poor assumption on which to base public policy. The simple rule is: *Hold power accountable.*

One means of protecting ourselves from exploitation by leaders is to deprive them of power. To a degree we have done that and will continue to do it, but the strategy has its limits. At the same time that we diminish the power of leaders, we are forever calling for leaders who "can get the job done." For the society to get its work done, leaders and the systems over which they preside must be granted some measure of power. It is a common experience for leaders today to have far less power than they need to accomplish the tasks we hand them.

But those who are granted power must be held accountable. Not just leaders but power holders in general must be held to account. It is a hard fact that most of the people whose actions affect our lives are power holders rather than leaders. An entrenched government bureaucrat utterly unknown to the public can profoundly affect public policy. In the economic sphere, a land developer, a specialist in corporate takeovers, a gifted marketer, a greedy banker may affect the course of events and the lives of a great many people without the slightest pretense of leadership.

Systems That Ensure Accountability

It comes down to the task of designing the system in such a way as to *ensure* accountability. The most effective strategy ever devised is, of course, the rule of law. The emergence of the principle so well expressed by Pliny in the first century, "Non est princeps super leges, sed leges super principem" [The prince is not above the laws but the laws above the prince], was a historic breakthrough in the domestication of power. The rule of law requires that power be exercised within a set of explicit and universally applicable constraints.

Thomas Jefferson said, "In questions of power . . . let us hear no more of confidence in man, but bind him down from mischief by the chains of the Constitution."

Less celebrated as a social strategy, but equally effective is the dispersion of power: break it up, spread it around, never allow it to become too highly concentrated in one person, one institution or one group. The barons at Runnymede had a rough and ready grasp of both strategies, though their concept of accountability was quite limited. The primary purpose of the Magna Carta was to hold the king accountable to the barons, not to hold either of them accountable to the people.

In our society, as indicated earlier, we have carried the dispersion of power to some length. The Founding Fathers started with the structure of government itself. The separation of powers, the reservation of power to the states, and similar measures did about as much as could be done to insure that no one element within the governmental structure would gain excessive power.

Our eighteenth-century leaders like the admonition, "Eternal vigilance is the price of liberty," but it turns out that free citizens are not eternally vigilant. They keep dozing off, and on one or another front their liberties are infringed on. If they are lucky, they wake up and combat the threat to their liberties before it is too late. But if success attends their efforts, they promptly doze off again. Citizens must make the most of the moments of wakefulness to build (or rebuild) sleepless monitoring systems that warn of the erosion of liberty and the abuse of power—a free press, the guarantees of free speech, an uncorrupted judiciary, an educated citizenry, and so on.

Government and the Private Sector

The primary focus must be on government because a properly functioning government can help hold power accountable in the rest of society. We can never make government wholly efficient or pure. But we can go far toward making it accessible, responsive and accountable—giving a measure of reality to that universally quoted, sporadically honored phrase, "the consent of the governed."

The concern for accountability, however, cannot be focused on government alone. It must include all spheres of life. Over the course of the centuries many private groups—powerful families or clans, the churches, guilds or unions, corporations, political parties, professionals—have demonstrated by their excesses that nongovernmental power must also be held accountable.

The dilemma is that although the power of such groups presents a problem for the society, their very existence may be a source of strength for the society. Dictators have found it much easier to subjugate an unorganized populace than to cope with the organized power of the churches, the corporations, the universities, the unions. Against a potential dictator, these elements of private power may serve as bulwarks of freedom. The power of "the people" is too broadly and thinly spread to cope with certain kinds of threats.

So the problem is complicated. A vigorous government is needed to keep private power centers from tyrannizing, but a vigorous private sector is needed to hold government accountable.

Power must be held accountable—accountable to someone, somehow. The corporate chief executive officer should be accountable to the board of directors and to the shareholders, which is often not the case. Stanley Hiller, Jr., chief executive officer of York International, says that the most serious weakness in American business is "the flaw in corporate governance" that permits the CEO to escape strict accountability and to cling to power despite gross failures of leadership.[13]

In nonprofit organizations as well one encounters flaws in the arrangements for accountability. Even organizations that are designed for wide participation tend to be run by "the active few," and all too often those few create arrangements that protect their positions.

Citizen Action

Of central importance in holding power accountable is the existence of well-established modes of citizen participation. The prime instrument of political accountability is the electoral process, so it must be protected with jealous concern. That means removing obstacles to voter registration, getting out the vote, ensuring an open nominating process and guarding the integrity of elections.

The gravest threat to the integrity of the electoral process today is the capacity of money to buy political outcomes. The politician becomes accountable to the donor rather than to the voter. Campaign gifts are the preferred mode today, but there are many other ways to pass money. The late Mayor Daley, who had his own small law firm, undertook to advise a young legislator who had a small real estate business. "Don't take a nickel. Just hand them your business card."[14]

It is desirable that the political parties be open to rank-and-file participation, that there be citizen access to litigation to correct government excesses or inaction, and that other procedures for the redress of grievances be readily available.

Openness is a necessary condition. Citizens cannot give "the consent of the governed" if they do not know what is going on. Hence the importance of statutes on conflict of interest, and freedom of information. It is a universal characteristic of human systems, governmental or not, that those running the system, over time, devise ways of keeping inside information inside. Over years, governing bodies design institutional arrangements that make it difficult for citizens to obtain the information needed for independent judgment. There is, of course, in any government agency a small body of information that should not be divulged for reasons of security or invasion of privacy, but the agency's natural impulse is to withhold information far beyond that perimeter.

Citizen action beyond the ballot is essential if government is to be held to account. All of the special interests that influence government have found ways of "voting between elections." So must citizens. They must organize themselves to advance their various concerns. Citizen action is not only good for government; it is good for the citizens doing the acting. It cannot be emphasized too often that an alert citizenry with a tradition of citizen action is our ultimate guaranty against the abuse of power. Our system provides many well-designed protections, but if citizens neglect their duties, we risk dangers from which the system cannot save us.

14

LEADERSHIP DEVELOPMENT: THE EARLY YEARS

I have deliberately postponed attention to one of the most important subjects of all. I did not want to introduce it until we had had the opportunity to examine and reflect on the realities of leadership in the contemporary world.

All who have studied and thought about leadership development recognize that we know too little to permit definitive treatment of the subject. The best we can hope is to offer provisional clarification on the way to something better.

The answer to the question "Can leadership be taught?" is an emphatic but qualified "Yes"—emphatic because most of the ingredients of leadership can be taught, qualified because the ingredients that cannot be taught may be quite important. The notion that all the attributes of a leader are innate is demonstrably false. No doubt certain characteristics are genetically determined—level of energy, for example. But the individual's hereditary gifts, however notable, leave the issue of future leadership performance undecided, to be settled by later events and influences.

Most of the capabilities that enable an outstanding leader to lead are learned. Ronald Reagan's extraordinary communication skills were the product of many decades of professional experience. Douglas MacArthur's strategic and tactical brilliance in World War II was the product of a lifetime of study and action.

Young people with substantial native gifts for leadership often fail to achieve what is in them to achieve. So part of our task is to develop what is naturally there but in need of cultivation. Talent is one thing; its triumphant expression is quite another. Some talents express themselves freely and with little need for encouragement. Leopold Mozart did not have to struggle to uncover buried gifts in little Wolfgang. But generally speaking, the maturing of any complex talent requires a happy combination of motivation, character and opportunity. *Most human talent remains undeveloped.*

We cannot design a production line that turns out leaders. But we can offer promising young people opportunities and challenges favorable to the flowering of whatever leadership gifts they may have. Some will become leaders, partly from what we enabled them to learn and from challenges we set before them, partly from the self-knowledge we helped them achieve. Beyond that, time and events will teach them. Mistakes and failures will teach them. And with respect to the very greatest leaders, a decent humility should remind us that we do not fully understand—may never fully understand—their emergence.

Obstacles to Leadership

Creeping Crises

What are the circumstances that account for the diminished supply of leaders today?

One way of accounting for the extraordinary quality of America's first generation of leaders is to point to the impact of crisis. The American Revolution occurred before crisis became one of our favorite words, but it meets any criterion. So do the Civil War, the Depression, and World War II. Each produced great leaders.

Many people believe we are living through a crisis today, but it is slow moving. The generalization may be that explosive crises produce great leaders, creeping crises do not.

Size and Complexity

Large organizations and communities have a suppressive effect on the incidence of leaders in the system. The painstaking research of Roger Barker has demonstrated that the number of *significant functions per individual* tends to be greater in small social units than in large.[1] A very small school must struggle to get together enough students to put on the school play. There are more than enough significant functions for anyone sufficiently motivated. In the very large high school, there is no way to use all the students who want to participate in the play. The number of students available far exceeds the number of significant functions. Many have *no* function. That is not the soil in which leadership develops.

Our young people are born into a society that is huge, impersonal and intricately organized. Far from calling them to leadership, it appears totally indifferent. Far from providing the challenge that young leaders require, it is apt to create puzzlement and a sense of powerlessness.

Even for adults the complexity is daunting. Untutored good judgment, the main reliance of leaders since the beginning, is no longer enough. Effective leadership demands understanding of the complex systems and processes by which our communities and our nation function. Complexity is difficult enough, but bureaucratized complexity—in government, in great corporations, large hospitals, big universities, and so on—discourages initiative, innovation, and boldness.

We cannot change the realities of size and complexity, but we can spare ourselves some of their ill consequences by devising new modes of organization. Industry is leading the way in reexamining the impact of size of unit on the initiative and involvement of individuals, and is experimenting with the creation of smaller units within the whole. In the same spirit, there have been many attempts—some quite successful—to enhance the vitality of state and local government and neighborhood organizations. Anyone interested in leadership development must applaud such efforts. They ensure platforms for early leadership experiences closer to home and less intimidating than national roles.

The nonprofit institutions of the private sector are still inadequately explored as a testing ground for young leaders. Such institutions proliferate at the grass roots so they are within easy reach, and local voluntary organizations are sufficiently small so that they can provide valuable early experiences for young leaders.

Specialization

The prestige of professional training drains off potential leaders into marvelously profitable nonleadership roles. The colleges and universities, particularly the graduate and professional schools, drive students down the road to specialization.

Leaders have always been generalists. Tomorrow's leaders will, very likely, have begun life as trained specialists, but to mature as leaders they must sooner or later climb out of the trenches of specialization and rise above the boundaries that separate the various segments of society. Young potential leaders must be able to see how whole systems function, and how interactions with neighboring systems may be constructively managed.

The Anti-Leadership Vaccine

If, despite all the discouragements, a spark of enthusiasm for leadership is ignited in any of our young people, our educational system may well snuff it out. It does this in two ways. First, it places enormous emphasis on individual performance, and virtually none on the young person's capacity to work with the group.

Second, the educational system—not necessarily with conscious intent—persuades the young person that what society needs are experts and professionals, not leaders. Thomas Jefferson envisaged an aristocracy of talent, but most of today's aristocrats of talent feel no responsibility either to lead or to help develop leaders. Even if young men and women escape discouragement at the hands of their mentors, they are likely to absorb the contemporary skepticism toward all symbols and institutions of authority. Far from wishing to be leaders, they may conclude that they do not even wish to associate with them.

The Rigors of Public Life

With respect to the possibility of attracting leaders into government, an obvious impediment is the withering criticism heaped on our public figures. Some contemporary commentators seem to believe that this is a post-Watergate phenomenon. They forget the stormy years of Lyndon B. Johnson and the scathing criticism of Harry Truman during his presidency.

I have already mentioned the savage attacks on George Washington. Thomas Jefferson was not spared. In the September 15, 1800, issue of the *Hartford Courant*, "Burleigh" suggested the consequences that would follow the election of Jefferson:

> Neighbors will become enemies of neighbors, brothers of brothers, fathers of their sons, and sons of their fathers. Murder, robbery, rape, adultery and incest will be openly taught and practiced, the air will be rent with the cries of distress, the soil soaked with blood, and the nation black with crimes.[2]

Unfortunately, it would appear that such intemperate criticism is one of the costs of democracy. Perhaps the best we can hope for is the healthy attitude of Harry Truman, who said: "I became quite used to being vilified. It has its stimulating aspects and, for all I know, it may even be good for the liver."[3]

I regret to say that one must be similarly fatalistic about the modesty of financial rewards. I have fought in behalf of higher pay for public servants, but it is an uphill battle. Not to mince words, the citizens of a democracy are foolishly stingy in these matters.

Nor is there any way to ensure a decent measure of personal privacy for powerful public figures. We can and should fight to preserve it for them, but we shall never have more than partial success. Invasions of privacy go with the status and fame of public leaders. A character in Machiavelli's *La Mandragola* says, "Non e il mele senza le mosche" [You can't have the honey without the flies].

Still another complaint about public life is that when well-motivated individuals leave their comfortable private-sector occupations to take on elective or appointive office they find themselves all too often in hopelessly frustrating bureaucratic situations, strangled by red tape, thwarted by poorly designed public processes. This is *not* an unavoidable evil. If we put our minds to it, much can be done to make government a workable environment for able people.

I have not attempted to brighten a gloomy picture. But we can draw hope from the fact that most of the unfavorable realities have existed since the nation began. Our leaders emerged despite those realities. Apparently there is a supply of individuals with the necessary motivation, resilience and toughness of hide to do the job. I believe that we can markedly increase that supply.

It is my impression that the mind-set that turns many of our young people away from leadership is not even a conscious objection. A great many men and women with leadership potentialities simply do not recognize the possibilities within themselves.

Steps That Can Be Taken

Leaders must help bring younger leaders along. They can create the conditions and a climate of challenge, expectation and opportunity. They can remove the obstacles, unearth the buried gifts and release the world-renewing energies.

I mentioned earlier the assertion that leaders are born, not made. I take the same view of this claim that Dr. Samuel Johnson took of cucumbers, which he said should be carefully sliced, well seasoned with pepper and vinegar, and then thrown out.

Given the mysteries of human development, the role of luck, and the many paths to failure, we shall never succeed in devising a program of training that will with certainty turn a promising youngster into a leader. We can, however, produce a substantial cadre of young *potential* leaders from which the next generation of leaders will emerge.

Our thinking about leadership development for the nation must be broadly based and necessarily involve very large numbers. That is not at all what people have in mind when they say we need more and better leaders. But given the dispersed leadership so essential to the vitality of our society, we have no choice.

If we could produce a very large number of elementary and high school children who had been well trained to accept responsibility in group activities (the first step toward leadership); if we could produce substantial numbers of late adolescents who had been helped to understand and experience leadership in their youth organizations, churches, and schools; if we could produce a great many men and women in their early twenties who had not only developed the skills of leadership but also had tested those skills in community activities and political campaigns or in government and industry, then we could ensure a steady flow of mature leaders into all segments and all levels of our society.

If these young people could continue their development in industry, in government, in the unions, the professions and nonprofit organizations, we would have a plentiful supply of upper-middle-level people long schooled in the demanding tasks of leadership. And that would be a richer source of top-level leaders than this nation has ever enjoyed. We are very far from an effort of that magnitude today.

Early Influences

Not long ago after I had given a talk on leadership, a member of the audience asked, "How can a parent contribute to the development of a child's leadership potentialities?" I said "What age level do you have in mind?" and after an embarrassed pause he replied, "Well, actually he'll be two in April." The audience exploded with laughter, but it was not a foolish question. No doubt many attributes crucial to adult functioning have roots deep in childhood.

Seeking clues to the early emergence of qualities associated with leadership, I consulted Robert and Pauline Sears, two of the most distinguished child psychologists in the nation, who have had long experience in the tantalizing search for childhood precursors of adult behavior. They said the research on child development did not permit confident generalization, but they offered some tentative answers, which I paraphrase:

- Physical vitality and intelligence are probably primarily genetic, but intelligence is very likely influenced quite substantially by early childhood experience with respect to language usage.
- The capacity to understand others and skill in dealing with others has its most striking development in adolescence and especially young adulthood, but the beginnings are in the years before five.
- The need for achievement starts developing in the first two years of life, but it seems to be under constant change of strength from early school age to early adulthood.
- Confidence and assertiveness are strongly influenced by the adequacy of parental support of the attachment process during the first year of life. Like the other traits required for leadership, these attributes are somewhat situation-specific: The child, and later the adult, may be confident or assertive in one context and not in others. And other events—a severe disappointment in an important arena of life or the discovery of a fine mentor—can strengthen or weaken the attributes even in middle age.

Unfortunately, despite these significant clues, we know too little about the actual steps parents might take, so we must leave unanswered the question posed by the young father. All we can say is that behavior standards imposed in the home, the drives engendered there, the values inculcated, the models found in parents—all affect the later emergence of potentialities for leadership.

School and College

Given the fact that heredity and early home life have already had an influence by the time the child enters school, some of the questions of leadership potential will already have been settled for good or ill. By school age some qualities that may contribute to future leadership are clearly visible.

Catherine M. Cox, in her study of eminent historical figures, found that early in life they displayed qualities that would serve them well in adulthood—qualities such as intelligence, high self-regard, eagerness to excel, and forcefulness.[4]

At the school level, values are still being shaped, and teachers have their impact through precept and example. Not only the ethos of the school but also the patterns of interpersonal behavior exhibited by teachers and administrators have their effect.

If we extend our time horizon and look at both school and college years, we must deal with the issue of specialization mentioned earlier. *Versatility is built into the species, but the modern world diminishes it drastically through specialization. Young potential leaders would do well to hold on to their birthright.* We must persuade our high schools and colleges that whatever they may teach young people in the way of specialized skills, they must also equip them with something broader—and not just for the sake of future leadership. The students are to be citizens, the most generalist of occupations. Specialization is an integral feature of contemporary social organization, not to be denigrated; but breadth and versatility are important, too. Molière said, "Where the goat is tethered, there it must browse." Young citizens-to-be need long tethers; and young potential leaders even longer ones.

Liberal Arts

At college level, the best preparation is a liberal arts education. It is essential to broaden and deepen the understanding of those individuals who will have in their hands the future of our communities and our society. That means covering the whole range of the liberal arts, from science to literature, from mathematics to history.

Leaders today, at whatever level, in whatever segment of society, live with the reality of unceasing change. They cannot prevent it, they can only hope to channel it in such a way as to preserve values and other essential continuities. And they cannot do that unless they understand the larger framework in which change is occurring, and unless they know their own history. They cannot know what they want to preserve against the buffeting of change, or what sources of strength they can draw on to channel change, unless they know the path already traveled. Justice Holmes said, "Continuity with the past is not a duty, it is only a necessity."

Today's leaders must have some grasp of economic realities and some comprehension of the basic framework within which scientific and technological change takes place. They must gain an understanding of the political process. They must comprehend the pitfalls of power and the sources of human conflict.

Corporate executives must understand the relationship between government and the private sector and must comprehend the national and world economy. In this interdependent world, leaders should come to know some culture other than their own, and all high-level leaders must understand international issues in depth.

In earlier chapters I have emphasized that we expect our leaders to function within a framework of values. They find themselves continuously weighing and balancing competing values. By absorbing, through literature, religion, psychology, sociology, drama and the like, the hopes, fears, aspirations and dilemmas of their people and of the species; by coming to understand what our ancestors valued and fought for; by coming to know through history and biography the extraordinary outlines of the human story, they may hope to discharge their duties with wisdom.

How a group moves to meet universal human needs is determined by the culture; and how leaders conduct themselves must take the culture into account. The bearing, presence, and tactics of Bismarck that proved so effective in mid-nineteenth-century Prussia would not have gotten him elected mayor of late-twentieth-century Los Angeles. (Bismarck might be relieved to know this.) The style and tactics of a hard-driving sales manager would not be suitable for the dean of a great university faculty.

In short, leaders must understand culture. Much of the culture is latent. It exists in the minds of its members, in their dreams, in their unconscious. It can be discerned in their legends, in the art and drama of the day, in religious themes, in their history as a people, in their seminal documents, in the stories of their heroes.

Our Founding Fathers had varying levels of formal education but through reading they shared the best thought of the ages. They knew Plutarch and Thucydides. They had read and discussed Bacon, Hume, Locke and Montesquieu. And they were deeply interested in the science of their day—incomparably more interested than American leaders today.

At the graduate and professional level, specialization is inevitable and valuable. Even the future generalist benefits by knowing one subject in depth. Most future leaders will be specialists turned generalists. But graduate and professional schools should persuade their students that a certain percentage of each class must keep some form of leadership as a lively option in thinking about their own futures—even if it takes them beyond the field for which they are being trained.

So far we have been talking about the conventional liberal arts curriculum. Somewhat more controversial is the idea of a college course devoted explicitly to leadership, an idea that provokes skepticism in many faculty members. They object that there does not exist the underlying body of rigorous scholarly work on which university-level courses are customarily based. The fact that the course must range over a number of academic specialties goes against the grain in colleges that resist interdepartmental programs.

There is something to be said for the faculty resistance. A good many leadership courses have yet to lift themselves out of mediocrity. But a number of existing programs are excellent. There is ample material in the fields of political science, history, psychology, and sociology to build a course solidly grounded in scholarship.

The value of such courses does not depend solely or even primarily on their effectiveness in developing leaders. The nature of leadership should be of interest to all thinking people.

Communication

If one had to name a single, all-purpose instrument of leadership, it would be communication. It may be that the peaks of performance in communication can only be scaled by leaders of impressive native gifts. But most of the communication necessary for leadership can be taught. Young potential leaders should gain exceptional command, in both writing and speaking, of their own language and—in an interdependent world—workable knowledge of a second language. Courses in public speaking and debating do not enjoy high status in the academic world today. But the plain truth is that most bright young people are poor speakers, and it is a skill that leaders need.

Churchill and DeGaulle, two of the greatest leaders of this century, illustrate the fact that adult excellence in language has early roots. As a boy, Winston Churchill was defiant and his school performance suffered, yet he stood at the top of his class in classics, and near the top in English, French and the Scriptures. DeGaulle's chief interests as a schoolboy were in history, literature and philosophy. He memorized the whole of Rostand's *Cyrano de Bergerac*, and substantial passages of *Antigone* in Greek. He loved Corneille, Racine and Molière.

Outside the Classroom

Not long ago a young man asked me, "What is the most important thing to have in mind if I think I have it in me to lead?" I said "The most important thing to have in mind is that leaders need followers." I was not being flippant. Most young people in professional and executive ranks have had long training—literally since elementary school—in individual performance. They learn that it is how they perform as individuals that counts, not how they relate to others. So it is not surprising that many young executives—even middle-aged executives—are still pirouetting for some scorekeeper, real or imagined, with little thought of their possible constituency. Their gaze is directed upward, at the executive staff meetings they want to worm their way into, at the executive vice-presidents they want to impress. They are not even paying attention to the people at their own level or below, whom they might hope to lead.

The stress on individual performance in the classroom does not need to be as intense as it is. Some classroom instruction can readily be set up in group situations. But no doubt the opportunities are much greater outside the classroom. Student government presents interesting possibilities but, all too often, the functioning of student government exhibits a fatal air of unreality. Sports, dramatics, the school newspaper and a range of other opportunities are available.

Off-campus public service offers further possibilities. One of the best university programs is at Stanford University where President Donald Kennedy has created a Public Service Center. The director of the center, Catherine Milton, has assembled a remarkable group of gifted and dedicated students to conduct the program, the goal of which is to provide significant public service experiences for students. Such service does not always have a leadership ingredient, but it can strengthen motivation for public service and it may substantially extend the students' capacity to relate to unfamiliar constituencies.

Programs that bring young potential leaders together for a shared experience have an effect over and above the nature of the particular program. Just the fact of having been singled out has a motivating effect, and contact with peers may have considerable impact. Just such an experience brought a major change in the perspective and career plans of young Henry Cisneros. As a junior at Texas A&M he was chosen to attend a Conference on United States Affairs at West Point, and the meeting plus a visit to New York City proved to be immensely challenging. Of the conference he said "I was completely outclassed," but there is reason to doubt that youthful conclusion. Only a few years later he emerged as one of the ablest young political figures in the country—and was elected mayor of San Antonio in 1981.[5]

Outward Bound and a number of other programs based on outdoor activities are designed to provide leadership and teamwork experiences and to build self-confidence and self-reliance.

The program called *Leadership America*, sponsored by the International Leadership Center, provides college students between their junior and senior years with a rewarding and demanding ten-week program combining classwork and field experience.

The Untidy World

One hopes that well-conceived out-of-classroom experiences provide one or more of the following:

- Opportunities for students to experience the shared responsibilities of group action, and to learn the skills required to make a group function effectively.
- Opportunities for students to test their judgment under pressure, in the face of opposition, and in the fluid, swiftly changing circumstances characteristic of action.
- Opportunities for students to test and sharpen their intuitive gifts and to judge their impact on others.
- Exposure to new constituencies.
- Exposure to the untidy world, where decisions must be made on inadequate information and the soundest argument does not always win, where problems rarely get fully solved or, once solved, surface anew in another form.

Unfortunately, many of the real-life experiences designed for young potential leaders are trivial. Students assigned as interns to executives sometimes find themselves fetching coffee and playing the ignorant observer at events they do not understand. To prevent just such outcomes, the National Council of La Raza, a civil rights and community development organization, places its interns in regular staff positions and works them hard. The interns are paired up with more experienced staff members for the first month and then must fly on their own. Raul Yzaguirre, president of La Raza and one of the nation's ablest Hispanic leaders, told me, "We make the point strongly that there is no distinction between interns and regular staff."

The best off-campus or real-life experiences are linked to some form of instruction or counseling, so that the young person dropped into a strange milieu is helped to comprehend it. For example, internship in a legislature can be profitably linked to a seminar on the legislative process. Experience, thought to be the best teacher, is sometimes a confusing teacher. Robert Benchley said that having a dog teaches a boy fidelity, perseverance, and to turn around three times before lying down.

However imperfect these out-of-classroom experiences may be, they have a special relevance. College and post-graduate programs move young people steadily away from the mainstream of American experience. The young men and women selected for our more demanding institutions have exceptional skill in the manipulation of verbal and numerical symbols. That is what the tests test and that is what it takes to get good grades. With each passing year they find themselves with a more and more highly selected group of young people, who have been trained to approach life in terms of those skills, and who have almost certainly lost touch with most of their less-gifted friends. As they move through university and graduate school, they drift further and further out of touch with those Americans who would rather play Bingo than watch "Masterpiece Theatre," who bowl on Thursday nights and elect presidents of the United States on the first Tuesday after the first Monday in November. It is not good for the students or for the society.

Exemplars and Mentors

Short of giving young people actual experience in leading, it is useful to place them in situations in which they can observe leaders at close range and find the role models so helpful to further growth. Internship programs such as the White House Fellows program expose young people to seasoned leaders and exemplary figures so that they can perceive and understand those dimensions of leadership that cannot be put into words. There is much about leadership that is best learned from living examples.

Mature people can do much more than serve as exemplars or role models. They can play the role of mentor, actively helping young people along the road to leadership—as friends, advisors, teachers, coaches, listeners, or resource persons. Mentoring may be as formal as a master-apprentice relationship or as informal as an older friend helping a younger one.

Mature people are not all equally motivated to play the role of mentors nor equally capable of it. Some are people developers by nature, others are not. When Robert Greenleaf studied the careers of the twelve top people in AT&T, he found that four of the twelve had come up through the same middle manager (who was 1 of 900 at his level).

Mentors are "growers," good farmers rather than inventors or mechanics. Growers have to accept that the main ingredients and processes with which they work are not under their own control. They are in a patient partnership with nature, with an eye to the weather and a feeling for cultivation. A recognition that seeds sometimes fall on barren ground, a willingness to keep trying, a concern for the growing thing, patience—such are the virtues of the grower. And the mentor.

A great many programs send young people out as interns in government, business or the nonprofit world. Not one in ten such programs, perhaps not one in a hundred, bothers to build a network of effective mentors to whom such young people can be assigned.

Self-Knowledge

One hopes that self-knowledge is a consequence not just of leadership programs but of all education. La Fontaine said, "Il connaît l'univers, et ne se connaît pas" [He knows the universe; himself he knows not]. Somewhere, somehow, with all the courses, the extracurricular activities, the lessons learned from contemporaries, the help from wise elders, the young person must gain the necessary knowledge of self.

LEADERSHIP DEVELOPMENT: LIFELONG GROWTH

We cannot design an assessment procedure that yields a leadership aptitude score that is adequately predictive at age twenty or thirty. Nor can we expect our graduate and professional schools to send their graduates out with their future greatness prepackaged. One can prepackage a good deal, but the future will bring what it brings. Leadership development is a process that extends over many years.

The realities of life require (and justify) selection and training that occur early in the individual's career, but that is only a first step. Leadership development calls for repeated assessments and repeated opportunities for training. In some individuals leadership gifts are well hidden until mature years; and even in the case of early bloomers, what shows itself early may offer no more than hints of what will emerge later. All talent develops through an interplay—sometimes over many years—between native gifts on the one hand and opportunities and challenges on the other.

Churchill offers an instructive example. Knowing how the story comes out, one can easily imagine that in the accounts of bumptious, willful childhood behavior one glimpses the claw of the young lion. But the evidence, carefully studied, suggests that in his case the promise of greatness was deeply hidden. Even during his later youth and early middle years, the verdict was "brilliant, but"—erratic, lacking in judgment, not steady, not dependable. He had only himself to blame. A friend described him as a man who jaywalked through life. He was sixty-six before his moment of flowering came. They say it's all right to be a late bloomer so long as you don't miss the flower show. Churchill did not miss it.

Selecting and Recruiting

The many programs whose purpose is to select able young people are not necessarily well-designed to identify potential leaders. Some of the qualities required for leadership are hard to discern, and conventional selection processes tend to screen for other kinds of talent. We may expect better selection procedures. Some of the tests of achievement motivation and management skills pioneered by David McClelland are promising. The work of the Center for Creative Leadership in Greensboro, North Carolina, has gone beyond conventional procedures.

Difficulties in assessment stem from the very nature of leadership. For example, measurements of steadiness and courage in a test that lasts an hour (or a day) may be useful, but not necessarily predictive of steadiness and courage over weeks and months of stress—a very common circumstance for leaders. We had better face the necessity for multiple assessments over the course of a career.

The Culture Selects

Those concerned with selecting leaders must never forget that consciously designed selection processes do not have the field to themselves. The culture selects, the workplace selects, the system selects. The famous British public school system provided the nation's leadership for generations, but not by teaching leadership. They inducted their boys into a ruling class ethos and way of life. Most of the graduates eventually entered the bureaucratic and professional elite from which leaders were chosen. The fact that Churchill was molded by the class that had supplied leadership in the great days of the Empire may have powerfully reinforced his leadership when Britain had to call on every ounce of traditional patriotism. And perhaps it just as powerfully limited his leadership in the postwar world.

We have all become aware of how our own culture selected on the basis of gender, economic status and race in the past. To some extent, that is still true. If we succeed—as we must—in eliminating those biases, many subtle questions still remain concerning the paths to leadership. Every human society constructs obstacle courses over which potential leaders must travel. The obstacle course serves the society well if it yields only to those of superior wisdom, talent and vigor. But that is rarely the case. In the winner's circle one also finds conformists, sycophants and others skilled in the arts of self-advancement. Some of these turn out to be able leaders. Most do not.

The chairman of a large and famous corporation once said to me, "We recruit young people fresh out of college, and for thirty years we reward them for keeping their noses to the grindstone, doing their narrow jobs unquestioningly. Then when a top post opens up, we look around in frustration and say 'Where are the statesmen?' " No one consciously intended to eliminate the statesmen; but the organizational culture produced that result.

It is equally easy—without anyone intending it—for the organizational culture to allow those with opportunistic, "careerist" motivations to get through the gate ahead of those most sincerely committed to the group and its shared purposes. I asked a friend about the selection and advancement of leaders in a particular minority group organization, and he said, "The flashy ones get there first." Anyone concerned for the supply of leaders will want to ask what unseen selective processes are at work in the system.

On the Job

Industry and the military services spend large sums on leadership training programs, create centers for advanced work, and send their people to universities for graduate degrees. But where leadership development is the goal, the most effective arena for growth continues to be the workplace. As Norman Douglas put it, "There are some things you can't learn from others. You have to pass through the fire."

Most of what an organization does in behalf of leadership development is done within the context of its normal, day-to-day work supervision. The first requirement is that supervisors not squelch potential leaders or drive them out of the organization. The second requirement is that they provide challenge. Promising future leaders are apt to be both restless and marketable. They are not given to prolonged loitering in an unchallenging environment. They do not produce a confrontation, they just leave; and top management does not even know the event occurred. No organization can afford such losses.

Entry into the world of work is a major milestone for all young people, and the scene of unexpected defeat for some who seemed most promising. Sir Arthur Pinero said, "So many coming young men! Where do they all go?" It is not really a mystery that so many coming young men and women fade before fulfilling their promise. The fulfillment of promise in "real life" is dependent on attributes other than talent: courage, resolve, emotional stability, steadiness, capacity to stay the course.

Learning on the job is enhanced by the fact that any workplace generates a certain amount of pressure, and ambitious young people generate inner pressures of their own. Seeking recognition, fearing failure, working against deadlines, experiencing the urgencies of life in the real world, they learn lessons they do not soon forget.

Interaction with peers is a vital ingredient of learning for young people. After the first few experiences in which an important endeavor is derailed by interpersonal conflict, they learn to detect the signs of trouble to come. They learn teamwork. They learn to deal with hostility. They learn when to compromise and when to stand firm.

If they are to be leaders, they must come to know how other workers feel about their jobs, how they regard those above them in the hierarchy, what motivates them, what lifts their morale and what lowers it. For all of that, the workplace is a learning laboratory.

In such a setting young people deepen the self-knowledge I spoke of earlier. As David De Vries of the Center for Creative Leadership put it, they cannot manage others until they learn to manage themselves. And they must come to understand the impact they have on others. It is a curious fact that from infancy on we accumulate an extensive knowledge of the effect others have on us, but we are far into adulthood before we begin to comprehend the impact we have on others. It is a lesson young leaders must learn. It will be their stock in trade.

In the workplace the young person finds role models, and—as Thomas Cronin suggests—reverse role models: the ones who demonstrate in their own behavior "how *not* to do it." As in all learning, evaluations of performance and feedback are important. The young person's fellow workers usually provide both—promptly, candidly, and free of charge. But supervisors and mentors can often perform the function in a more discriminating and thoughtful way.

If young people are exceptionally lucky in their mentors, they learn to respect those whom they hope to lead. Leaders, managers and teachers must wage a constant battle within themselves against the impulse to underestimate their people and condescend to them. Condescension does not release energies or stir people to give the best that is in them.

Reassignment

I commented in chapter 12 on the good consequences of reassignment. The organization concerned to develop its young potential leaders reassigns them periodically with a view to posing new challenges, testing new skills, and introducing them to new constituencies. Able young people learn rapidly, then the learning curve levels off, and performance may even drop as boredom sets in. No leadership course can affect young men and women so powerfully as a well-designed sequence of reassignments.

The tenure in any one assignment must be long enough so that the young leader is forced to take it seriously and to master it. During the Vietnam War there was a period when the military's system of officer rotation became counterproductive. Tours of duty were so brief that many officers did not really gain command of their field assignments before they were rotated.

Cross-Boundary Experience

Contemporary social organization is rich in boundaries. Professions spawn subprofessions, each with its arcane knowledge. The great organizations, corporate and governmental, that dominate modern life have their internal divisions and subdivisions, each with its own identity and turf. Our great universities are made up of scores of academic departments, each proud of its autonomy, jealous of its territory. We have regional, religious and ethnic subcultures.

The higher the young leaders rise, the more they find themselves dealing with a diversity of subcultures. As I pointed out earlier, they should be introduced soon to the boundary-crossing experience. They should learn to find their way into an unfamiliar organizational culture, to honor that culture's sensitivities, and to develop empathy for its values and assumptions. They should learn early how to mediate disputes among subcultures, to build coalitions, to negotiate. In today's interdependent world, national boundaries are among those that young potential leaders must learn to cross.

Off-Site Experiences

Most organizations whose managers have thought long and hard about leadership development turn sooner or later to off-site learning experiences for their people, lifting individuals out of their all-too-familiar organizational settings and exposing them to other kinds of growth possibilities.

The most conventional programs are essentially advanced courses in management. The military services offer them at many sites. College and university business schools provide programs to which corporations send their executives. Major corporations sometimes have their own centers.

The Federal Executive Institute at Charlottesville, Virginia, and other centers provide programs for civil servants.

Quite another approach is offered by the Aspen Institute and by programs such as the Stanford University Executive Program in the Humanities. Their purpose is to provide intellectual refreshment and an opportunity to view the world more broadly and deeply than is possible in the pressure cooker of daily work.

The Center for Creative Leadership conducts seminars and workshops for corporate clients, assesses leadership skills, and provides training sessions designed for the development of leaders.

The American Leadership Forum brings together highly selected men and women who are at the threshold of top leadership (generally in their forties or fifties) and provides a program designed to develop their leadership skills. The trainees, who are drawn from diverse segments of the community, learn modes of collaborative action.

Of course, young executives can plan their own off-site learning experiences. In the richly diverse voluntary sector of American life they can test themselves in tasks that they would never encounter on the job. Bruce Adams has pointed out that the young executive who serves on a citizen advisory commission or any organization concerned with community development is gaining invaluable experience for future leadership.[1]

A particularly interesting opportunity is provided by the numerous cities that have city leadership programs (Leadership Atlanta, Leadership Cincinnati, and the like). In these programs young potential leaders are exposed to experiences designed to increase their understanding of their own community and to enhance their leadership capabilities. Just bringing such groups together can be valuable in itself, particularly if they are truly representative of all segments of the community. Unfortunately, some of the programs use up the time of the young people with fairly low-grade show-and-tell activities of the sort that led one observer to describe them as "meet the sheriff" programs.

Midcareer Renewal

If we accept the fact that leadership development is a lifelong process, much remains to be done for men and women in midcareer. Irwin Miller put the matter in its starkest light when he said, "By the time you are in midcareer your 'experience' will have been gained in a world that no longer exists."[2]

Leaders who have functioned effectively over the early years sometimes experience a midlife slump. All too many grow stale or burn out or lose their sense of direction. Many, with appropriate help, can come through the slump and go on to important work. Sabbaticals, new assignments, off-site training experiences and extracurricular activities are all possible paths to renewal. In some cases, of course, the problem may lie deeper—in failing energies or illness.

If we were sensible about these things, we would create midcareer clinics staffed with experienced counselors to whom mature individuals could go for consultation. Leaders and managers have a special problem: the higher they rise, the harder it is to talk to anyone about their career problems. It should not require a very high order of social inventiveness to serve that need.

It is my belief that all graduate schools of business, education, public administration, and the like should create midcareer training and refresher experiences that acknowledge the continuing nature of personal growth. I would like to see it widely accepted that no leader manager should go longer than five years without a two-week university refresher, and perhaps every seven years, a sabbatical semester. Such refresher programs might consider three possible ingredients: (1) a review of the newest perspectives and techniques in one's field; (2) a Great Books ingredient along the lines of the Aspen Institute's traditional program, to raise sights and stir intellectual depths; and (3) career counseling for anyone who wants it. With respect to the last item, it has been my experience that careers fall into a state of disrepair just as automobiles and television sets do and need attention.

Political Leadership

Developing elective political leadership is a separate subject. I have observed leadership development programs all over the country, and it is unusual to encounter a young man or woman who is seriously considering life as an elective official.

When we think of public sector service, we tend to think of the part-time public leader—the distinguished citizen who does a "tour of duty" in public life. But we have to remind ourselves that most of our great public leaders served long, full-time apprenticeships.

Most of our Founding Fathers entered public life in their twenties. Franklin Delano Roosevelt did not, as some seem to imagine, graciously emerge from the patrician life to become governor. He was elected to the New York Senate when he was 28, and served as assistant secretary of the Navy at age 31. His life was politics. And incidentally, Eleanor Roosevelt, thought by many to have entered public life when her husband entered the White House in 1933, was an effective and experienced political organizer in the early 1920s.

I would urge able young men and women to have an experience in elective politics—for example, helping out in an election campaign—quite early in their careers. Political science departments should insist on it. The farther young people move toward the stable environments of adulthood, the less likely they are to expose themselves to the instability of politics.

Another introductory experience is an internship or junior staff position in the office of an elected official or on a legislative committee staff. If enough young people could in this fashion be introduced to the rigorous life of elective politicians, then a reasonable fraction—self-selected by temperament or circumstance—might choose to remain on that path.

Women as Leaders

The strong presence of women in the work force, the acceleration of their entry into the professions, and the steady advance in recognition of women's rights make the increasing prominence of women in leadership ranks inevitable.

Even so, there continue to be substantial obstacles, and leadership development programs for women must deal with them. Family responsibilities pose familiar and difficult choices that can and must be eased by new arrangements for part-time work, flexible work schedules, maternity leave, and child care.

Discrimination

More serious are the barriers of prejudice and discrimination that still confront young women who have leadership potentialities. Research bears out the existence of such barriers. On the upward path to leadership most of the gatekeepers are men and many still cannot fully accept women as leaders. The obstacles are giving way, but mainly at the lower and middle levels of organization. Research suggests that for women the last third of the journey to top leadership roles is still immensely difficult. In an article published in the fall of 1987, Slater and Glazer cited the following:

Thirteen of the 185 law schools in the Association of American Law

Schools have deans who are women. . . . Women constitute about 20 percent of the faculties at four-year institutions, but less than 10 percent of the full professors. . . . In 1975, 5.4 percent of the presidents of four-year colleges were women. By 1982 the number had risen to only 7.7 percent.

In the federal judiciary, the court of appeals had 154 circuit judges as of May 1987, and only 17 were women. Of the 529 judges sitting in the district courts, only 48 were women. . . . In the *Fortune* 500 companies women represent a mere 1.7 percent of corporate officers.[3]

Gender Differences in Performance

A number of able feminist scholars assert that there are marked differences between men and women in their styles of leadership and, indeed, in their whole approach to the task of leadership, stemming from the sharply differing character of women's and men's life experiences. Sara Ruddick, for example, says that the experience of mothering leads to special leadership concerns on the part of women. "Mothers must not only preserve fragile life. They must also foster growth and welcome change."[4]

Nancy Chodorow says, "Women's lives . . . define them as embedded in social interaction and personal relations in a way that men are not."[5] This gives women a greater sense of relational involvement.[6]

Other feminist writers suggest that women are particularly well fitted to emerging patterns of leadership because, compared to men, they are more intuitive, creative, adaptive, flexible, oriented toward people, and sensitive to the needs of others.

Unfortunately, the considerable research on gender differences in leadership style has yielded conflicting results on many points. Researchers at the Center for Creative Leadership, after reviewing the literature and conducting research of their own, found little support for the proposition that there are substantial differences. Specifically, they did not find differences in dominance, confidence, or sense of security; nor differences in the capacity to lead, influence, or motivate; nor differences in understanding, humanitarian approach, or capacity to reduce interpersonal friction.[7]

I do not see the need, at this point, for a definitive judgment on whether or not there are gender differences in leadership style. No doubt there is more and better research to come. And in any case I do not see the issue as crucial. Women have diverse leadership styles, as do men, and in my judgment there are plenty of women capable of filling leadership roles in whatever style the culture requires. Theirs is a problem not of performance but of opportunity.

The historical record offers extraordinary examples of leadership by women. And as with men they were diverse in their attributes and their contributions. Some, like Anne Hutchinson, were fearless; some, like Mary Woolley, were intellectually brilliant; some, like Jane Addams, had an unshakable commitment to visionary goals. Carrie Chapman Catt and Frances Perkins had exceptional executive gifts. Susan B. Anthony was a natural organizer with a gift for command. Mary Baker Eddy and Mary McLeod Bethune were charismatic.

One of the most dramatic examples of leadership by a woman is that of Elizabeth I. Life was hazardous in the ruling circles of sixteenth-century Europe, and not least in England. When Elizabeth was three, her mother (Anne Boleyn) was beheaded. Parliament recognized Elizabeth as heir to the throne in 1534, then proclaimed her illegitimate in 1536 (after her mother's execution), and then, reversing itself again, recognized her and her half-sister Mary as heirs to the Crown if their brother Edward died without issue.

In 1549, when Elizabeth was 16, her suitor, Lord Seymour, was executed for treason; and at age 21 she was imprisoned in the Tower by her half-sister, Queen Mary. When she came to the throne at age 25, court circles had widely shared doubts about women monarchs. Mary had had a tumultuous and unpopular five-year reign, and Mary's predecessor, Lady Jane Grey, was finally beheaded.

Into that world of fierce plots and sudden death stepped the young and attractive Elizabeth. Ruling circles were arrogantly masculine, rivalries venomous, the stakes high. Men of immense power and personal force took turns trying to influence, manipulate, or control the young queen. It was an uneven match, but not in the direction they had anticipated. She played one off against the other, sought out disinterested advisors, allowed powerful opponents to overestimate her malleability, and reigned triumphantly for forty-five years. She had extraordinary strength, inner security, nimbleness of mind and above all, judgment.

I share the view of those who believe that even her famed indecisiveness was more often than not a tool of policy. When apparent indecisiveness ends in a sound final judgment or at any rate a favorable outcome, not occasionally but usually, perhaps some label other than indecisiveness is in order.

Elizabeth did not succeed by making herself a carbon copy of the male leaders of her day. She led in her own style, on her own terms.

Further Progress

In their excellent review of women's role in higher educational leadership, Shavlik and Touchton point out that much has been accomplished in legislation over the past quarter century, many useful programs for leadership development in women have come into existence, and good results are already visible.[8] But they also point out that there is a long way to go. No doubt male attitudes are changing, and one could argue that if we would only be patient, women will eventually reach a point of fair-minded acceptance. My guess is that this would take us well into the later years of the twenty-first century. The preferable path is unrelenting legal and social pressure on all institutions to speed the pace.

Where Are They Now?

The men who founded this nation saw far into the future. But there is one thing they did not foresee: It never really crossed their minds that the day might come when our best people would avoid leadership roles, particularly roles of public leadership.

At the time this nation was formed, our population stood at around 3 million. And we produced out of that 3 million perhaps six leaders of world class—Washington, Adams, Jefferson, Franklin, Madison, and Hamilton. Today our population stands at 245 million, so we might expect at least 80 times as many world-class leaders—480 Jeffersons, Madisons, Adams', Washingtons, Hamiltons, Franklins.

It becomes harder and harder to believe that we once had a president who, long before coming to office, drafted the Declaration of Independence. And another capable of composing the Gettysburg Address.

Where are the Jeffersons and Lincolns of today? The answer, I am convinced, is that they are among us. Out there in the settings with which we are all familiar are the unawakened leaders, feeling no overpowering call to lead and hardly aware of the potential within.

Would we be overwhelmed if we had 480 men and women with the historical perspective, concern for the national interest and depth of political understanding of James Madison or John Adams? Not at all. Scattered throughout our society at all levels of government, in the corporations, unions, professions and nonprofit groups, they would set a new tone and new standards in our national life.

How do you send out a call to the unawakened leaders? How do you make them aware of their leadership potential? How do you make leadership feasible and tolerable for leaders? Are these just questions to be tossed into the box that lies beyond the in-box and the out-box? (Dean Acheson said there should be a third box, labeled Too Hard.) I am not prepared to dispose of the questions so easily. We have barely scratched the surface in our feeble efforts toward leadership development.

Great gifts unused, even unsuspected, are hardly a rarity. No doubt there have always been a great many men and women of extraordinary talent who have died "with all their music in them." But it is my belief that with some imagination and social inventiveness we could tap those hidden reserves—not just for government, not just for business, but for all the diverse leadership needs of a dynamic society.

16

MOTIVATING

Charles Trotter, sixteen, had jacked up the rear of the family's station wagon and was working underneath it when the jack slipped and the car dropped, pinning down his right leg. While his stepfather tried to put the jack back in place, his mother took direct action. A woman of thirty-nine years, five feet, seven inches and 123 pounds, recovering from a rheumatic disorder of the left knee and an attack of thrombophlebitis in her right leg, she grasped the rear bumper in the middle and gave a tremendous heave. The rear of the 3,300-pound vehicle rose enough for Charles to get out. X rays of his mother's back showed that she had incurred a compression fracture with one vertebra crushed.[1]

We have all heard such stories of extraordinary performance under intense motivation. One cannot build leadership philosophy or practice around such rare circumstances, but the tales are useful reminders of the power of motives.

The world is moved by highly motivated people—people who believe very strongly or who want something very much. Such people can get out of hand: we are familiar with the excesses born of fanaticism, hatred, greed and lust for power. But no human venture succeeds without strongly motivated men and women. It is said that horse sense is the good judgment horses have that keeps them from betting on people. But we have no choice—we have to bet on people, and when I make that bet I look for high motivation more than any attribute other than judgment.

I do not deal here with the motivation that drives individuals to seek leadership roles. For those concerned to pursue that subject, I recommend the writings of David McClelland and his associates.[2] I deal here with the leader's task of motivating others.

The Leader as Motivator

Anything that humans expend effort for can be a source of motivation. They expend effort in behalf of their physiological needs, family and group loyalties, money, security, and deeply held beliefs. They expend effort in behalf of things that foster their pride and self-esteem, their sense of their own dignity.

The tasks of the leader with respect to motivation are many and varied. A good introductory discussion is provided by Bernard M. Bass in *Leadership and Performance Beyond Expectations.*[3] Among other things, a leader must recognize the needs of followers or constituents, help them see how those needs can be met, and give them confidence that they can accomplish that result through their own efforts. Sometimes the leader helps to remove constraints or inhibitions that had been impeding the full play of motivation.

Except in very rare circumstances of total control (and even then only in moments of emergency), leaders are not puppeteers who make constituents dance. Humans are too complex for that. Life and the world are too complex. Motivation is affected by environmental circumstances over which the leader has no control. It is affected by idiosyncratic impulses in followers, by chance events, and by deeply rooted belief systems. Yet leaders can accomplish a great deal if they understand the needs of their constituents. There are, in any population, enormous energies to be tapped by those who understand how to reach them.

In evoking group performance over any considerable period of time, coercion is grossly inefficient. There are too many ways for group members to give less than their best, too many invisible ways to frustrate group action, too many ways to let up as soon as the pressure lets up. In contrast, if the leader can help people to see how both personal and group needs can be met by appropriate shared action, pressure is no longer necessary.

Needs

A great deal of motivational research focuses on biological needs. Much of it involves experimental work with animals, and some of it has been useful in thinking about human motivation. Individual behavior is substantially affected by physical needs. But biological motives take us only a short distance along the road to understanding a matter of social behavior such as leadership. Social behavior is overwhelmingly affected by what goes on in people's minds—by ideas and attitudes and values.

Research on organizations has taught us much about the motivation of workers. Traditional incentives such as pay and promotion are effective, but beginning with the Hawthorne studies more than fifty years ago we learned that workers have needs and expectations other than rational and economic.[4] We learned, for example, to accept the reality of an informal social organization among workers.

The small work group fills important social and emotional needs, and such groups develop attitudes and norms that affect productivity, morale and quality of product. It is now generally accepted that these realities must be recognized and dealt with if a highly motivated work force is to be achieved. Worker participation in decisions on the setting of goals, the assignment of tasks and the like heightens productivity. To the degree that workers have a sense of involvement, their pride and dignity are enhanced, and they are more likely to feel personal responsibility for a good outcome. Similarly, feedback on performance can heighten motivation.

Leaders must understand the needs of the people they work with—their needs at the most basic level for income, jobs, housing and health care; their need for a measure of security; their need for confidence in the stability of the system of which they are a part, including the capacity of the system to solve the problems that threaten it (crime, inflation, social disintegration, economic collapse and the like); their need for a sense of community, of identity and belonging, of mutual trust, of loyalty to one another; their need for recognition, for the respect of others, for reassurance that they as individuals are needed; their need for new challenges and a conviction that their competences are being well used.

Research suggests that workers are more effective if they can take pride in the product, or the quality of the services rendered, or the known integrity of their organization. In a great many people today there is deep resentment of the huge and impersonal systems that dominate their lives, and anger at the unknown controllers and gatekeepers of those systems. There is hostility toward the unseen administrator in an administered age. People feel powerless. They want to have their say and regain command of their lives. Anything leaders can do to help them in that quest serves a good purpose.

Any group has many competing motives. The leader tries to increase the salience of those motives that enhance group performance. Each member has other motivations, sometimes at odds with the group effort. The leader has the task of keeping the shared motives on top, and persuading members that the shared goals are as important as (or at least not incompatible with) individual goals. Leaders who are acceptable by our lights appeal to those motives most likely to serve the highest conception of the community's good.

Unexpressed Needs

The most gifted leaders understand that the needs of people cannot be fully plumbed by asking them what they want or why they want it. One of the deepest of truths about the cry of the human heart is that it is so often muted, so often a cry that is never uttered. To be sure, there are needs and feelings that we express quite openly; lying deeper are emotions we share only with loved ones, and deeper still the things we tell no one. We die with much unsaid. It is strange that members of a species renowned for communicative gifts should leave unexpressed some of their deepest yearnings, their smoldering resentments, their worries and secret hopes, their longing to serve a higher purpose.

As a consequence, beneath the surface of most constituencies are dormant volcanoes of emotion and motivation. Oddly, when leaders tap those geothermal sources and evoke intense responses, we attribute the intensity not to the subterranean fires but to charisma in the leader.

The greatest poets, novelists and playwrights have always tapped those underground sources. They have always given expression to the unexpressed, have always had transactions with the hidden element in the souls of their audiences. The ablest leaders share that gift of understanding and carry on similar transactions. So do the most inspired religious teachers.

Some of the dormant emotions can be extremely destructive, and we are rightfully apprehensive of leaders who evoke them for political advantage. But leaders should know what is there.

In 1987 the media reported in lurid detail the sexual escapades of TV evangelist Jim Bakker. Observing him and his weepy, doll-like wife, Tammy Faye, one had an inescapable impression of juvenility. Given the extraordinary gullibility of his followers, it appeared to be a matter of children leading children. But a question intrudes: What is missing in our culture that left the followers so undernourished that even a Jim Bakker could satisfy their spiritual and emotional hunger?

Individual and Group

Because leadership requires working with shared values and goals, the task grows difficult—eventually impossible—as shared values disintegrate. Leaders seek to bring about group action, and that can occur only when individual members are willing to lend themselves to common purposes. Descriptions of effective leadership rarely mention the extent to which group attitudes make leadership possible. People talk of the legendary leader "you would follow over a cliff," not mentioning that it happens only when those doing the following are deeply committed to something the leader symbolizes.

Regenerative Processes

The disintegration of communities and belief systems has been going on since the Renaissance or—at the latest—since the scientific revolution in the sixteenth century. If it has been going on that long how can there be any coherence left? The answer is that there are always processes of regeneration at work to counter disintegrative forces. As old social groupings break down, new groupings tend to form. At the same time that coherent systems were breaking down in nineteenth-century Europe, new communities were forming in the American West, communities that are now looked back on nostalgically as models of cohesion.

The regenerative powers of human society, the capacity of humankind to create and re-create social coherence, are always there, enduring and irrepressible.

Human beings have a strong need to stabilize their environment. They do not like unpredictability, insecurity or disorder. They create communities with a framework of rules to keep at bay the lawless element that exists in every community (and in the hearts and minds of most of us). When order is destroyed and elements of savagery reemerge, the community embraces and empowers almost any regime that promises to end the chaos and reimpose order. No one understood that better than Hitler, and he was skilled at heightening the disorder that led people to welcome a coercive steadying hand. Before events reach that point of desperation, leaders must take active steps to rebuild community at all levels—and must enlist their constituencies as rebuilders.

Mutual Dependence

Leaders today are going to have to help people recover an understanding of the mutual dependence of individual and group that has existed in all healthy communities from the beginning of time. Implicit in that mutual dependence is some measure of commitment on the part of the individual to the society's shared purposes.

Obviously, the expression of such a view is not the preferred formula for leadership in many circles today. God forbid that you should tell citizens they owe anything to anybody. You tell them that society owes them just about everything and you are going to see that the debt is paid. In Shaw's *The Apple Cart*, the demagogue says, "I talk democracy to these men and women. I tell them that they have the vote, and that theirs is the kingdom and the power and the glory. They say 'That's right, tell us what to do'; and I say 'Vote for me.' "[5]

No doubt that formula will remain popular with political leaders. But it is not good enough. Voters are not only supreme, they are obligated. Constituents not only have needs, they have duties. You are owed something, and you owe something. We cannot respect anarchic individualism. Aristotle expected that the youth of Athens would be committed to the community. We must expect it of our young people today.

The mutual dependence between individual and group is ancient. But today if our communities are to survive, and if we are to survive as social beings, we must alter somewhat the nature of the relationship. Historically the society supplied most of the continuity and coherence through its long-established belief systems and nurturing institutions. In return the individual gave allegiance, but except in time of war it was a rather passive allegiance. Individuals accepted their culture as infants accept their cradle. It was the nurturing environment that enveloped them.

Passive allegiance is not enough today. Individuals must see themselves as having a positive duty to nurture and continuously reconstruct the community of which they are a part. They must be committed to a continuous reweaving of the social fabric, and leaders have an important role in bringing that about. It is not the usual task that has faced humans throughout history, but it is not unprecedented. John Winthrop, first governor of the Massachusetts Bay Colony, talked to his fellow colonists about community building: "We must delight in eache other, make others condicions our own, rejoice together, mourne together, labour, suffer together, alwayes haveing before our eyes our Community."[6] Winthrop was no friend of pluralism, as Roger Williams discovered, but a community builder he was.

After wars and other disasters, humans have demonstrated over and over that they have a considerable talent for community building and rebuilding. Leaders must encourage those processes.

Note that the task is not one of uncritical reaffirmation; it is a task of renewal. The process of renewal encompasses both continuity and change, reinterpreting tradition to meet new conditions, building a better future on an acknowledged heritage.

Having said that humans are community builders, one must acknowledge another side of our nature: We are great excluders. As far back as the record runs, we have been defining those outside our tribe as the enemy; and as I pointed our earlier, it is an impulse we can no longer afford.

Commitment and Meaning

Commitment to community is not unrelated to the problem of finding meaning in life—an ancient problem but never more widespread than today.

I once lived in a house where I could look out a window as I worked at my desk and observe a small herd of cattle browsing in a neighboring field. And I was struck with a thought that must have occurred to the earliest herdsmen tens of thousands of years ago. You never get the impression that a cow is about to have a nervous breakdown. Or puzzling about the meaning of life.

Humans have never mastered that kind of complacency. We are worriers and puzzlers, and we want meaning in our lives. For many this life is a vale of tears; for no one is it free of pain. But we are so designed that we deal with it if we can live in some context of meaning. Given that powerful help, we can draw on the deep springs of the human spirit to bear with the things we cannot change, to see our suffering in the framework of all human suffering, to accept the gifts of life with thanks and endure life's indignities with dignity.

The meaning in your life is not just handed to you, as a wayward motorist might be provided with a set of directions. Young people run around searching for identity, but it is not handed out free any more—not in this transient, rootless, pluralistic society. Your identity is what you have committed yourself to—whether the commitment is to your religion, to an ethical order, to your life work, to loved ones, to the common good, or to coming generations.

Today we have to build meaning into our lives, and we build it through our commitments. These must be not only the commitments already discussed, but also generation-spanning commitments—keeping faith with the future, with our children, and our children's children; and keeping faith with the best of the past, the models that guide and inspire, and the stories that tell us who we are—accepted not unthinkingly but with what Ralph Barton Perry called "a discriminating and forward-looking fidelity."[7]

Commitments Beyond the Self

To rehabilitate the idea of commitments beyond the self reverses a century of fruitless search for happiness in an ever more insatiable shattering of limits, so that the self might soar free and unrestrained. Commitments involve self-discipline. They involve constraints—but freely chosen constraints.

Because we are all too familiar with the pathologies of commitment—for example, with mindless allegiance of the sort favored in totalitarian states and in certain cults—we had better pause for clarification. Leaders must share the profound respect for a mature individuality that has evolved in Western culture over centuries. We want no mindless submersion in an individuality-destroying cult or movement. We seek the freely given commitments of mature individuals. We have had unhappy experiences with the bigotry and militant violence of zealots, so we expect that commitments, however ardent, will be pursued within the framework of law and custom, and with the tolerance that makes civilized life possible.

And since we rule out mindless commitment, we are duty-bound to give attention to those educational pursuits that prepare our young people to understand their own tradition and to see in perspective the value choices they must make.

Commitment requires hard work in the heat of the day; it requires faithful exertion in behalf of chosen purposes and the enhancement of chosen values. In return it gives meaning to our lives and joint endeavors and lends dignity and continuity to living. Commitments motivate. Values motivate. The hunger for justice, for liberty, for equality of opportunity, and for dignity as an individual has overthrown coercive systems and toppled proud regimes.

In recent years a good many American corporations have concluded that workers who make commitments to their work and find meaning in it perform more effectively.[8] The likelihood of such commitments is increased if they come to see quality of product as a source of self-respect and ultimately respect from the community; if they see service to customers as a source of pride; if they value the mutual trust and loyalty that exist among fellow workers; if they feel proudly involved in decisions concerning their work; if they believe that the company cares about their development as individuals; if they see competition with other firms as an invigorating challenge; and if the company's loyalty to them convinces them that their own security is linked to the firm's well-being. Obviously whether or not they hold any of these views depends on the philosophy and practice of the corporation as well as the qualities workers bring to the workplace.

The Role of Leaders

In any functioning society everything—leadership and everything else—takes place within a set of shared beliefs concerning the standards of acceptable behavior that must govern individual members. One of the tasks of leadership—at all levels—is to revitalize those shared beliefs and values, and to draw on them as sources of motivation for the exertions required of the group. Leaders can help to keep the values fresh. They can combat the hypocrisy that proclaims values at the same time that it violates them. They can help us understand our history and our present dilemmas. They have a role in creating the state of mind that is the society. Leaders must conceive and articulate goals in ways that lift people out of their petty preoccupations and unite them toward higher ends.

Leaders must not only have their own commitments, they must move the rest of us toward commitment. They call us to the sacrifices necessary to achieve our goals. They do not ask more than the community can give, but often ask more than it intended to give or thought it possible to give.

Leaders have a variety of ways of accomplishing all of these tasks. What they say, the policy decisions they make, the kinds of people with whom they surround themselves—all are part of the message they send out. And in this dimension the impact of leaders derives only in part from performance and in part from what they are and represent as human beings. Although Saint Francis of Assisi was a moving speaker, the most eloquent message he offered was not in what he said but in what he was—a truly devout man, a lover of life, of nature, of humankind, a giver and thanksgiver, a humble man of soaring spirit.

Of course, all leaders are not moral, and all who are moral do not live by the same code. There are leaders who reach for the worst in us. All leadership must be judged within the framework of values that represents the civilization at its best.

History will judge leaders on—among other things—how well they understand the traditional framework of values, and on how they renew the tradition by adapting it to contemporary dilemmas. On occasion they may have to suggest hitherto neglected values (as Elizabeth Cady Stanton and Susan B. Anthony did) or revive forgotten values (as the environmentalists did).

Only living values count. They must be reflected in actual behavior, embedded in our laws and institutions. Values decay "out there"—in the marketplace, the law office, the press—and they must be regenerated out there.

In any community, some people are more or less irretrievably bad and others more or less consistently good. But the behavior of most people is profoundly influenced by the moral climate of the moment. One of the leader's tasks is to help ensure the soundness of that moral climate.

Freedom and Obligation

We have learned through hard experience that without commitments, freedom is not possible. Something has to hold the society together. If that something is not dictatorial rule, it must be a commitment to the constitutional framework and web of custom that characterize the open society. We must freely give our allegiance to the society that gives us freedom. Montesquieu said that a republic can survive only as long as its citizens love it.

I made the point in *Excellence:* "Liberty and duty. Freedom and obligation. That's the deal." You are free within a framework of obligations—to your family, community, nation, species; in Shaw's words, to "the posterity that has no vote and the tradition that never had any"; to your God, to your conception of an ethical order. The obligations you accept may be different from mine. But it is not in the grand design that we can have freedom without obligation. Not for long.

17

THE RELEASE OF HUMAN POSSIBILITIES

Many factors contribute to the rise of a civilization—accidents of resource availability, geographical considerations, preeminence in trade or military power, and so on. But whatever the other ingredients, a civilization rises to greatness when something happens in human minds.

Reflecting on Pericles, Socrates, Sophocles and the other great citizens of Athens in that most golden of golden ages, the fifth century B.C.; reflecting on figures so extraordinarily diverse as William Shakespeare, Francis Drake, Thomas More, Francis Bacon and Queen Elizabeth in sixteenth-century England; reflecting on Cortes, St. Teresa, Cervantes, St. John of the Cross and others in sixteenth- to seventeenth-century Spain, one is bound to believe that there occurs at breathtaking moments in history an exhilarating burst of energy and motivation, of hope and zest and imagination, and a severing of the bonds that normally hold in check the full release of human possibilities. A door is opened and the caged eagle soars.

When a golden age subsides, the genetic possibilities in the population have not changed. The human material remains. But the dream and the drama have ended.

Sooner or later all leaders find themselves trying to build confidence. It is not an entirely easy task today. Paul Valery's wry comment that the future isn't what it used to be seems to be confirmed by the following passage from an essay by John Galsworthy:

> On the 8th day of July in the year 1401, the Dean and Chapter of Seville assembled in the Court of the Elms and solemnly resolved: "Let us build a church so great that those who come after us may think us mad to have attempted it." The church took 150 years to build.

The passage bespeaks depth of faith and a grand intent to celebrate that faith, but even more it reflects confidence in the long future.

Attitudes Toward the Future

At the heart of sustained morale and motivation lie two ingredients that appear somewhat contradictory: on the one hand, positive attitudes toward the future and toward what one can accomplish through one's own intentional acts, and on the other hand, recognition that life is not easy and that nothing is ever finally safe.

Students of the American westward movement are familiar with the powerful sense of the future that characterized so many of the pioneers. It was more than a positive belief in their own personal future. They felt that they were part of an immensely exciting drama just begun. When I was a boy growing up in California around the time of World War I, most people were quite sure of a good future. It is not that we had a clear vision of what the future would be, it is just that we felt the excitement of it. It was always there, beckoning, reflecting a confidence that many find hard to recapture today.

In the mid-twentieth century communists gained immense emotional support from the conviction that history was on their side. Hitler, seeking to gain comparable support, talked grandly of a Thousand Year Reich. Both views ran counter to the Spenglerian gloom that has dominated this century. Spengler wrote *The Decline of the West* at the end of World War I, and though his theory of history never gained a commanding position, his pessimism has echoed through the intellectual world ever since—and is very much alive today.[1]

A friend of mine living in Japan when that nation was still getting used to the rewards of its industrial rise said in a letter written in 1971, "They feel that they are riding the wave of the future and it is unbelievably exhilarating."

Of course, any reference to positive attitudes to the future calls to mind the fatuous optimism of those who close their eyes to the harsh realities of life. We need not slip into that foolishness. Recognition of the realities must be part of any mature approach to life.

What is needed is tough-minded optimism. Leaders must instill in their people a hard-bitten morale that mixes our natural American optimism with a measure of realism. To sustain hope one need not blind oneself to reality. People need to know the worst—about the evils to be remedied, the injustices to be dealt with, the catastrophes to be averted.

High hopes that are dashed by the first failure are precisely what we do not need. We need to believe in ourselves and our future but not to believe that life is easy. Life is painful and rain falls on the just. Leaders must help us see failure and frustration not as reason to doubt ourselves but as reason to strengthen resolve. As I said in *No Easy Victories* (1968), "The first and last task of a leader is to keep hope alive."[2] Never denying the difficulties, they must keep confidence unimpaired.

Life requires unrelenting effort, a willingness to try—and contrary to a widely held conception, humans are well fitted for the effort. In humans the long process of evolution has produced a species of problem solvers, happiest when engaged in tasks that require not only physical effort but also the engagement of mind and heart. We are not only problem solvers but problem seekers. If a suitable problem is not at hand, we invent one. Most games are invented problems. We are designed for the climb, not for taking our ease, either in the valley or at the summit.

Somewhat more complex than simple attitudes toward the future are the attitudes individuals have toward their own capacity to affect that future. Psychologists have ways of measuring the extent to which people believe they control (or can influence) the circumstances of their lives and the world around them. Some feel utterly powerless: victims of fate, leaves in the wind. Others have varying degrees of conviction that they do, indeed, have some capacity to control their own lives and to influence the world around them; and this confidence greatly increases the likelihood of sustained, highly motivated effort. Teachers instructing small children in a new task know that they have to divide their time between teaching the youngsters *how* to do it and convincing them they are *able* to do it.

Generally speaking, fatalists do not have much impact on events. The future is shaped by people who believe in the future—and in themselves. In *Excellence* I described a conversation I had with Martin Luther King, Jr. at a seminar on education. The black woman leading the seminar had entitled her talk "First, Teach Them to Read." King leaned over to me and said "First, teach them to believe in themselves."

Leaders must help people believe that they can be effective, that their goals are possible of accomplishment, that there is a better future that they can move toward through their own efforts. An employee of the

John Deere company said of Bill Hewitt, then the chief executive officer, "He made us realize how good we were."

Confidence

Any athlete or coach can testify to the importance of confidence, which is after all one kind of attitude toward the future. When athletes say they have psyched themselves up for a contest, they mean that they have coached themselves in certain positive expectations. When Vince Lombardi said, "We never lose, but sometimes the clock runs out on us," he was manifesting the aversion of the intense competitor to anything approaching admission of defeat.

Harlan Cleveland points out that the leader has little choice but to be optimistic. The analyst, the critic, the journalist can afford not to be. But taking a positive view is not something that effective leaders have to work at: It is in their temperament, and no doubt had much to do with their attainment of a leadership role. It may have been a leader who said, "I'd be a pessimist but it would never work." Out of a positive attitude toward the future comes much of the boldness and courage to risk failure so characteristic of the ablest leaders. They must not only have confidence but also the capacity to communicate that confidence.

The opposite of positive attitudes is not adequately captured by the word *pessimism*. Loss of confidence brings images of defeat and failure, helplessness, even self-contempt. Among the direct consequences are an incapacity to summon energy in behalf of purposeful effort, an unwillingness to take risks, and a fatal timidity when the moment of opportunity breaks. The effect on an organization can be devastating. As negative attitudes rise, bureaucratic defensiveness rises along with them and the whole system rigidifies.

Those who have worked with populations living in deep poverty in the less-developed nations of the world know the fatalism and passivity that exist when people do not believe they can affect their future in any significant way. Malnutrition, debilitating diseases and other factors are implicated in the passivity of people living in deep poverty, but lack of hope ranks as a major ingredient.

I mention the extreme example of people in deep poverty because it makes the point vividly. But the principles involved affect purposeful effort at all income levels. They affect all employee morale, all learning, all performance. People have to believe in their capacity to bring about a good result. Leaders must help them keep that enlivening belief.

Michael Walsh, one of the ablest leaders in American industry today, came to the Union Pacific Railroad as chief executive officer in 1986 and brought about remarkable improvements in the company's performance. One of his first tasks was to deal with pessimism within the company itself. "We had to persuade ourselves that we had a future. Frankly, I encountered many who doubted it."[3]

Of course, leaders must not only help their followers take a positive view of the future, they must seek to correct the objective circumstances that are producing negative attitudes. In dealing with children in poverty, for example, society must not only help children to believe in themselves, but must break the web of imprisoning circumstances that engender defeatism. It is not enough for corporate managers to advocate positive attitudes; they must correct conditions in the work environment that leave workers feeling hopelessly frustrated.

It is hard to have a sense of responsibility if one feels wholly powerless and unconnected to events. That is why many corporations today are striving to give workers down the line a feeling of involvement in decisions—"a sense of ownership" of the problems. And that is why many of us who worry about the continued vitality of our political system seek to increase citizen involvement in public life.

Expectations

As I pointed out in *Excellence*,[4] teachers and leaders share a trade secret—that when they expect high performance of their charges, they increase the likelihood of high performance.[5] If you expect me to hold myself to standards of excellence and discipline, you increase the likelihood that I will do so.

High expectations, then—of all our young people. That means standards. That means a respect for excellence. Our educational system is preeminently the instrument through which we express our expectations. May the expectations never diminish! Obviously the goal is not an indiscriminate cultivation of all human capacities, but individual fulfillment within a moral framework.

It is just as important for adults as for young people. There is much to be said for the leader stating goals and expectations in the most explicit terms. Students of presidential leadership often cite Franklin D. Roosevelt's announcement on May 16, 1940, that he had set a production goal of 50,000 planes a year, and John F. Kennedy's announcement that we would put a man on the moon within the decade. Both goals were breathtaking and both goals were met. And no one can doubt that in each case the achievement was hastened by the dramatic announcement.

Leaders cannot hope to have that kind of impact unless they themselves have a high level of morale. There is a famous story about a general on George C. Marshall's staff who reported to Marshall that some of the officers had morale problems. Marshall said, "Officers don't have morale problems. Officers cure morale problems in others. No one is looking after my morale." It is a sound principle. Low morale is unbecoming to a leader.

The Will to Act

Recently a speaker, discussing the economic competition the United States is facing externally, cited the great difficulty of mobilizing the national will. The reason for the difficulty may be that the various levels of leadership that should perform the task do not give much attention to the side of human nature that feeds the will.

A friend of mine assures me that we will soon have robots that can think in more complex ways than humans think. And that raises the interesting question, "Are we simply organisms whose functions can be performed by thinking robots, or are we something more?" Most of us, no doubt, are on the side of something more, something that does not spring only from reason, nor from miniaturized circuits that mimic reason, but also from the spirit, from our belief in truth greater than ourselves, from our hopes and our tears, from the stories of the great remembered dead, from our need for one another.

If I may, with tongue in cheek, explore the future of the robots, I predict that as they tackle more and more problems, and think more and more independently, they will come eventually to an interesting milestone. Some day they will take a long look at the world (not the physical globe but the human world), they will calculate the rationally possible ways of making it all work, and they will conclude that you cannot get there from here. Some racetrack philosopher said that all things considered, life is nine-to-five against; if that is true, the robots will make the calculation instantly. It would be excessively dramatic to say that their circuits will droop in despair, but it is clear they will be facing something that is not entirely their kind of problem.

It is the kind of problem appropriate to human beings—creatures who cheerfully act against the odds if they believe strongly enough, creatures who reach for unreachable stars and dream of impossible victories—and have at the same time the marvelously rational ingenuity to design thinking robots.

This points toward a comfortable division of labor. We can work with the robots on the rational things they do so well, and we can continue on our own to bring into play various other qualities—qualities that mark the species as human and may have helped it to survive. I am speaking of hope in a world that often gives little ground for hope; the quest for justice in a world only fitfully committed to justice; love in a world that is often unlovely and unloving; the hunger to understand things that elude understanding; the capacity for awe, wonder, reverence . . . I invite the reader to extend the list.

My point is that if leaders are to deal effectively with motivation, they are going to have to be on familiar terms with that side of our nature. If they are, they will understand that even in the most apathetic, the most materialistic, or the most unimaginative members of a group there is something waiting to be awakened, wanting to be awakened.

Leaders must understand that for most men and women the driving energies are latent. Some individuals are unaware of their potentialities, some are sleepwalking through the routines of life, some have succumbed to a sense of defeat. What leaders see on the surface can be discouraging—people, even very able people, caught in the routines of life, thinking short-term, plowing narrow self-beneficial furrows through life. What leaders have to remember is that somewhere under that somnolent surface is the creature that builds civilizations, the dreamer of dreams, the risk taker. And, remembering that, the leader must reach down to the springs that never dry up, the ever-fresh springs of the human spirit.

If one is leading, teaching, dealing with young people or engaged in any other activity that involves influencing, directing, guiding, helping or nurturing, the whole tone of the relationship is conditioned by one's faith in human possibilities. That is the generative element, the source of the current that gives life to the relationship. William James pointed out that just as our courage is so often a reflex of another's courage, so our faith is often in someone else's faith.

When the faith is present in the leader, it communicates itself to followers with powerful effect. *In the conventional mode people want to know whether the followers believe in the leader; a more searching question is whether the leader believes in the followers.*

If our leaders at all levels are to be capable of lifting us and moving us, they are going to have to believe in the people of this nation—a people so able to perform splendidly and so inclined to perform indifferently, so troubled in their efforts to find a future worthy of their past, so capable of greatness and so desperately in need of encouragement to achieve that greatness.

NOTES

CHAPTER 1
The Nature of Leadership

1. Niccolò Machiavelli, *The Prince* (New York: New American Library, 1952).

2. Sidney Hook, *The Hero in History* (Boston: Beacon Press, 1955).

3. Thomas E. Cronin, *Chronicle of Higher Education* (February 1, 1989), pp. B1–B2.

4. Jeffrey Pfeffer, "The Ambiguity of Leadership" in *Leadership: Where Else Can We Go?* ed. Morgan W. McCall, Jr., and Michael Lombardo (Durham, N.C.: Duke University Press, 1978).

5. William J. Cirone and Barbara Margerum, "Models of Citizen Involvement and Community Education," *National Civic Review* 76, no. 3 (May–June 1987).

6. John W. Gardner, *Excellence*, rev. ed. (New York: W. W. Norton, 1984).

CHAPTER 2
The Tasks of Leadership

1. Philip Rieff, *The Triumph of the Therapeutic* (New York: Harper and Row, 1966).

2. Elisabeth Griffith, *In Her Own Right: The Life of Elizabeth Cady Stanton* (New York: Oxford University Press, 1984).

3. Jean Monnet, *Memoirs*, trans. Richard Mayne (New York: Doubleday Publishing, 1978).

4. Elspeth Huxley, *Florence Nightingale* (New York: G. P. Putnam's Sons, 1975).

5. Aaron Wildavsky, *The Nursing Father: Moses as a Political Leader* (Tuscaloosa: University of Alabama Press, 1984).

6. William Cabell Bruce, *John Randolph of Roanoke* (New York: Putnam, 1922).

7. Niccolò Machiavelli, *The Prince* (New York: New American Library, 1952), p. 93.

8. Thurman Arnold, *The Folklore of Capitalism* (New Haven: Yale University Press, 1937).

9. Rachel Carson, *Silent Spring* (New York: Houghton Mifflin, 1963).

10. Betty Friedan, *The Feminine Mystique* (New York: Dell, 1963).

11. Merrill D. Peterson, *The Jefferson Image in the American Mind* (New York: Oxford University Press, 1960).

12. Erik Erikson, *Gandhi's Truth* (New York: W. W. Norton, 1969); Mohandas D. Gandhi, *An Autobiography* (Boston Beacon Press, 1957).

13. Monnet, *Memoirs*, p. 147.

14. Charles DeGaulle, *The War Memoirs, 1940–1946* (New York: Simon & Schuster, 1964), I:7.

15. Donald M. Michael, "Competence and Compassion in an Age of Uncertainty," *World Future Society Bulletin*, January–February 1983.

CHAPTER 3
The Heart of the Matter: Leader–Constituent Interaction

1. Max Weber, *The Theory of Social and Economic Organization*, trans. A. M. Henderson and Talcott Parsons (New York: Oxford University Press, 1947).

2. Georg Simmel, *The Sociology of Georg Simmel*, ed. and trans. Kurt Wolff (Glencoe, Ill. Free Press, 1950).

3. Excellent reviews of the research literature are available in B. M. Bass, *Stogdill's Handbook of Leadership* (New York: Free Press, 1981); B. M. Bass, *Leadership and Performance Beyond Expectations* (New York: Free Press, 1985); and Edwin Hollander, "Leadership and Power," in *The Handbook of Social Psychology*, 3d. ed., G. Lindzey and E. Aronson (New York: Random House, 1985).

4. Erik Erikson, *Gandhi's Truth* (New York: W. W. Norton, 1969).

5. ———, *Young Man Luther* (New York: W. W. Norton, 1958).

6. Edmund Wilson, *Patriotic Gore* (New York: Oxford University Press, 1962).

7. Woodrow Wilson, *Leaders of Men* (Princeton, N.J.: Princeton University Press, 1952), p. 43.

8. John F. Kennedy, *Profiles in Courage* (New York: Harper and Row, 1964), p. 134.

9. Weber, *The Theory of Social and Economic Organization*, pp. 358–59.

10. Robert C. Tucker, "The Theory of Charismatic Leadership," *Daedalus*, Summer 1968: 731–56.

11. James MacGregor Burns, *Leadership* (New York: Harper and Row, 1978).

CHAPTER 4
Contexts

1. R. M. Stogdill, "Personal Factors Associated with Leadership," *Journal of Psychology* 25 (1948):35–71.

2. F. E. Fiedler, *A Theory of Leadership Effectiveness* (New York: McGraw-Hill, 1967).

3. Abigail Adams, Letter to Thomas Jefferson, 1790.

4. Henry Steele Commager, "Leadership in 18th-Century America and Today," *Daedalus*, Fall 1961: 652–73.

5. James Flexner, *Washington: The Indispensable Man* (New York: American Heritage Publishing Co., 1968), 2:864.

6. *American Heritage History of the Presidents* (New York: American Heritage Publishing Co., 1968), 2:864.

7. Jean Monnet, *Memoirs*, trans. Richard Mayner (New York: Doubleday Publishing, 1978).

8. Ibid.

9. Theodore N. Vail, "Public Utilities and Public Policy," *Atlantic Monthly* III, March 1913.

10. Ibid.

11. Peter F. Drucker, *The Effective Executive* (New York: Harper and Row, 1966).

12. George F. Kennan, *Memoirs 1925–1950* (Boston: Little, Brown, 1967).

CHAPTER 5
Attributes

1. B. M. Bass, *Stogdill's Handbook of Leadership* (New York: Free Press, 1981).

2. Edwin P. Hollander, *Leadership Dynamics: A Practical Guide to Effective Relationships* (New York: Free Press, 1978).

3. Golda Meir, *My Life* (New York: G. P. Putnam's Sons, 1975).

4. *The Journal of Christopher Columbus*, ed. Clements P. Markham, trans. for the Hakluyt Society, London, 1893.

5. William Manchester, *The Last Lion: Winston Spencer Churchill 1874–1932* (New York: Dell, 1983).

6. Abraham Lincoln, Address before the Young Men's Lyceum of Springfield, Illinois, January 27, 1838.

7. John Adams, "Diary 1755–1770," in *The Adams Papers*, ed. L. H. Butterfield (New York: Atheneum Publishers 1964).

8. Manchester, *The Last Lion.*

9. Quoted in John F. Kennedy, *Profiles in Courage* (N.Y.: Harper and Row, 1964), p. 62.

10. Ibid., p. 67.

11. Comments at a leadership conference sponsored by the Association of American Colleges, November 20, 1986.

12. James Flexner, *Washington: The Indispensable Man* (New York: New American Library, 1974).

13. Attributed to John Morley in Richard Hofstadter, *The American Political Tradition* (New York: Alfred A. Knopf, 1951), p. 225.

14. Thomas B. Edsall, "Dole's Transformations," *Washington Post*, 9 March 1987.

15. Barbara Gamerekian, "TV Coaches: Success Is Appearing to Be in Charge," *New York Times*, 25 August 1988.

CHAPTER 6
Power

1. Tip O'Neill, *Man of the House* (New York: St. Martin's Press, 1987), pp. 222–23.

2. Studs Terkel, *Working* (New York: Pantheon Books, 1974), p. 38.

3. Mao Tse-tung, *Quotations from Chairman Mao Tse-tung* (Beijing: Foreign Languages Press, 1972).

4. Nikita Khrushchev, *Khrushchev Remembers* (Boston: Little, Brown, 1970).

5. David Mathews et al., *The Promise of Democracy* (Dayton, Ohio: The Kettering Foundation, 1989).

6. Herodotus, *The Histories*, trans. Aubrey de Selincourt (London: Penguin Books, 1954).

7. Woodrow Wilson, *Leaders of Men* (Princeton, N.J.: Princeton University Press, 1952), pp. 20–21.

8. Robert M. LaFollette, *Autobiography* (Madison: University of Wisconsin Press, 1960), pp. 83–84.

9. David C. McClelland, *Power: The Inner Experience* (New York: Irvington Publishers, Inc., 1975).

CHAPTER 7

The Moral Dimension

1. Robert Conquest, *The Harvest of Sorrow* (Oxford University Press, 1986). Reliable recent reports from Moscow indicate that Soviet officials themselves acknowledge the 10 million figure. Other estimates from U.S. and European sources range up to 15 million.

2. Gordon W. Prange, *Hitler's Words* (*Speeches* 1922–1943). Washington, 1944, cited in Alan Bullock's *Hitler: A Study in Tyranny*, rev. ed. (New York: Harper and Row, 1962), p. 398.

3. Bullock, *Hitler*, p. 527.

4. Adolf Hitler, *Mein Kampf* (Boston: Houghton Mifflin, 1943).

5. Prange, *Hitler's Words*.

6. Hitler, *Mein Kampf*.

7. Ibid.

8. Otto Strasser, *Hitler and I* (Boston: Houghton, 1940).

9. Mike Royko, *Boss: Richard J. Daley of Chicago* (New York: E. P. Dutton, 1971).

10. James D. Barber, "Adult Identity and Presidential Style: The Rhetorical Emphasis," *Daedalus* 97, no. 3 (Summer 1968).

11. James Flexner, *Washington: The Indispensable Man* (New York: New American Library, 1984).

12. Thomas Jefferson, *Notes on Virginia*, 1782.

13. Gilbert Murray, *Five Stages on Greek Religion* (New York: Doubleday Publishing, 1955).

14. Gerald Grant, "The Character of Education and the Education of Character," *Kettering Review*, Fall 1983: 26.

15. Lyman Bryson, *The Next America* (New York: Harper and Brothers, 1952), p. 9.

16. Caryl P. Haskins, *Report of the President of Carnegie Institution of Washington 1961–1962*. (Washington, D.C., 1962).

CHAPTER 8

Large-Scale Organized Systems

1. Steven Muller, "The University Presidency Today," *Science* 237, 14 August 1987.

2. Max Weber, *The Theory of Social and Economic Organization*, trans. A. M. Henderson and Talcott Parsons (New York: Oxford University Press, 1947).

3. For example, Elton Mayo, an industrial psychologist at the Harvard Graduate School of Business, did pioneering work on the morale and motivation of workers. In 1938, Chester Barnard, in his book *The Functions of the Executive* (republished by Harvard University Press in 1984) contributed importantly to a new understanding. In the 1950s and 1960s writers such as Rensis Likert, *New Patterns of Management* (New York: McGraw-Hill, 1961) and Douglas McGregor, *The Professional Manager* (New York: McGraw-Hill, 1967) pursued the same questions.

4. *Business Week*, 6 December 1982.

5. *Forbes Magazine*, 30 May 1988.

6. Daniel Yankelovich, *Work and Human Values* (New York: Public Agenda Foundation, 1983).

7. Richard M. Cyert and James G. March, *A Behavioral Theory of the Firm* (Englewood Cliffs, N.J.: Prentice-Hall, 1963).

8. Warren Bennis and Burt Nanus, *Leaders* (New York: Harper and Row, 1965).

CHAPTER 9
Fragmentation and the Common Good

1. Garrett Hardin, "The Tragedy of the Commons," *Science* 62 (1968) 1243–48.

2. Elliott Jacques, Stephen Clement, Carlos Rigdy, and T. O. Jacobs, *Senior Leadership Performance Requirements at the Executive Level* (U.S. Army Research Institute for the Behavioral Sciences, January 1986), p. 26.

3. Emmett John Hughes, *The Ordeal of Power* (New York: Atheneum Publishers, 1962), p. 124.

4. Bruce Murray, *Journey into Space* (New York: W. W. Norton, 1989).

CHAPTER 10
The Knitting Together

1. Adolf Hitler, *Mein Kampf* (Boston: Houghton Mifflin, 1943).

2. Comments at a seminar on the United Nations sponsored by the Aspen Institute for Humanistic Studies, Wye Plantation, Maryland, December 4, 1982.

3. Remarks at memorial service for Wilber Cohen, June 17, 1987.

4. The story may have improved in the telling. True or apocryphal, most early Office of Strategy Services officers repeated it as gospel.

5. *The Chicago Project: A Report on Civic Life in Chicago*, 1986. Staff director for the study was Professor Pastora San Juan Cafferty, University of Chicago. The report was signed by H. Laurance Fuller, President, Amoco Corporation and Duane R. Kullberg, Managing Partner and CEO, Arthur Andersen and Co.

CHAPTER 11
Community

1. Oscar Handlin, *The Uprooted* (Boston: Little, Brown, 1952)

2. Emile Durkheim, *Le Suicide* (Paris: Alcan, 1897).

3. Daniel Bell, "The Return of the Sacred? The Argument on the Future of Religion," *British Journal of Sociology*, 28, no. 4 (December 1977).

4. In the explorations that I undertook before writing this section I was greatly aided by my friends Bruce Adams, Loren Mead, and John Parr.

5. Jeff S. Luke, "Managing Interconnectedness: The Need for Catalytic Leadership," *Futures Research Quarterly*, Winter 1986.

CHAPTER 12
Renewing

1. James MacGregor Burns, *Leadership* (New York: Harper and Row, 1978).

2. Nelson W. Polsby, *Political Innovation in America* (New Haven: Yale University Press, 1984).

3. Harlan Cleveland, *The Knowledge Executive* (New York: E. P. Dutton, 1985).

4. Francis Bacon, *Essays* (New York: Macmillan, 1930).

5. Harold Leavitt, *Corporate Pathfinders* (New York: Penguin Books, 1986).

6. John W. Gardner, *Self-Renewal* (New York: W. W. Norton, 1981).

7. Lord Moran, *The Anatomy of Courage* (London: Constable, 1945).

8. *The Complete Essays of Montaigne*, trans. Donald Frame (Stanford, Calif.: Stanford University Press, 1958).

9. James Michener, quoted in Gilber Brim, "Losing and Winning," *Psychology Today*, September 1988.

10. Aaron Wildavsky, *The Nursing Father: Moses as a Political Leader* (Tuscaloosa: University of Alabama Press, 1984).

11. Sigmund Freud, *On the History of the Psychoanalytic Movement* (London: Hogarth Press, 1916), p. 21.

CHAPTER 13
Sharing Leadership Tasks

1. Robert A. Nisbet, "Leadership and Social Crisis" in Alvin W. Gouldner's *Studies in Leadership* (Russell, 1965), p. 711.

2. Daniel Yankelovich, "How the Public Learns the Public Business," *Kettering Review*, Winter 1985, pp. 8–18.

3. Benjamin Barber, *Strong Democracy: Participatory Politics for a New Age* (Berkeley: University of California Press, 1984).

4. Robert K. Greenleaf, *The Servant as Leader* (Peterborough, N.H.: Center for Applied Sciences, 1973).

5. Douglas McGregor, as quoted in Clark Kerr and Adrian Gade, *The Many Lives of Academic Presidents*, (Washington, D.C.: Association of Governing Boards of Universities and Colleges, 1986), pp. 133–34.

6. For a summary of the literature, see Donald R. Kinder and David O. Sears, "Public Opinion and Political Action," in *The Handbook of Social Psychology*, 3d ed., Gardner Lindzey and Elliot Aronson (New York: Random House, 1985).

7. William Watts and Lloyd A. Free, *State of the Nation III* (Lexington, Mass.: Lexington Books, 1978).

8. Neal R. Peirce and Carol F. Steinach, *Corrective Capitalism: The Rise of America's Community Development Corporation* (New York: Ford Foundation, 1987).

9. *Community-Based Development: Investing in Renewal*. Report of the Task Force on Community-Based Development. September 1987, p. 35.

10. Kenneth Benne and Paul Sheats, "Functional Roles of Group Members," *Journal of Social Issues* II (1948): 41–49.

11. Alex Bavelas, "Leadership: Man and Function," *Administrative Science Quarterly*, March 1960.

12. Edgar H. Schein, *Organizational Psychology* (Englewood Cliffs, N.J.: Prentice-Hall, 1980), p. 251.

13. Stanley Hiller, Jr., "Corporate Governance: The Flaw in America's Reconstruction." (Address to the Commonwealth Club, San Francisco, May 21, 1988.)

14. Mike Royko, *Boss: Richard J. Daley of Chicago* (New York: E. P. Dutton, 1971).

CHAPTER 14
Leadership Development: The Early Years

1. Roger Barker and Associates, *Habitats, Environments and Human Behavior* (San Francisco: Jossey Bass), p. 346.

2. J. Eugene Smith, *One Hundred Years of Hartford's Courant* (New Haven, Conn.: Yale University Press, 1949).

3. Merle Miller, *Plain Speaking: An Oral Biography of Harry S. Truman*. (New York: G. P. Putnam's Sons, 1973), p. 307.

4. Catherine M. Cox, *The Early Mental Traits of Three Hundred Geniuses*, vol. III of the *Genetic Studies of Genius* (Stanford, Calif.: Stanford University Press, 1926).

5. Kemper Diehl and Jan Jarboe, *Henry Cisneros* (San Antonio, Texas: Corona Publishing Co., 1984), p. 37.

CHAPTER 15
Leadership Development: Lifelong Growth

1. In a memorandum to the author, May 1988.
2. Irwin Miller, lecture at Yale School of Organization and Management, November 14, 1986.
3. Miriam Slater and Penina Migdal Glazer, "Prescription for Professional Survival," in *Learning About Women: Gender, Politics and Power: Daedalus*, Fall 1987: 119–35.
4. Sara Ruddick, "Maternal Thinking," in *Mothering: Essays in Feminist Theory*, ed. Joyce Trebilcot (Towota, N.J.: Rowman and Allanheld, 1983).
5. Nancy Chodorow, *The Reproduction of Mothering* (Berkeley: University of California Press, 1978).
6. Carol Gilligan, *In a Different Voice* (Cambridge, Mass.: Harvard University Press, 1982).
7. Ann M. Morrison, Randall P. White, and Ellen Van Volsor, "The Narrow Band," in *Issues and Observations*, Spring 1987, Center for Creative Leadership, Greensboro, North Carolina.
8. Donna L. Shavlik and Judith G. Touchton, "Women as Leaders" in Madeleine F. Green, *Leaders for a New Era* (New York: Macmillan, 1988), pp. 98–117.

CHAPTER 16
Motivating

1. *Time Magazine*, 9 May 1960.
2. D. C. McClelland et al., *The Achievement Motive* (New York: Appleton-Century-Crofts, 1953); D. C. McClelland, *Power: The Inner Experience* (New York: Irvington Publishers, 1975); Richard E. Boyatzis, *The Competent Manager* (New York: John Wiley and Sons, 1982).
3. Bernard M. Bass, *Leadership and Performance Beyond Expectations* (New York: The Free Press, 1985).
4. F. J. Roethlisberger and William J. Dickson, *Management and the Worker* (Cambridge, Mass., Harvard University Press, 1949). Summaries may be found in Edgar H. Schein, *Organizational Psychology* (Englewood Cliffs, N.J.: Prentice-Hall, 1980) and Robert H. Waterman, Jr., *The Renewal Factor* (New York: Bantam Books, 1987).
5. G. B. Shaw, *The Apple Cart* (Penguin Books, 1956), p. 47.
6. John Winthrop, "A Model of Christian Charity." Sermon delivered on board ship in Salem harbor just before landing in 1630.

7. Ralph Barton Perry, *Puritanism and Democracy* (New York: Vanguard Press, 1944).

8. Robert H. Waterman, *The Renewal Factor* (New York: Bantam Books, 1987).

CHAPTER 17
The Release of Human Possibilities

1. Oswald Spengler, *The Decline of the West* (New York: Alfred A. Knopf, vol. I, 1926; vol. II, 1928).

2. John W. Gardner, *No Easy Victories* (New York: Harper and Row, 1968), p. 134.

3. Michael Walsh, "Dialogue with the Chairman," *Info Magazine*, Union Pacific Railroad, October 1988.

4. John W. Gardner, *Excellence*, rev. ed. (New York: W. W. Norton, 1984).

5. Unfortunately, assertions have been made in the psychological literature that carry the notion beyond good sense or available evidence. There is no scientific evidence that high teacher expectations raise pupil IQ, and it is dangerous to view teacher expectations as inexpensive means of compensating for profound social disadvantage as a factor in performance.

INDEX